"*Fundamentals of New Testament Textual Criticism* is an excellent treatise on a vitally important subject. Stanley Porter and Andrew Pitts were seeking to produce a textbook that falls midway between Bruce Metzger's *Text of the New Testament* and my own *New Testament Textual Criticism: A Concise Guide,* and they have succeeded brilliantly. . . . Their careful research deepens our understanding of the role of textual criticism in exegesis, and I am confident that this book of theirs will be widely used both inside and outside of the classroom."

— DAVID ALAN BLACK
Southeastern Baptist
Theological Seminary

"Porter and Pitts have admirably achieved what they set out to do — provide a succinct introduction to the manuscript tradition of the Greek New Testament for first- and second-year students of Koine Greek. . . . This book is ideal both for students in classrooms and for general readers who seek reliable information about the origins and the text of the New Testament."

— ECKHARD SCHNABEL
Gordon-Conwell
Theological Seminary

"In this book Stanley E. Porter and Andrew W. Pitts take interested students by the hand and introduce them to the *essentials* of New Testament textual criticism. . . . They provide welcome, concise assessments of external and internal evidence for judging textual variants. . . . A very useful tool for instructing students in New Testament textual criticism."

— THOMAS J. KRAUS
University of Zurich

Fundamentals of New Testament Textual Criticism

Stanley E. Porter & Andrew W. Pitts

WILLIAM B. EERDMANS PUBLISHING COMPANY
GRAND RAPIDS, MICHIGAN / CAMBRIDGE, U.K.

© 2015 Stanley E. Porter and Andrew W. Pitts

Published 2015 by
Wm. B. Eerdmans Publishing Co.
2140 Oak Industrial Drive N.E., Grand Rapids, Michigan 49505 /
P.O. Box 163, Cambridge CB3 9PU U.K.

Printed in the United States of America

21 20 19 18 17 16 15   7 6 5 4 3 2 1

Library of Congress Cataloging-in-Publication Data

Porter, Stanley E., 1956-
    Fundamentals of New Testament textual criticism /
    Stanley E. Porter & Andrew W. Pitts.
        pages   cm
    Includes bibliographical references and index.
    ISBN 978-0-8028-7224-1 (pbk.: alk. paper)
    1. Bible. New Testament — Criticism, Textual.   I. Title.

BS2325.P67   2015
225.4'86 — dc23

                                        2014049876

www.eerdmans.com

Contents

Acknowledgments

This book is the product of two people interested in a common task — teaching others about textual criticism, within the context of advancing knowledge of New Testament Greek — working together to achieve that aim. We leave others to decide whether we have accomplished that goal. However, we have enjoyed the process from start to finish, as we have refined this work and developed it according to our goals of providing the fundamentals of textual criticism for those who are interested and serious about learning this important area. As the notes and bibliography make clear, we are very interested in this topic, as well as the Greek language in general, and come to the writing of this book on the basis of having done serious work in textual criticism. We hope that we have learned enough along the way to make the process of learning easier for others.

We realize that the writing of a book like this is never the work of just one or, in this case, two people. We would also like to thank a number of people for their work with us in trying to ensure that we have got our facts straight, and, more importantly, that we have pitched this book at the right level to provide the kind of book that we have envisioned. Thus we would like to thank Will Varner, Karl Armstrong, Bryan Fletcher, and Cliff Kvidahl, who read the entire manuscript and offered thoughtful comments and ideas that made the volume better in many ways. Cliff was especially helpful in working on issues related to the format and images for the volume.

This volume, as its title — *Fundamentals of New Testament Textual Criticism* — indicates, is designed as part of the series of Greek language resources being published by Eerdmans. Previous volumes in that series include Stanley E. Porter, Jeffrey T. Reed, and Matthew Brook O'Donnell,

Fundamentals of New Testament Greek (2010) and Porter and Reed, *Fundamentals of New Testament Greek: Workbook* (2010). We are in the process of writing an intermediate grammar that continues to develop this learning curriculum, as well as a book on exegesis and interpretation. We wish to thank Eerdmans for their support of this entire project, including all of its component volumes. To this end, we wish to thank Michael Thomson at Eerdmans, as well as his excellent colleagues there.

Finally, we wish to thank our various supporting institutions for their help in making this work possible. We also wish to thank our wives, Wendy and Amber, for their love and unstinting support. We could not do what we do without them — and it would not be nearly as rewarding or pleasurable.

STANLEY E. PORTER & ANDREW W. PITTS

The Reason for This Book and How to Use It:
A Note to Professors and Students

Both of the authors of this book have taught Greek language and exegesis for a number of years — one of them over the course of a career of twenty-five years at undergraduate, seminary, and graduate levels. One consistent challenge to us as we have selected textbooks for these classes is the lack of a book that addresses the fundamentals of New Testament textual criticism and important related issues that is neither too advanced nor too elementary. In other words, we have written this distinctly midlevel textbook on New Testament textual criticism for interested and serious students and with recent scholarly discussion in pertinent areas in mind. Books like Bruce Metzger's classic, *The Text of the New Testament* (4th ed., rev. Bart D. Ehrman; Oxford: Oxford University Press, 2005 [1964]), and Kurt and Barbara Aland's *Text of the New Testament* (2nd ed.; Grand Rapids: Eerdmans, 1989), or more recently David Parker's *Introduction to the New Testament Manuscripts and Their Texts* (Cambridge: Cambridge University Press, 2008), while all very helpful, are far too detailed for the first-year or second-year Greek student. At the same time, books like David Alan Black's *New Testament Textual Criticism: A Concise Guide* (Grand Rapids: Baker, 1994) or J. Harold Greenlee's *Introduction to New Testament Textual Criticism* (rev. ed., 1993; repr. Peabody: Hendrickson, 1995) seem too abbreviated to us, not providing enough detailed information or exposure to major issues for the student. Paul Wegner's *Textual Criticism of the Bible* (Downers Grove, IL: InterVarsity Press, 2006) in some ways improves upon these but, probably due to its focus upon both Testaments, leaves many areas in *New Testament* textual criticism untouched. Not only were the textbooks with which we were familiar either too detailed or too abbreviated, but we observed no midlevel textbooks that introduced students to the main debates within textual criticism and addressed issues such as canon and translation theory, discussions that we like to include in our first- and second-year Greek courses (especially for first-year students in a seminary context).

Out of a desire to use a book that captures these many elements for our first- and second-year Greek students, this book was born. It is intended for students who are in the process of studying or have had at least one year of New Testament Greek or its equivalent (e.g., Classical Greek) and desire to begin learning the principles of Greek exegesis, and specifically textual criticism. This book has been written to function as an excellent companion for Stanley Porter, Jeffrey Reed, and Matthew Brook O'Donnell's *Fundamentals of New Testament Greek* (Grand Rapids: Eerdmans, 2010) and, when it appears, an intermediate grammar of New Testament Greek by Stanley Porter, Christopher Land, and Andrew Pitts, all in the same series from Eerdmans. This is all designed to be part of a coordinated Greek study curriculum, with attention to learning the language and learning about the text of that language. We are also in the process of developing a book on exegesis and interpretation to help round out the curriculum. We hope that this book on the fundamentals of textual criticism might also stand on its own for someone who desires to learn New Testament textual criticism apart from a classroom context (and has ideally had at least some prior instruction in New Testament Greek or its equivalent, or is ambitious!).

Teachers should especially note a few features of this book. First, at the end of each chapter a list of key vocabulary is included with definitions directly following the emboldened text within the chapter itself. These key words can serve as quiz material since they are intended to incorporate the central concepts and technical terminology found within each lesson. Second, each chapter also includes a select bibliography of our sources. These bibliographies are also intended to provide students with a starting point for research papers or text-critical exercises related to any of the given chapters. Third, and finally, an appendix introduces students to the tools of textual criticism and could provide a great opportunity to discuss how these tools could be used by the students in a future classroom or ministry setting.

Abbreviations

Aeg	*Aegyptus*
ASV	American Standard Version
AV (= KJV)	Authorized Version
Bib	*Biblica*
BZNW	Beihefte zur Zeitschrift für die neutestamentliche Wissenschaft
CBET	Contributions to Biblical Exegesis and Theology
CBQ	*Catholic Biblical Quarterly*
CEB	Common English Bible
CEV	Contemporary English Version
ConBNT	Coniectanea Biblica New Testament Series
CQ	*Classical Quarterly*
Ebib	Études bibliques
ECHC	Early Christianity in Its Hellenistic Context
ESV	English Standard Version
GNB (= GNT)	Good News Bible
GNT (= GNB)	Good News Translation
HCSB	Holman Christian Standard Bible
HTB	Histoire du texte biblique
HTR	*Harvard Theological Review*
JBL	*Journal of Biblical Literature*
JGRChJ	*Journal of Greco-Roman Christianity and Judaism*
JRASup	Journal of Roman Archaeology Supplement Series
JSNTSup	Journal for the Study of the New Testament Supplement Series
JTS	*Journal of Theological Studies*
KJV (= AV)	King James Version
LBS	Linguistic Biblical Studies

LNTS	Library of New Testament Studies
LXX	Septuagint
NA	Eberhard Nestle, Kurt Aland, et al., *Novum Testamentum Graece* (various editions)
NASB	New American Standard Bible
NAU	New American Standard Bible 1995 Update
NET	New English Translation
NIV	New International Version
NKJV	New King James Version
NovT	*Novum Testamentum*
NovTSup	Novum Testamentum Supplement
NRSV	New Revised Standard Version
NTS	*New Testament Studies*
NTTS	New Testament Tools and Studies
NTTSD	New Testament Tools, Studies and Documents
PAST	Pauline Studies
RSV	Revised Standard Version
RV	Revised Version
SBLTCS	Society of Biblical Literature Text-Critical Studies
SD	Studies and Documents
SNTSMS	Society for New Testament Studies Monograph Series
TENTS	Texts and Editions for New Testament Study
TEV	Today's English Version
TNIV	Today's New International Version
TSAJ	Texte und Studien zum antiken Judentum
TynBul	*Tyndale Bulletin*
UBS	United Bible Societies
UBSGNT	*United Bible Societies' Greek New Testament* (various editions)

CHAPTER 1

What Is Textual Criticism? Definitions and Aims

The goal of textual criticism is defined in two distinct ways in contemporary New Testament (henceforth NT) scholarship. Textual criticism is traditionally seen as the science and art of reconstructing the original Greek autographs as closely as possible. More recent scholars, however, tend to perceive textual criticism as a means of tracking the history of textual transmission in order to gain insight into the social history of early Christianity, especially as Christianity and its texts developed in the second century. We shall refer to these two positions as the **traditional model** and the **sociohistorical model** of textual criticism. The traditional model begins from the standpoint of there being an original form of the text, whereas the sociohistorical model places attention on the transmission process itself and often doubts whether there is an original text to be discovered. Each school of thought is briefly considered below, followed by a summary and evaluation.

1. Textual Criticism as Textual Reconstruction: The Traditional Model

Textual criticism is traditionally defined by its concern to recover the original form of the text by means of applying rigorous text-critical methodology to the available manuscript tradition. This is the aim of the text-critical methodologies developed and practiced by early text-critical scholars, such as Constantine Tischendorf, J. J. Griesbach, F. J. A. Hort, Frederic Kenyon, and Kirsopp Lake, and by more recent textual critics such as Kurt Aland, Bruce Metzger, Leon Vaganay, E. C. Colwell, J. Harold Greenlee,

1

Gordon Fee, and Phillip Comfort, to name some of the more significant figures. Greenlee's definition is typical: *"Textual criticism is the study of copies of any work of which the autograph (the original) is unknown, with the purpose of ascertaining the original text."*[1] B. F. Westcott and F. J. A. Hort conceive of the discipline similarly, as an "attempt to present exactly the original words of the New Testament, so far as they can now be determined from surviving documents."[2] Such definitions are legion, in both introductory and scholarly works on textual criticism. This model is so firmly established throughout the history of the discipline that it is not an exaggeration for J. H. Petzer to identify the entire history of NT text-critical theory and practice as a concentrated effort aimed at reconstructing the original Greek text:

> Looking at practical reconstructions of this history [of the NT text] over the past two and a half centuries, however, it becomes clear that it can more or less be defined as the attempt to identify and explain the different forms of text in the extant witnesses to the New Testament by means of relating them to each other, with the purpose of identifying the most trustworthy witness(es), which can be used as the basis of the reconstructed text of the New Testament. This is more or less what has been in the center of the ongoing attention to the witnesses to the Greek New Testament since the inception of New Testament textual criticism as a modern discipline.[3]

According to the **traditional model**, the history of manuscript transmission is viewed as the primary resource for reconstructing the original text. The manuscript tradition is understood to be the primary means to the end of recovering the autograph, rather than being an end in itself. From Erasmus, the seventeenth-century Dutch scholar who published the first "modern" Greek edition of the NT in 1516, to the Nestle-Aland[28] (NA) text published in 2012 (the standard critical edition used by most NT scholars),

---

1. J. Harold Greenlee, *Introduction to New Testament Textual Criticism* (Grand Rapids: Eerdmans, 1964), 11.

2. B. F. Westcott and F. J. A. Hort, *Introduction to the New Testament in the Original Greek with Notes on Selected Readings* (1882; repr. Peabody, MA: Hendrickson, 1988), 3.

3. Jacobus H. Petzer, "The History of the New Testament Text — Its Reconstruction, Significance and Use in New Testament Textual Criticism," in *New Testament Textual Criticism, Exegesis and Church History: A Discussion of Methods* (ed. Barbara Aland and Joël Delobel; CBET 7; Kampen: Kok Pharos, 1994), 11.

modern editions[4] of the NT have been developed on the basis of this traditional model.

Textual criticism, defined along these traditional lines, may be contrasted with **higher criticism**. In such a framework of higher and lower criticism, **lower criticism** (an older label for textual criticism) provides the foundation (thus it is lower or more fundamental) for other types of critical study. The term *lower criticism*, though not widely used in contemporary scholarship, describes the logical relationship between textual criticism and the wider interpretive enterprise. In other words, lower criticism functions as the logical prerequisite to higher criticism in attempting to reconstruct the text that becomes the subject of investigation through the use of "higher" critical interpretive methods. In the modern period, at least up until the end of the last half of the twentieth century, these higher-critical methods were essentially confined to source, form, redaction, and tradition-history criticism. Textual criticism undergirds these diachronic[5] or historical-critical modes of interpretation with a reconstructed final form of the text. This form of the text, according to these methods, serves as a basis for exploration of a number of preliterary stages, independent sources, editorial emendations (changes), and earlier traditions to be discovered behind the text's final form. Textual criticism, in this sense, serves as a window into what is behind the text, rather than providing a methodological basis for investigating the characteristics of the final form of the text itself. By contrast, more contemporary synchronic[6] or text-focused modes of interpretation, such as literary, linguistic, canonical, rhetorical, and, to a more limited degree, social-scientific criticism, are characterized by detailed attention to the final form of the text. For most biblical scholars, this means analysis simply of the text provided by one of the popular critical editions (NA$^{27/28}$ or *UBSGNT*$^{4/5}$).

---

4. The Greek NT in current use (NA$^{27/28}$; *UBSGNT*$^{4/5}$) is an *eclectic text*. That means it does not follow a single manuscript but evaluates and selects readings from all of the ancient manuscripts.

5. *Diachronic* refers to methods that unfold through time, and are concerned with the historical development of a subject.

6. *Synchronic* refers to methods that are treated as occurring on the same temporal plane, as a cross-section of current practice and experience.

2. Textual Criticism as Tracking Textual Transmission: The Sociohistorical Model

The **sociohistorical model** of textual criticism, a fairly recent development in text-critical methodology, traces the transmission history of the
text within various scribal traditions and communities, as a means of
studying the social history of early Christianity. This method is in many
ways a reaction to Hort's view that the transmission process remained
unaffected by the theological biases of the scribes who transmitted the
text. In a frequently quoted passage, Hort suggests, "Even among the numerous unquestionably spurious readings of the New Testament there
are no signs of deliberate falsification of the text for dogmatic purposes."[7]
Although he had some significant predecessors, Eldon Epp's monograph,
The Theological Tendency of Codex Bezae Cantabrigiensis in Acts, was the
first among a series of works that seriously attempted to call these assumptions into question by bringing attention to the doctrinal tendencies
of the scribes who transmitted the Western text of Acts. The central thesis
of his work is that the Western tradition as exemplified in the fifth-century
bilingual (Greek and Latin) manuscript Codex Bezae represents a clear
anti-Judaic tendency in around 40 percent of the text's variant readings
in Acts.

A number of recent scholars have followed Epp's lead. One current
project has been initiated by Josep Rius-Camps along with Jenny Read-
Heimerdinger, who systematically assess the message of Codex Bezae in
Acts in comparison with the Alexandrian tradition.[8] While the authors
grant that the Bezan Acts text represents the ideological proclivities of
its compiler, against Epp they insist that the text reflects Jewish rather
than Gentile editorial emendations. Bart Ehrman has devoted numerous

---

7. Westcott and Hort, *Introduction,* 282. Hort continues: "The license of paraphrase
occasionally assumes the appearance of willful corruption, where scribes allowed themselves to change language which they thought capable of dangerous misconstruction; or
attempted to correct apparent errors which they doubtless assumed to be due to previous
transcription; or embodied in explicit words a meaning which they supposed to be im-
plied. . . . Accusations of willful tampering with the text are not infrequent in Christian
antiquity: but, with a single exception [Marcion], wherever they can be verified they prove
to be groundless, being in fact hasty and unjust inferences from mere diversities of inherited text" (pp. 282-83).

8. Josep Rius-Camps and Jenny Read-Heimerdinger, *The Message of Acts in Codex Bezae*
(4 vols.; LNTS 257, 302, 365, 415; London: Continuum, 2004-2009).

publications to attempting to show how ideological conflicts within early Christian communities have resulted in theologically driven alterations of the texts by the scribes transmitting them. The thesis governing Ehrman's *Orthodox Corruption of Scripture,* for example, is that "scribes occasionally altered the words of their sacred texts to make them more patently orthodox and to prevent their misuse by Christians who espoused aberrant views."[9] The underlying goal of text-critical theory and practice, according to Ehrman, should be to recover the ideological and intellectual contexts that motivated early Christian scribes to make such changes. Regarding the traditional objective of textual criticism to recover the original text, Ehrman contends that one of the most significant recent developments "has been the widespread realization that an exclusive concentration on the autographs is myopic, as it overlooks the value of variant forms of the text for historians interested in matters other than exegesis."[10] For Ehrman:

> Changes that scribes made in their texts frequently reflect their own sociohistorical contexts. By examining these changes, one can, theoretically, reconstruct the context within which they were created, contexts that are otherwise sparsely attested in our surviving sources. When viewed in this way, variant readings are not merely chaff to be discarded en route to the original text, as they were for Hort and others of his ilk; they are instead valuable evidence for the history of the early Christian movement. The New Testament manuscripts can thus serve as a window into the social world of early Christianity.[11]

This sociohistorical objective has thus become the major goal of text-critical studies for a number of scholars. In yet another example of this approach, David Parker focuses upon the various "stories" or "narratives" behind scribal alterations in Gospel texts. Parker's provocative book goes so far as to suggest that, due to varying preliterary forms and editorial stages of much early Christian literature, "there is no definitive text to be

---

9. Bart D. Ehrman, *The Orthodox Corruption of Scripture: The Effect of Early Christological Controversies on the Text of the New Testament* (Oxford: Oxford University Press, 1993), xi.

10. Bart D. Ehrman, "The Text as Window: New Testament Manuscripts and the Social History of Early Christianity," in *The Text of the New Testament in Contemporary Research: Essays on the Status Quaestionis* (2nd ed.; ed. Bart D. Ehrman and Michael W. Holmes; NTTSD 42; Leiden: Brill, 2013), 803.

11. Ibid., 804.

discovered." The goal of textual criticism, therefore, must be the transmission process itself rather than recovering the original.[12]

3. Summary

The principal objective of text-critical studies, and its traditional aim, must continue to be reconstruction of the original text of the NT documents based upon the manuscript traditions currently available. While a study of the textual transmission process and its sociohistorical contexts may provide important windows into the historical development of early Christianity, this must always remain a secondary goal. The reason for this lies in the foundational role that textual criticism plays in NT studies. Apart from a carefully constructed Greek text, there is no basis for textual interpretation. The textual critic must ascertain the text itself before the exegete can begin to interpret the meaning of that text. But a carefully reconstructed original text, or perhaps an ancient text such as Sinaiticus (see ch. 7), not only is logically prior to critical interpretation but must precede sociohistorical text-critical analysis itself. There must be a representative base text to provide a basis for assessing theologically and culturally driven scribal "alterations." These scribal changes must be considered against an original text that can serve as the basis for judging posited changes in the text under analysis. The Alexandrian tradition has commended itself to most scholars as providing the most secure platform for discussing textual variants, whether they are alterations in the Western tradition or the later Byzantine tradition (see ch. 7). Therefore, although variant readings may provide helpful and interesting insights into the social development of early Christianity, reconstructing the original text must remain the principal aim of text-critical studies. The focus of this book will be upon this traditional text-critical aim.

KEY TERMINOLOGY
Textual Criticism: Traditional Model
Textual Criticism: Sociohistorical Model
Lower Criticism
Higher Criticism

---

12. David C. Parker, *The Living Text of the Gospels* (Cambridge: Cambridge University Press, 1997), 6.

BIBLIOGRAPHY

Traditional Model

Aland, Kurt, and Barbara Aland. *The Text of the New Testament: An Introduction to the Critical Editions and to the Theory and Practice of Modern Textual Criticism.* Trans. Erroll F. Rhodes. 2nd ed. Grand Rapids: Eerdmans, 1989.

Bruce, F. F. *The New Testament Documents: Are They Reliable?* 6th ed. 1981. Repr. Downers Grove, IL: InterVarsity Press, 1988.

Colwell, E. C. *Studies in Methodology in Textual Criticism of the New Testament.* NTTS 9. Leiden: Brill, 1969.

Comfort, Philip W. *Encountering the Manuscripts: Introduction to New Testament Paleography and Textual Criticism.* Nashville: Broadman & Holman, 2005.

Comfort, Philip, and David Barrett. *The Text of the Earliest New Testament Greek Manuscripts.* Wheaton, IL: Tyndale House, 2001.

Fee, Gordon D. "Textual Criticism of the New Testament." Pages 3-16 in Eldon Jay Epp and Gordon D. Fee, *Studies in the Theory and Method of New Testament Textual Criticism.* SD 45. Grand Rapids: Eerdmans, 1993.

Greenlee, J. Harold. *Introduction to New Testament Textual Criticism.* Grand Rapids: Eerdmans, 1964.

————. *Scribes, Scrolls, and Scripture: A Student's Guide to New Testament Textual Criticism.* Grand Rapids: Eerdmans, 1985.

Griesbach, Johann Jakob. *Novum Testamentum Graece.* London: Mackinlay, et Cuthell et Martin, 1809-1810.

Lake, Kirsopp. *The Text of the New Testament.* Rev. Silva New. 6th ed. London: Rivingtons, 1928.

Metzger, Bruce M. *The Text of the New Testament: Its Transmission, Corruption, and Restoration.* 4th ed. Rev. Bart D. Ehrman. Oxford: Oxford University Press, 2005.

Petzer, J. H. "The History of the New Testament Text — Its Reconstruction, Significance and Use in New Testament Textual Criticism." Pages 11-36 in *New Testament Textual Criticism, Exegesis and Church History: A Discussion of Methods.* Ed. Barbara Aland and Joël Delobel. CBET 7. Kampen: Kok Pharos, 1994.

Porter, Stanley E. *How We Got the New Testament: Text, Transmission, Translation.* Grand Rapids: Baker, 2013.

Tischendorf, Constantine. *Novum Testamentum Graece.* 8th ed. Leipzig: Giesecke and Devrient, 1869-72.

Westcott, B. F., and F. J. A. Hort. *Introduction to the New Testament in the Original Greek with Notes on Selected Readings.* 1882. Repr. Peabody, MA: Hendrickson, 1988.

Sociohistorical Model

Bovon, François. "Fragment Oxyrhynchus 840, Fragment of a Lost Gospel, Witness of an Early Christian Controversy over Purity." *JBL* 119 (2000): 705-28.

Ehrman, Bart D. *The Orthodox Corruption of Scripture: The Effect of Early Christological Controversies on the Text of the New Testament.* Oxford: Oxford University Press, 1993.

———. *Misquoting Jesus: The Story Behind Who Changed the Bible and Why.* San Francisco: HarperSanFrancisco, 2005.

———. *Studies in the Textual Criticism of the New Testament.* NTTS 33. Leiden: Brill, 2006.

Epp, Eldon Jay. "The 'Ignorance Motif' in Acts and Anti-Judaic Tendencies in Codex Bezae." *HTR* 55 (1962): 51-62.

———. *The Theological Tendency of Codex Bezae Cantabrigiensis in Acts.* SNTSMS 3. Cambridge: Cambridge University Press, 1966.

———. "The New Testament Papyri at Oxyrhynchus in Their Social and Intellectual Context." Pages 47-68 in *Sayings of Jesus: Canonical and Non-Canonical: Essays in Honour of Tjitze Baarda.* Ed. William L. Petersen, Johann S. Vos, and H. J. de Jonge. NovTSup 89. Leiden: Brill, 1997. Repr. as pp. 497-520 in Eldon Jay Epp, *Perspectives on New Testament Textual Criticism: Collected Essays, 1962-2004.* NovTSup 116. Leiden: Brill, 2005.

———. "Anti-Judaic Tendencies in the D-Text of Acts: Forty Years of Conversation." Pages 111-46 in *The Book of Acts as Church History: Text, Textual Traditions and Ancient Interpretations.* Ed. Tobias Nicklas and Michael Tilly. BZNW 120. Berlin: de Gruyter, 2003.

Parker, David C. *The Living Text of the Gospels.* Cambridge: Cambridge University Press, 1997.

Rius-Camps, Josep, and Jenny Read-Heimerdinger. *The Message of Acts in Codex Bezae.* 4 vols. LNTS 257, 302, 365, 415. London: Continuum, 2004-2009.

CHAPTER 2

Canon: The Domain of New Testament Textual Criticism

The *domain* of NT textual criticism must be established before we can undertake the *task* of NT textual criticism. Therefore, it is necessary to determine the proper domain of the discipline, that is, to determine the works that constitute the NT and how they came to be considered part of this body of writings. Determination of the books within the domain of textual criticism is directly related to the issue of the NT **canon**. The canon can be defined as the body of writings that came to be recognized by the early church as authoritative in matters of doctrine and liturgical practice (this definition is clarified and defended in section 3 of this chapter). These canonical books can be distinguished from other writings that were only *useful* for or supplementary to these purposes (such as the *Didache*, an early worship manual). The term canon comes from the Greek word κανών, which originally referred to a rod or measure or list, but which, by at least the fourth century, was used metaphorically by Christians to denote the collection of writings that were considered to be inspired Scripture[1] (but see below). The process whereby these works were chosen to be part of the canon is often referred to as **canonization**.

In this chapter, we shall see that, in addition to the canon providing a foundation for textual criticism, the canon is also informed by textual criticism, since much of the early evidence for the Christian canon is derived from an analysis of early manuscripts and their contents.

---

1. This distinction is sometimes referred to as *norma normata* ("the rule that is ruled," i.e., by Scripture). The canonized Scriptures, by contrast, are referred to as *norma normans* ("the rule that rules").

1. Evidence for an Early Canon:
The New Testament Canon in the First Three Centuries

There are essentially two views concerning the formation of the NT canon. The first view, espoused by both older and more recent scholars, asserts that, in response to Marcion and the Montanists (see below), the NT canon emerged quickly under the leadership of the church of Rome during the second half of the second century A.D. This view became an established consensus in NT scholarship that held until relatively recently. The second view, adopted by a number of contemporary scholars, insists that the decisive period in the canonization of the NT was not the second century but the fourth and fifth centuries, when the canonical councils convened.

Two types of evidence are usually weighed in assessing the existence of a canon in the first few centuries of Christianity: (1) manuscript evidence and (2) ancient canonical lists. In this chapter we argue for the traditional view, insisting that these two categories of evidence support an early development for the NT canon in the second and third centuries, which was affirmed by the councils of the fourth century.

a. Evidence from the New Testament: Canon in the First Century

Were Paul and the other NT authors aware that they were writing Scripture? In other words, did Paul and the other writers have what has been called a **canonical awareness** (i.e., knowledge that they were writing what would be recognized as canonical material)? Did they think that their narratives and letters would one day be collected and made into a multiauthored work that we call the NT? It is highly unlikely that these early authors held to such a developed view of the canon. However, this does not mean that Paul and the other NT writers were oblivious to the fact that they were writing divinely inspired authoritative literature. Let us consider some examples from Paul's Letters. In Gal 1:12 Paul claims that he received his gospel through a revelation of Jesus Christ (cf. also Gal 1:1, 11). Romans 16:25-27 indicates that Paul thought of his entire letter on the same level as Old Testament (henceforth OT) prophetic writings.[2] In 1 Cor

---

2. Some debate the status of Rom 16:25-27 within the history of the transmission of the text of Romans, although most recent scholarship endorses its (Pauline) authenticity. See

7:25 Paul temporarily steps outside his apostolic authority, saying that the Lord is not commanding the Corinthians on this point, but that he is. Later he states clearly, in a discussion of spiritual gifts, that "the things that I am writing to you are a command from the Lord" (1 Cor 14:37). In 1 Thess 2:13 Paul equates his message with the word of God rather than with a human word. Paul's command in Col 4:16 for the Colossian letter to be read among the Laodiceans indicates that he intended his letter for a wider audience than those strictly addressed within the letter. Others within the early church appear to have had this same conception. For example, 2 Pet 3:16 speaks of a group of Pauline letters (plural) that people were finding hard to understand, just like the "other scriptures." The singular form of the same word that is used for "scriptures" here (γραφή) is used in 2 Pet 1:20 to describe OT prophetic writings. While Paul may not have had the entire result of the canonical process within his purview, he certainly seemed aware — as was Peter — that he was producing documents that the early church received as authoritative, inspired writings, worthy of being collected and used in the church.

The Gospels and the book of Revelation were written in different literary contexts than the Epistles, but they are similar in that they record the words of Jesus, the figure from whom the apostles derive their authority. In their recording of Jesus' words, the authors indicate that they are recording the words of a divinely inspired and uniquely authoritative person. Matthew records Jesus' words of commissioning (28:16-20), including his call to make disciples, as an authoritative message both for Matthew's original audience and for the church. John records the commission of the early followers of Jesus to be led by and to communicate the message of the Holy Spirit (John 14 and 16). The book of Revelation is even more direct than the Gospels, since it records a firsthand account of a revelation of the risen Jesus Christ.

In other words, a number of the canonical authors of the first century — including at least Paul; the authors of the Gospels; Peter; and John, the author of Revelation — seem to perceive of their writings as Scripture, that is, as conveying the authority of Jesus Christ and as an extension of OT revelation, even if it is unlikely that they viewed their writings as part of a complete body of literature that we now call the NT.

Harry Y. Gamble, *The Textual History of the Letter to the Romans: A Study in Textual and Literary Criticism* (SD 42; Grand Rapids: Eerdmans, 1977).

b. Early Collections and the Formation of the Canon

The evidence of an early formation of the NT canon is attested in a range of early church testimony. A collection of thirteen Pauline letters, the four Gospels, and Acts, as well as a few other apostolic letters, is confirmed by some of the earliest church fathers. A view held by many earlier scholars suggests that these pronouncements regarding the NT writings by the early fathers were a direct response to the views of the second-century teacher **Marcion** (A.D. 140). Marcion believed that the God of Jesus was distinct from the OT God of judgment, making the OT obsolete for Christians and therefore noncanonical. Marcion also believed that there should only be one authoritative Gospel, Luke, and only one set of letters, those of Paul (excluding 1-2 Timothy and Titus). The **Marcionite canon**, then, included only Luke's Gospel and ten Pauline letters. This view is not held as widely today, because it is more likely that, instead of the early fathers reacting to Marcion, who was the first to form a canon, Marcion was reacting to an established canon of Christian writings. In modern scholarship this idea goes back at least as far as the nineteenth- and early-twentieth-century scholar Theodor Zahn, and has been advocated by Adolf Harnack and a number of recent scholars as well (e.g., T. C. Skeat, Graham Stanton, T. K. Heckel, and Martin Hengel).

The mainstream view of the establishment of the NT canon during the second or (even) first century is supported to varying degrees by at least five of the early church fathers: (1) Tatian (A.D. 110-180), (2) **Justin Martyr** (A.D. 100-165), (3) **Irenaeus** (second and third centuries A.D.), (4) **Clement of Alexandria** (A.D. 150-215), and (5) **Tertullian** (A.D. 160-225). Tatian's *Diatessaron* (ca. A.D. 170; see ch. 4 below) was a harmony of the four now-canonical Gospels and predates virtually all of the earliest manuscripts of the NT that we currently possess, including the major codices.[3] That the four canonical Gospels were used as the basis for the harmony indicates an early authoritative reception of this collection. Justin Martyr refers to the singular *Gospel* (*Dial.* 10.2; 100.1) and to the plural *Gospels* (*1 Apol.* 66), which may indicate that he had the four canonical Gospels in mind, but this is by no means certain. More suggestive is that he refers to "memoirs" (*Dial.* 106.3) composed by the apostles and those who followed, which probably refers to the two Gospels written by the

---

3. The codex was an early book form, made from folded pages bound together. The early Christians were instrumental in the development and widespread use of the codex.

apostles, Matthew and John, and the two that were written by those who followed them (Luke and Mark).

Around A.D. 180 Irenaeus argued at length for the four canonical Gospels and no more. Skeat has plausibly suggested that his argument is based on an earlier tradition of argumentation for a four-Gospel collection based in Ezek 1:1-21 and the Apocalypse.[4] F. F. Bruce thinks that the analogy that Irenaeus uses regarding the four winds and the four Gospels indicates how widespread their use and acceptance was; that is, they were like natural phenomena in their pervasiveness.[5] In addition to his references to the Gospels, Irenaeus calls the following works "Scripture": "Acts and the thirteen letters of Paul." However, while "1 Peter and the two Johannine letters (1 and 2) are appraised like the Pauline letters . . . James and Hebrews are probably not so highly esteemed" (*Haer.* 1.9.4; cf. 2.26.1-2; 3.1.1).

Clement of Alexandria refers directly to "four Gospels" (*Strom.* 3.91). He understands Hebrews to be written by Paul in Hebrew for the Jews, but later translated into Greek by Luke for use in Greek communities (Eusebius, *Hist. eccl.* 6.14.1-3). So he affirms fourteen Pauline letters and cites 1 Peter, 1-2 John, Jude, and Revelation as Scripture.

While Clement cites other early Christian documents in support of his ideas as well, including noncanonical Gospels, Hengel is correct when he observes that (citing Clement), "the New Testament, Gospels and apostolic writings, is the 'supreme authority.'"[6] For Clement, in terms of authority, it is "the four Gospels that have been handed down to us" (*Strom.* 3.13.93).

Tertullian, often deemed the father of Latin theology, draws a distinction between the Gospels written by apostles and those written by the disciples of the apostles: "Of the apostles, therefore, John and Matthew first instil faith into us; whilst of apostolic men, Luke and Mark renew it afterwards" (*Marc.* 4.2.2). Tertullian refers to the four Gospels, Acts, thirteen Pauline letters, 1 John, 1 Peter, Jude, and Revelation as an "entire" authoritative "volume" (*Praescr.* 32).

Adducing from these second-century authors a mainstream view that has its origins in an earlier period is a methodological principle first employed by Zahn that scholars such as Graham Stanton and Peter Balla con-

---

4. T. C. Skeat, "Irenaeus and the Four-Gospel Canon," *NovT* 34 (1992): 194-99.

5. F. F. Bruce, *The Canon of Scripture* (Downers Grove: InterVarsity, 1988), 175.

6. Martin Hengel, *The Four Gospels and the One Gospel of Jesus Christ: An Investigation of the Collection and Origin of the Canonical Gospels* (trans. John Bowden; Harrisburg: Trinity Press International, 2000), 15-16.

tinue to use. This principle essentially involves working "back from the full flowering of a concept or a development to its earlier roots."[7] Thus, according to Balla, "If we find no sign of a major change in the view of the church reflected in the previous sources, it can be argued that the situation clearly expressed around 180 C.E. by Irenaeus applies to earlier decades as well."[8]

This basic picture from the church fathers of an early canon consisting of at least four Gospels and Acts plus thirteen or fourteen Pauline letters is confirmed by the manuscript evidence. Although Paul may not have located his writings within the larger canonical development of the post-apostolic church, there is good evidence that he and/or his close associates may have been involved in collecting his letters, resulting in the formation of a Pauline canon within the first century. $\mathfrak{P}^{46}$, a significant papyrus manuscript (dated A.D. 180-200), provides support for this thesis, as the manuscript contains Hebrews and all of the letters attributed to Paul in the NT, with the exception of 2 Thessalonians, the Pastorals, and Philemon. This provides clear evidence that a Pauline canon was in existence by the end of the second century. The most likely way to account for this is to posit some type of systematized collecting of these letters within the first century. The most likely candidates for undertaking this collection process would have been either Paul himself or his close traveling companions, which would have included secretaries, fellow missionaries, and church planters. With this portrayal of the formation of the Pauline canon, Paul composed his mix of personal and ecclesial letters, during the course of his several missionary journeys. For each of them he used scribes, and for many if not most of them he made copies, according to the letter-writing customs of the time. These copies were kept in the possession of either Paul or his companions, which often meant the same thing, as they traveled together. Regardless of where he wrote his prison letters, eventually Paul was imprisoned in Rome. This means that Paul and his closest companions may have been directly responsible for collecting together his letters — not as an afterthought by means of someone visiting all of the various cities and gathering the letters together (and hence running the risk of certain ones being lost), but by virtue of their having copies of the letters in their possession. In essence, this means that the collection of Paul's letters also seems

---

7. Graham N. Stanton, "The Fourfold Gospel," *NTS* 43 (1997): 318. See also idem, *Jesus and Gospel* (Cambridge: Cambridge University Press, 2004), 77-79.

8. Peter Balla, "Evidence for an Early Christian Canon (Second and Third Century)," in *The Canon Debate* (ed. Lee Martin McDonald and James A. Sanders; Peabody, MA: Hendrickson, 2002), 380.

to imply the publication of his letters, as they were made more widely known first perhaps by Paul and then by successive generations of Paul's followers. One might expect on this basis to have all of the letters that Paul is reported to have written, including other letters to the Corinthians and to the Laodiceans (but it is possible that the letter to the Laodiceans is the Letter to the Ephesians). It is not certain why these letters are missing, unless they simply were not copied originally (perhaps because the letter to the Corinthians [cf. 2 Cor 2:4] was so severe) or were themselves lost in the course of Paul's travels, which included shipwrecks.

The question remains as to why the Pastorals and Philemon were not included in the papyrus manuscript $\mathfrak{P}^{46}$. Were these books not included in the early Pauline canon? Did the early church understand them to be **pseudepigraphal** (written in an author's name [Paul in this case] by another author)? A few considerations help clarify this question. To begin with, the entire original document is not preserved in what remains in $\mathfrak{P}^{46}$. The manuscript begins in Romans 5 and breaks off in 1 Thessalonians. Some scholars have argued, based upon the size of the script and the anticipated size of the codex, that these letters were probably not included in the original form.

Two proposals provide plausible explanations of this situation. First, according to Jeremy Duff, we must keep in mind that toward the end of the papyrus the size of the script is reduced, apparently in hopes of conserving space. He insists that this may indicate that the author realized that he was running out of space and that he wrote with smaller letters so that the missing Pauline letters could be included in the manuscript (if the author ran out, he could also add a sheet or more).[9] Second, according to Jerome Quinn, while some scholars attribute the exclusion of the Pastorals from $\mathfrak{P}^{46}$ to an early recognition within the church that these letters were pseudonymous, this still would not explain the exclusion here of Philemon, which was generally accepted as being Pauline. Quinn suggests that the most likely explanation is that $\mathfrak{P}^{46}$ represents one of two collections of the Pauline literature that circulated in the early church: (1) the letters addressed to the churches **(ecclesial letters)** and (2) the letters addressed to individuals **(personal letters)**. He offers the following evidence in support of this division: (a) The papyrus $\mathfrak{P}^{32}$ is a fragment of Titus dated no later than A.D. 200 that originally contained

---

9. Jeremy Duff, "P46 and the Pastorals: A Misleading Consensus?" *NTS* 44 (1998): 578-90.

more than Titus, but there is no way to know which letters, showing at the very least that a collection including Titus was in circulation before the turn of the second century; (b) around the same time, Tertullian responds to Marcion's exclusion of the Pastorals, referring to an apparently well-known distinction between ecclesial and personal Pauline letters (*Marc.* 21); and (c) the Muratorian fragment (see below) maintains a distinction between ecclesial and personal letters. There were, then, three collections of Pauline literature circulating in the early church: (1) a collection of personal letters, (2) a collection of ecclesial letters, and (3) a Marcionite collection with ten Pauline letters (excluding the Pastorals). The reason the Marcionite canon was inevitably rejected by Tertullian and the early church is that the received thirteen-letter collection and the four Gospels and Acts were in circulation prior to it. And Tertullian's point against Marcion was that he was inconsistent in including Philemon in his collection, but not the Pastorals, since he arbitrarily selects one letter from the collection of personal letters. So if $\mathfrak{P}^{46}$ did not originally include the Pastorals and Philemon, the reason may well be found in the fact that these letters were personal letters and the intention of the scribe was to put together a collection of ecclesial letters.[10]

Because of Paul's firsthand involvement with his letters and their collection, Paul's letter collection was probably formed first, so it is not surprising that some of the earliest evidence for a canon is a canon of Pauline literature. However, we also have evidence of a collection of the canonical Gospels and Acts shortly thereafter in the papyrus manuscript $\mathfrak{P}^{45}$ (early third century), which contains portions of all four Gospels and Acts. It is not hard to envision how the Gospels and Acts could have been formed in a way similar to the formation of the Pauline corpus. If Luke kept copies of his works (the Gospel and Acts) and apparently had a copy of Mark, then only copies of John and Matthew would need to be added to the collection as it circulated within the early church. There is evidence of the gathering of such collections in the first two centuries. $\mathfrak{P}^{4}$ is a fragmentary papyrus of Luke, $\mathfrak{P}^{64}$ is a fragmentary papyrus of Matthew, and $\mathfrak{P}^{67}$ is a fragmentary papyrus of Matthew. At first considered three separate manuscripts, their similarities in paleographical characteristics and provenance (origin) have led a number of scholars to believe that they came from the same Gospel manuscript, copied around A.D. 150-175. It seems that this manuscript apparently contained at least two of the Gospels in circulation together. $\mathfrak{P}^{75}$,

10. Jerome D. Quinn, "P46 — The Pauline Canon," *CBQ* 36 (1974): 379-85.

which contains parts of Luke and John and is dated to the late second or early third century, has the Gospel title at the end of Luke's Gospel and at the beginning of John's Gospel, back to back. It is possible that just these two Gospels circulated together, although the use of the titles indicates that probably all four of the Gospels were included.[11] As Eldon Epp notes, referring to the work of T. C. Skeat, "plausible arguments have been made that both $\mathfrak{P}^{64}$ + $\mathfrak{P}^{67}$ + $\mathfrak{P}^{4}$ [A.D. 150-157] and $\mathfrak{P}^{75}$ [late second or early third century] are parts of original fourfold Gospel manuscripts."[12] The Gospel titles are important in this discussion. Hengel argues that the titles ("The Gospel according to X") must have been inserted at an early date in order to distinguish the Gospels from one another in the liturgical libraries and archives of early church communities.[13] These titles, then, provide evidence for early liturgical use of multiple canonical Gospels. Through this usage these Gospels gained authority and value as they were used individually within various churches. Finally, with the invention of the codex, they began to circulate in collections of two and three during the early second century until by the mid-second century all four Gospels had begun to circulate together, resulting in a manuscript like $\mathfrak{P}^{45}$.

So it seems quite likely, based upon the evidence from the early church fathers and manuscripts, that by the second century there was something like a recognized canon(s) of authoritative Christian writings. This is not to say that all of the now canonical writings were bound into the same volume by this time or even viewed directly in relation to one another. Lack of circulation of all of the literature in all parts of the ancient world certainly would have prevented this. Instead, during this early period, Christians would probably have thought of their sacred writings in terms of canons associated with particular authors and/or content. We see that 2 Peter's community apparently had access to a collection

11. The presumption is that the titles, probably at the beginning and end of each Gospel, indicate more than simply the two Gospels. With John included, there is strong evidence that the manuscript originally included all four Gospels, rather than, for example, just the Synoptics.

12. Eldon Jay Epp, "Issues in the Interrelation of New Testament Textual Criticism and Canon," in *Canon Debate*, ed. McDonald and Sanders, 489. There have been questions raised by Martin Hengel, for example ("The Titles of the Gospels and the Gospel of Mark," in *Studies in the Gospel of Mark* [London: SCM, 1985], 66), whether $\mathfrak{P}^{64}$, $\mathfrak{P}^{67}$, and $\mathfrak{P}^{4}$ belong to the same manuscript due to the physical features of the papyrus. However, these arguments are not decisive, and have been questioned by Stanley E. Porter, *How We Got the New Testament: Text, Transmission, Translation* (Grand Rapids: Baker, 2013), 95-99.

13. Hengel, "Titles," 64-84.

of Paul's writings, as did a number of others, and people were having a difficult time understanding them (2 Pet 3:16). Paul's literature was also apparently being circulated and copied (Col 4:16). There was probably, then, something like a Pauline canon at a very early stage. The earliest Gospels (Mark and Matthew) would have provided the first written records of Jesus, followed closely by Luke and then John. Acts was naturally associated with the Gospel of Luke, as Luke was the author of both (although Acts originally circulated independently, often with the Catholic Letters, i.e., James, 1-2 Peter, 1-3 John, and/or Jude), until ultimately this collection of writings was viewed as the authoritative apostolic deposit of Jesus tradition. Early in this process, Christians may have viewed one or two of these Gospels together until all four of the Gospels plus Acts came into wide circulation, as we have in $\mathfrak{P}^{45}$.

Within this canon, however, an assumed canonical framework seems to have been in place, where collections of apostolic writings were collected on the one hand and collections of Gospel writings composed by apostolic witnesses (to the work of the apostles) were collected on the other. The writers of these documents appear to have perceived their literature as an extension of the OT revelation, and those in the early church appear to have viewed them with the same authority.[14]

François Bovon argues that such an early canon was a natural consequence of the twofold pattern of the literature of the NT itself. He suggests that there is a **Gospel and apostle structure** — a twofold canonical structure consisting of the story of the message and mission of Jesus (Gospels) told and interpreted by his commissioned disciples (apostles) — to the literature of the NT that provided an intrinsic framework that naturally led to the emergence of the canon within the second century. Paul's commission was apparently viewed as a revelation from Jesus Christ (the *gospel*) to proclaim him among the Gentiles (Gal 1:15-16) (*apostolic* commission). The Johannine tradition (literature ascribed to the apostle John) is similar, with the Gospel emphasizing the Word in its prologue and 1 John adding to this the apostolic witness. Jesus' commission of the disciples and promise of the Holy Spirit as their teacher in John 14 and 16 supports this. The book of Revelation combines both elements in its introduction, focusing upon

---

14. There definitely was discussion over a few books (most notably Hebrews, 2 Peter, James, and Revelation), but the issue here was whether they really were an extension of the apostolic tradition or whether they were pseudonymous, not whether such a question was appropriate.

the revelation to John to be shared with Jesus' other servants. We also see the Gospel-apostle pattern in the structure of Luke-Acts, where we have a Gospel account followed by a record of the early apostolic ministry. The Gospels themselves favor this structure too, including pre- and post-Easter narrative accounts, providing information about Jesus' message and ministry, but also describing the apostolic commissioning. The apostolic fathers and early apologists (defenders of the faith) apparently grasped this structure and began bringing the various currents of early Christian tradition into more comprehensive collections. As Bovon states:

> the Gospel-Apostle structure, manifest from the first generation of Christians, prepares the way for the formation of a new body of scriptures as a complement or counterpart to the holy scriptures (the Septuagint) inherited by the church. The formation of a New Testament canon was therefore the logical materialization of this theological structure. The presence of the Gospel-Apostle pair during the time of the Apostolic Fathers and the apologists assured the transition from the parameters set by Paul, Luke, and John to the witnesses to the New Testament from the time of Irenaeus of Lyon and beyond.[15]

For example, Tertullian acknowledges the importance of this connection when he says (already quoted above): "Of the apostles, therefore, John and Matthew first instil faith into us; whilst of apostolic men, Luke and Mark renew it afterwards" (*Marc.* 4.2.2). He makes this connection more explicit in another writing where he divides the NT into "Gospels" and "the Apostles" (*Prax.* 15). Eusebius's (see below) account of Papias, bishop of Hierapolis in the early second century, already sees a need to connect Mark directly with the apostolic tradition (*Hist. eccl.* 3.39.15-16):

> And the presbyter used to say this: Mark became Peter's interpreter and wrote accurately all that he remembered, not indeed in order, of the things said or done by the Lord. For he had not heard the Lord, nor had he followed him, but later on, as I said, followed Peter, who used to give teaching as necessity demanded, but not making, as it were, an arrangement of the Lord's sayings, so that Mark did nothing wrong in thus writing down single points as he remembered them. For to one

---

15. François Bovon, "The Canonical Structure of Gospel and Apostle," in *Canon Debate,* ed. McDonald and Sanders, 522.

thing he gave attention, to leave nothing of what he had heard and to make no false statements in them.

This only leaves Luke and Hebrews. Bovon rightly places Luke with the Pauline school, but Hebrews is admittedly more difficult according to the criterion of strict apostolicity due to the uncertainty of its authorship. Nevertheless, its inclusion in $\mathfrak{P}^{46}$ among the Pauline Letters (after Romans and before 1 Corinthians) and the views of several early fathers that the document was composed by Paul or directly conveys Paul's thinking (e.g., transmitted by Luke) indicate that it was viewed, at least among particular sectors of the early church, as a Pauline document. This would have satisfied the apostolic criterion for canonicity and therefore allowed for its inclusion within the canon.

According to this hypothesis, the canon was not the result of pressures from Marcion or from other possible early influences such as Gnosticism (an early heresy emphasizing special knowledge and animism) or Montanism (an early prophetic movement), as some have assumed. As with Marcion, it appears that Gnosticism was a reaction to the writings of our NT canon, rather than a force that precipitated the formation of the canon.[16] There is even less known of Montanism, but it too appears to have been a reaction to the NT, in particular John's Gospel. Although these influences probably helped shape and speed up the process of generating official ecumenical statements on the nature and boundaries of the canon, the canon had begun to form much earlier within early Christian communities as the result of the literature's intrinsic structure, message, and authorship. These qualities caused the literature that later came to be pronounced as canonical to be grouped together in the minds of early Christians and therefore led them to collect it into multibook works at a fairly early stage within the development of early Christianity. This purpose and presupposition was greatly facilitated by the invention of the codex (see ch. 3), a book form (i.e., not a scroll) that allowed early Christians to assemble their sacred literature into appropriate collections, as we have evidenced within the second- and third-century papyri.

16. John's Gospel is often seen as being a reaction to Gnosticism. However, Charles E. Hill, *The Johannine Corpus in the Early Church* (Oxford: Oxford University Press, 2006), 205-93, has shown that John's Gospel was not a work in explicit or special dialogue with Gnosticism.

c. Ancient Canonical Lists

In addition to evidence from the NT itself, the early church fathers, and manuscript evidence from early papyrological collections of NT literature, the development of a stable canon — including the Pauline Letters, all four Gospels and Acts, and some of the Catholic Letters, with Revelation, James, and 2 Peter accepted by some — in the early second century is supported by ancient canonical lists. These lists correspond closely to the canon that was recognized in the fourth and fifth centuries by the official councils.

1. Muratorian Fragment

The **Muratorian Fragment**, discovered by Antonio Muratori in Milan, is a seventh- to eighth-century ancient canonical list, written in Latin, that includes all of the books of the NT, except Hebrews, James, and the Petrine Letters. It also explicitly dismisses other noncanonical books such as the *Shepherd of Hermas*. Although the possibility that Hebrews and James were originally included must be left open due to its fragmentary state, it is hard to see how they would have fit before the discussion, which begins with the four Gospels, or after it, since it ends with a discussion of non-canonical works. But the inclusion of Jude does seem to suggest that these documents may have been included within the fragment in an earlier form or at an earlier stage in the history of its transmission. At most, their exclusion is inconclusive. Scholars have traditionally maintained that this fragment provides the earliest list of canonical writings among early Eastern Christians, dating the fragment in the late second century (A.D. 180-200), but recently this view has been called into question. Scholars like Albert Sundberg and Geoffrey Hahneman argue for a late-fourth-century date.[17]

The strongest traditional arguments for a second-century date include the remark within the fragment that the *Shepherd of Hermas* (A.D. 100-145) was written "very recently, in our times" (lines 73-74), and that Pius is said to be bishop of Rome (line 75), which would seem to place the document no later than A.D. 200. Graham Stanton has put forward a number of argu-

---

17. Albert Sundberg Jr., "Canon Muratori: A Fourth-Century List," *HTR* 66 (1973): 1-41; Geoffrey Mark Hahneman, *The Muratorian Fragment and the Development of the Canon* (Oxford Theological Monographs; Oxford: Clarendon, 1992).

ments as well.[18] He shows that the Gospels are entitled using the second-century nomenclature similar to that of Irenaeus (e.g., "fourth of the Gospels"). He also notes that the relatively extensive discussion of John's Gospel would be expected in the second century, because of attacks on Johannine authorship from the Alogi,[19] but not in the fourth century, when the Gospel's authorship was not questioned. The primary contribution of Stanton's study, however, is in illustrating the literary differences between this list and those from councils in the fourth century. Other arguments, such as Roman catchwords and the exclusion of Hebrews and James, are also marshaled in favor of an early date, but these are not as convincing. Collectively, however, these arguments provide a strong cumulative case for the early date of the fragment.

There have, nevertheless, been responses to these suggestions and arguments put forward in favor of a fourth-century date. Lee McDonald summarizes nine such arguments.[20] First, he claims that such canonical lists were not present in the second century and the books mentioned were not yet included in the canon. This argument amounts to begging the question, by assuming a priori that such phenomena were not happening in the second century. This kind of strategy assumes without proof precisely what is under debate — whether the Muratorian Fragment is such a document. It is argued that we have no other parallels, but even in the fourth century we only have a few ecumenical lists, resulting from actual councils, although other lists are represented within diverse contexts (e.g., festal letters). Even if the basic argument here is granted — that ecumenical lists or catalogues were not a second-century phenomenon — we might still distinguish between "catalogues proper" that simply list authoritative literature and works that discuss why certain literature is accepted as authoritative. While it may be granted that the former category is limited to the fourth century, there is nothing to suggest that the latter type of catalogue did not emerge in the second century, as Peter Balla notes.[21]

Second, McDonald suggests that the date must be fourth century since the Gospels were not defended, as we find in Irenaeus. But what we have

18. Stanton, "Fourfold Gospel," 317-46.

19. The Alogi were a late-second-century A.D. heretical group in Asia Minor, attacked by Epiphanius, who accused them of being illogical and against the Logos (both plays on the term *Alogi*).

20. Lee Martin McDonald, *The Biblical Canon: Its Origin, Transmission, and Authority* (Peabody, MA: Hendrickson, 2007), 173-79.

21. Balla, "Evidence," 372-85.

in Irenaeus and other early apologists is precisely that, a defense, whereas the Muratorian Fragment appears to be no more than a simple statement of what was and was not received during the time that it was written.

Third, the Wisdom of Solomon is mentioned in the Muratorian Fragment, which mention has parallels only in the fourth century. This also begs the question since the claim is that the fragment represents precisely this phenomenon within the second century. The Wisdom of Solomon is referred to by second-century fathers such as Clement and Tertullian, in any case.

Fourth, the other two writings, *De Abraam* and *Expositio fidei catholice,* found with the Muratorian Fragment in the larger codex of which it is a part (the collection as a whole is known as Codex Muratori), date to the fourth century. However, it was not uncommon for codices to include documents that span more than one time period. Codex Sinaiticus, for example, has a great deal of diversity in terms of the dates of the documents found within the collection, since it includes the LXX, the NT, the *Epistle of Barnabas,* and the *Shepherd of Hermas.*

Fifth, it is suggested that the Latin style of the document is from the fourth rather than the second century. However, the Latin of the fragment is very poor, and has suffered from poor transcriptional practices.

Sixth, the Latin phrase *urbs Roma* (line 76), referring to the city of Rome, is said to be more common in the West. However, the language is represented in both the East and the West, so this point does not factor into the debate.

Seventh, the exclusion of Hebrews and James is not a strong argument for an Eastern origin, which we grant, or for a late date.

Eighth, the exclusion of Hebrews, James, and the Petrine Letters is odd in light of the inclusion of Jude and the rejection of other writings. This is indeed a mystery for an early or (perhaps more so) late date for the fragment and is, in any case, inconclusive evidence.

Ninth, finally, the statement, "very recently, in our times," requires too late a date for the *Shepherd of Hermas.* It was probably composed in the early second century, rather than the late second century when the fragment is said to have been written, and its exclusion from the canon must be a fourth-century development, since several early writers held it in high esteem. There is no serious obstacle to the writers cited as referring to the *Shepherd,* like Clement of Alexandria and Irenaeus, having access to this work, if we keep the traditional date of composition around A.D. 150. Regarding the rejection of the *Shepherd* as canonical, only Irenaeus explicitly refers to the work as "Scripture." It is by no means established that the second-century church held this work to be Scripture, even if they held it in high regard, as does the Muratorian Fragment, stating that it "ought indeed to be read" (line 77), just not among the prophets and apostles (lines 79-80).

So the arguments for a late date for the Muratorian Fragment are decidedly lacking, and usually end up begging the question at issue. The evidence for an early date remains persuasive.

What implications, then, does this second-century fragment have for tracing the development of the NT canon? As mentioned above, although certain modern canonical books are excluded, it is hard to tell whether their mention was lost within the history of textual transmission or through damage to the manuscript. The books that are included and excluded, however, are significant since the fragment evidences the reception of most of the NT canon within the late second century in the form of an actual discussion of received material. The mention of the "Wisdom of Solomon, composed by Solomon's colleagues," is an oddity but could easily refer to Proverbs. And the fragment does seem to confirm that a very similar group of documents, later approved in the fourth century, was already being received and used within the second century. That the *Shepherd of Hermas* is excluded, but read, offers further insight into early thinking on this document as well.

2. Eusebius

Eusebius, bishop of Caesarea in Palestine (A.D. 265-340) and a fourth-century church historian with a keen interest in documenting the development of the NT canon, discusses the positions of a number of the early church fathers on the status of scriptural books, often recording their views in the form of lists. Some scholars suggest that Eusebius frames his discussion with these lists to promote his interest in establishing an authoritative catalogue of Scripture. However, there is little reason to doubt that Eusebius did his best to document the views of the early church fathers, primarily in the interest of preserving the history of debate, rather than in an attempt to advance his own personal agenda.

In his *Ecclesiastical History,* written around A.D. 325, Eusebius (*Hist. eccl.* 6.14.5-7) records Clement of Alexandria's acceptance of four Gospels. The first ones written were those with genealogies. Then Peter's preaching in Rome was recorded by Mark as the third Gospel, and John was written last.

According to Eusebius, Origen (A.D. 185-254) distinguished between three groups of authoritative Christian writings: (1) **homologoumena** (writings that were generally acknowledged), (2) **amphiballomena** (writings that were doubted in certain parts of the church), and (3) **pseudē** (false writings that were composed by heretics). Origen, according to Eusebius's account, acknowledged in the first category an unspecified number of Pauline letters (more than likely the thirteen), as well as the four Gospels, Acts, Revelation, a short letter by John, and Hebrews, for which authorship is unknown. Both 2 and 3 John and 2 Peter fall within the second category. Our canon consists of the writings from Origen's first and second lists. Some scholars think that Eusebius is imposing his own fourth-century categories upon Origen at this point, but this is unlikely since Eusebius's own list employs different categories for classifying canonical material (*Hist. eccl.* 3.25). He distinguishes between (1) *homologoumenoi* (acknowledged works), (2) *antilegomenoi* (disputed books), and (3) spurious works. In the first category Eusebius includes the four Gospels, Acts, the thirteen Pauline letters (and Hebrews as a fourteenth, it seems), 1 John, 1 Peter, and perhaps the Revelation of John. In the second category he includes James, Jude, 2 Peter, and 2 and 3 John. The third category includes *Acts of Paul,* "the so-called" *Shepherd* [*of Hermas*], *Apocalypse of Peter, Epistle of Barnabas, Teachings of the Apostles* [*Didache*], and perhaps the Revelation of John.

2. The New Testament Canon in the Fourth and Fifth Centuries: Ecumenical Catalogues, Councils, and Codices

The fourth and fifth centuries of canonical development are characterized primarily by the attention of the church councils to discussing the nature and boundaries of the canon, composing lists of authoritative (i.e., canonical) material, and collecting this material into bound volumes (codices). The following are some of the more significant fourth- and fifth-century catalogues, councils, and codices that have relevance for understanding the NT canon.

a. Catalogue in Codex Claromontanus

Second only to the catalogue of canonical works listed in Eusebius's *Ecclesiastical History* (A.D. 325) (discussed at the end of the previous section), the catalogue contained in **Codex Claromontanus,** a bilingual Greek-Latin manuscript dating to the sixth century, is one of the earliest fourth-century canonical lists, preserving a document dating somewhere between A.D. 303 and 367. This list includes the four Gospels, ten letters of Paul (omitting 1-2 Thessalonians and Philippians), the seven Catholic Letters, Revelation, and a number of pseudepigraphal works (which are all marked, incidentally — probably indicating either doubt or the belief that these works were not authoritatively equal with the others).

b. Cheltenham List (Mommsen Catalogue)

Originating in North Africa around A.D. 360, the **Cheltenham List** was discovered by the great German classical scholar Theodor Mommsen in 1885 and therefore is sometimes referred to by scholars as the **Mommsen Catalogue.** It introduces its list with a quotation from Rev 4:10 about the twenty-four elders and, on the basis of allegorical interpretation, goes on to conclude that there are therefore twenty-four pieces of inspired literature: four Gospels, Acts, thirteen Pauline letters, three letters of John, two letters of Peter, and Revelation.

c. Epiphanius

In a treatise against heresies, **Epiphanius** of Salamis in Cyprus provides a list of canonical works (A.D. 374-377). Among the accepted NT writings, he includes the four Gospels, fourteen Pauline letters (including Hebrews), Acts, the Catholic Letters (James, 1-3 John, Peter, and Jude), and Revelation. Curiously, he also includes the Wisdom of Solomon and Ben Sira among the books of the NT.

d. Cyril, Gregory, and Amphilochius

Three lists were composed in a relatively brief time period, all between around A.D. 350 and 380. **Cyril of Jerusalem** (A.D. 350) produced a list of "divinely inspired Scriptures" in one of his catechetical lectures, which includes four Gospels (denouncing the Manichaean *Gospel of Thomas*), Acts, the seven Catholic Letters (James, 1-2 Peter, 1-3 John, and Jude), as well as fourteen Pauline letters (including Hebrews). A little later **Gregory** of Nazianzus (A.D. 380) produced a list of the books of the Christian Bible in verse for aid in memorization. His NT includes four Gospels, fourteen Pauline letters (including Hebrews), and seven Catholic Letters; and he claims that anything outside this list is not genuine. Finally, **Amphilochius of Iconium** (A.D. 380) produced a list around this time as well, including four Gospels, Acts, thirteen Pauline letters, Hebrews, the seven Catholic Letters, and Revelation — although he acknowledges that some question the status of Hebrews and Revelation.

e. Athanasius's Festal Letter

In A.D. 367 **Athanasius,** bishop of Alexandria (A.D. 328-73), read his thirty-ninth Festal Letter announcing the date of Easter. This is the first document to list precisely the twenty-seven books decided to be part of the NT by the councils late in the fourth century. He was the first author of the Eastern church since Origen to accept Revelation as authoritative. Hebrews is located among the Pauline Letters. No mention is made of the apocryphal books. The *Didache* and *Shepherd of Hermas,* while not canonical, are understood to be profitable for edification.

f. Latin Vulgate

Jerome translated (or better, revised from the Old Latin) the four Gospels into Latin in A.D. 383. His translation was later expanded to include the entire NT and would come to be known as the **Latin Vulgate** — there is agreement that Jerome produced the Gospels portion of this version, but his role in the production of the rest of the NT is open to question. The NT portion of this Latin Bible includes all twenty-seven books of the NT and was generally recognized by the Western church.

g. Rufinus and Pope Innocent

Rufinus of Aquileia (A.D. 345-410) is well known for his translation of Origen's works. He provided his generation with an exposition of the Apostles' Creed where he takes the opportunity to compile a list of books that he deemed to be inspired by the Holy Spirit. The list parallels those of Athanasius and Jerome, containing the twenty-seven books of the canonical NT. In A.D. 405, in a letter to Exsuperius, **Pope Innocent**, bishop of Toulouse (A.D. ?-417), affirmed these same twenty-seven books with the exception of Hebrews, which he omitted from his discussion.

h. Councils of Hippo and Carthage

In the East, under Augustine's influence, three councils convened that discussed the boundaries of the Christian canon. The first of these took place in A.D. 393 at the **Council of Hippo**, but the records from this council are no longer extant. Fortunately, its decisions were reaffirmed at the **Third Council of Carthage** in A.D. 397, where the twenty-seven books of the NT are acknowledged — a decision that was affirmed again at the **Sixth Council of Carthage** in A.D. 419.

i. Fourth- and Fifth-Century Codices

At least by the mid-fourth century A.D., entire codices of the NT were being assembled (see ch. 3). Two such documents are preserved in **Codex Vaticanus** and **Codex Sinaiticus**. By virtue of compiling a NT, scribes and officials were confronted with the decision of what properly belonged in this body of literature. Codex Sinaiticus is the only one of the early remaining codices to contain all twenty-seven books of the canonical NT, along with the *Epistle of Barnabas* and sections from the *Shepherd of Hermas* at the end. Codex Vaticanus contains most of the canonical NT; most of Hebrews (it breaks off in Heb 9), Paul's personal letters (the Pastorals and Philemon), and Revelation were presumably originally included but have not been preserved due to its fragmentary condition. Codex Alexandrinus, from the fifth century, preserves all four Gospels (but not all of Matthew), Acts, James, 1-2 Peter, 1-3 John, Jude, fourteen Pauline letters (including Hebrews), and Revelation, along with *1-2 Clement*.

3. Canon and Sacred Writings: Problems with Terminology

It is now appropriate to reflect further upon the definition of canon introduced at the beginning of this chapter. Eugene Ulrich notes three essential features in defining the concept of canon: (1) it is the book that is canonical, not its textual form; (2) it entails reflective judgment by officials and councils; and (3) it involves a closed list. Therefore, James Sanders, John Barton, and Albert Sundberg, along with a number of others working with the issue of NT canon,[22] emphasize the importance of distinguishing between **sacred writings**, writings recognized as holy and authoritative and used for liturgical practices, and **canonical writings**, books appearing in canonical lists based upon the decisions of official councils. Such a distinction is often maintained by advocates of a fourth/fifth-century development of the NT canon, based upon the decisions of the councils. The argument of those who hold to such a position is that, while "sacred writings" may have existed prior to the councils, these writings can only be viewed as "canonical"— in their sense of the term — within the late fourth century and beyond. The problem with this distinction is that it falsely circumscribes the discussion. The definitions are such that a second-century canon is inherently anachronistic. This is hardly convincing. Redefining "canon" so that its emergence is limited to a particular era the fourth to fifth centuries is far from proving that it did in fact emerge in that era. The evidence, as we have seen, is far from convincing.

4. Summary

The NT canon should be defined as the body of writings that the early church considered authoritative in matters of doctrine and liturgical practice. This definition has the advantage of not prejudging the date of the formation of the canon and allows all of the evidence to be weighed equally. According to this definition, there is evidence of something of a fixed canon already in the second century consisting of at least four Gospels and thirteen or fourteen Pauline letters (depending upon how Hebrews was viewed). Evidence for this is found in the circulation of these two bodies of materials together from an early date and in the content of the Muratorian Fragment. The status of other letters was apparently still being discussed according to how they fit into the basic Gospel-apostle framework, but the letters of James, John, and Peter, as well as Revelation, clearly had acceptance in many quarters of the church, even at a

---

22. Eugene Ulrich, "The Notion and Definition of Canon," in *Canon Debate,* ed. McDonald and Sanders, 31-33.

relatively early date. The councils and other documents of the fourth and fifth centuries merely provide an official statement on these matters in their respective geographical regions, affirming which books properly fit within the Gospel-apostle structure of canonical literature. Indeed, the canon was established intrinsically by what the church viewed as its own internal criteria as soon as the literature was written, and the canon was closed as soon as the last of the apostles died. The efforts of the church in (roughly) the first four centuries was then one of *discovering* which pieces of literature fit within the Gospel-apostle framework, not *deciding* on which pieces of literature were canonical. The criteria for canonicity rested within the writings themselves, not with the decision-making process of the church.

KEY TERMINOLOGY
canon
canonization
canonical awareness
Marcion
Marcionite canon
Tatian's *Diatessaron*
Justin Martyr
Irenaeus
Clement
Tertullian
pseudepigraphal
pseudonymous
ecclesial letters
personal letters
Gospel-apostle structure
codex
Muratorian Fragment
Eusebius
homologoumena
amphiballomena
pseudē
Codex Claromontanus
Cheltenham List (Mommsen Catalogue)
Epiphanius
Cyril of Jerusalem

Gregory of Nazianzus
Amphilochius of Iconium
Athanasius
Latin Vulgate
Pope Innocent
Council of Hippo
Third Council of Carthage
Sixth Council of Carthage
Codex Vaticanus
Codex Sinaiticus
sacred writings
canonical writings

BIBLIOGRAPHY

Balla, Peter. "Evidence for an Early Christian Canon (Second and Third Century)." Pages 372-85 in *The Canon Debate*. Ed. Lee Martin McDonald and James A. Sanders. Peabody, MA: Hendrickson, 2002.

Barton, John. *Holy Writings, Sacred Text: The Canon in Early Christianity*. Louisville: Westminster John Knox, 1997.

Blackman, E. C. *Marcion and His Influence*. London: SPCK, 1948.

Bovon, François. "The Canonical Structure of Gospel and Apostle." Pages 516-27 in *The Canon Debate*. Ed. Lee Martin McDonald and James A. Sanders. Peabody, MA: Hendrickson, 2002.

Bruce, F. F. *The Canon of Scripture*. Downers Grove, IL: InterVarsity Press, 1988.

Comfort, Philip W. *The Origin of the Bible*. Wheaton, IL: Tyndale House, 1992.

Duff, Jeremy. "P46 and the Pastorals: A Misleading Consensus?" *NTS* 44 (1998): 578-90.

Epp, Eldon Jay. "Issues in the Interrelation of New Testament Textual Criticism and Canon." Pages 485-516 in *The Canon Debate*. Ed. Lee Martin McDonald and James A. Sanders. Peabody, MA: Hendrickson, 2002.

Gamble, Harry Y. *The New Testament Canon: Its Making and Meaning*. Guides to Biblical Scholarship, New Testament Series. Philadelphia: Fortress, 1985.

Hengel, Martin. *The Four Gospels and the One Gospel of Jesus Christ: An Investigation of the Collection and Origin of the Canonical Gospels*. Trans. John Bowden. Harrisburg: Trinity Press International, 2000.

Kruger, Michael J. *Canon Revisited: Establishing the Origins and Authority of the New Testament Books*. Wheaton, IL: Crossway, 2012.

————. *The Question of Canon: Challenging the Status Quo in the New Testament Debate.* Downers Grove, IL: InterVarsity Press, 2013.

McDonald, Lee Martin. *The Biblical Canon: Its Origin, Transmission, and Authority.* Peabody, MA: Hendrickson, 2007.

McDonald, Lee Martin, and James A. Sanders, eds. *The Canon Debate.* Peabody, MA: Hendrickson, 2002.

Metzger, Bruce M. *The Canon of the New Testament: Its Origin, Development, and Significance.* Oxford: Clarendon, 1987.

Porter, Stanley E. *How We Got the New Testament: Text, Transmission, Translation.* Grand Rapids: Baker, 2013.

Quinn, Jerome D. "P46 — The Pauline Canon." *CBQ* 36 (1974): 379-85.

Sanders, James A. "Adaptable for Life: The Nature and Function of Canon." Pages 531-60 in *Magnalia Dei: The Mighty Acts of God: Essays on the Bible and Archaeology in Memory of G. Ernest Wright.* Ed. Frank Moore Cross, Werner E. Lemke, and Patrick D. Miller Jr. Garden City, NY: Doubleday, 1976.

Skeat, T. C. "Irenaeus and the Four-Gospel Canon." *NovT* 34 (1992): 194-99.

————. "The Origin of the Christian Codex." *Zeitschrift für Papyrologie und Epigraphik* 102 (1994): 263-68.

————. "The Oldest Manuscript of the Four Gospels?" *NTS* 43 (1997): 1-34.

Ulrich, Eugene. "The Notion and Definition of Canon." Pages 21-35 in *The Canon Debate.* Ed. Lee Martin McDonald and James A. Sanders. Peabody, MA: Hendrickson, 2002.

CHAPTER 3

Materials and Methods of Classification

The huge wealth of material available for the textual criticism of the NT is both a blessing and a curse. Although the number varies depending upon how they are counted, by one count there are over seventy-two hundred Greek manuscripts of various sizes and shapes representing different portions of the NT, in addition to hundreds of copies of various ancient versions or translations, and quotations of the NT in the early church fathers (see ch. 4). NT manuscripts range from the complete or close to complete major codices, such as Codex Sinaiticus or Codex Vaticanus, to much more fragmentary materials such as P. Vindob. G 42417 ($\mathfrak{P}^{116}$),[1] a recently discovered and published NT papyrus manuscript containing a few verses of Hebrews (Heb 2:9-11 on one side; 3:3-6 on the other). The original NT manuscripts unfortunately no longer exist. In their place, we have copies of copies made over the course of hundreds of years, as scribes copied these by hand and passed them down to others. The inevitable result of this process of copying and textual transmission is that a number of changes have been introduced either intentionally or unintentionally into the manuscripts. Some of the changes were made intentionally in order to correct or improve a manuscript (or so a scribe thought), while others were made unintentionally through carelessness or a slip of the pen. As a result, despite the large number, no two NT manuscripts are identical in all aspects.

---

1. Every NT manuscript has both its identification according to the collection in which it is held, and its designation in terms of the scheme used to identify all NT manuscripts, sometimes referred to as a Gregory-Aland identification (the two most important scholars who developed this scheme and classified manuscripts were Caspar René Gregory and Kurt Aland). In the example above, "P.Vindob. G" means that this is a papyrus in the Vindobonensis (Vienna) collection in Greek. It is known by the Gregory-Aland identification as $\mathfrak{P}^{116}$. We further discuss this system below and in chapter 4.

1. Books and Literacy in the First Century

In the Greco-Roman world in which the NT was written, there was a traditional emphasis upon orality (communication through spoken rather
than written media), such that the major ancient authors wrote for oral
performance in such media as Greek epic and tragedy. However, with the
growth of the Roman Empire there arose a need for record keeping that
led to a widespread scribal culture that developed into a full-blown literary culture. Thus Rosalind Thomas distinguishes between documents and
records.[2] All sorts of documents (e.g., business transaction, receipts) were
written for different purposes. However, there is a transition that takes
place when one recognizes that written documents may become records
of persons, possessions, or other things. With this recognition there comes
a certain power in literacy, to the point of developing systematized record
keeping. This is one of the hallmarks of the Roman Empire, especially as
evidenced in the papyri remains from Egypt (see the next section). The
confluence of record keeping and power can be clearly seen in the tax
records that were completed by the Romans every seven years up to A.D.
11/12 and then every fourteen years from A.D. 19/20 on. Even if an ancient
person was illiterate, he or she was not far removed from literate culture in
the need to use and have access to written documents. The power of record
keeping included the power to tax and the power to control the people. In
the Jewish world of the time, which functioned within the larger Greco-
Roman world, there was a similar phenomenon regarding the interplay of
orality and literacy. Birger Gerhardsson notes the creative and dynamic
role that oral tradition played in the rise of Judaism. He also notes that
early on, a number of centuries before the Christian era, written tradition
also began to play an important part in Judaism. Gerhardsson shows that
the written Torah, what we would equate with our OT, was complemented
by the oral Torah, which constitutes the oral interpretation that goes hand
in hand with it.[3]

Many students of the NT do not fully realize, however, the type of
book culture that was already flourishing in the first century A.D. Such a
book culture is often dismissed on the basis of a purported lack of means of

2. Rosalind Thomas, *Literacy and Orality in Ancient Greece* (Cambridge: Cambridge
University Press, 1992), 132-44.

3. Birger Gerhardsson, *Memory and Manuscript: Oral Tradition and Written Transmission in Rabbinic Judaism and Early Christianity; with, Tradition and Transmission in Early
Christianity* (Grand Rapids: Eerdmans, 1998), 19-32.

copying, the high cost of materials, and widespread illiteracy. The disparagement of writing and the book culture is, in some ways, an unfounded consequence of a way of thinking that draws a firm disjunction between orality and literacy. In other words, because the culture is posited as oral, the claim is that there must not be significant written sources. In fact, the standard assumptions regarding the lack of means of copying, expensive materials, and widespread illiteracy do not hold up in light of the evidence.

The copying and producing of handwritten copies of books was not as big an obstacle in the ancient world as many have assumed. How else do we account for such factors as Galen, a second-century A.D. doctor, wandering through a market and seeing books for sale, and his checking and seeing that some of those for sale were attributed to him and he knew that he had not written them? In other words, there was enough of a market for books that it made forgery a desirable option for some (clearly not for Galen, who was incensed). Similarly, the literary tradition associated with the ancient Greek orator Lysias is that a significant number of the works attributed to him even in ancient times were known to be forgeries, a problem that has kept scholars busy for years. Likewise, the Qumran community, though always a relatively small community living in isolation, was responsible for creating a significantly large number of books. There were also a number of large, well-known libraries, such as the ones at Alexandria and Ephesus, among others. There were a number of small private libraries as well, which may have been more important to the book culture than the larger libraries. In other words, books appear to have been so plentiful by the first century A.D. that the Latin author Seneca goes so far as to denounce what he sees as the ostentatious accumulation of books. Without minimizing the importance of orality — and that the major means of "publication" was in terms of oral performance, such as orations, the reading of poetry, lectures delivered in public, and theater — we must also recognize that there was a parallel book culture that was large and significant. There was no publishing industry as we would know it today, but there were means of getting books produced nevertheless.

The cost of book production was relatively cheap, at least cheaper than is often assumed. Papyrus, the paper of the ancient world, was widely available and so the cost was not high (on papyrus, see below). As Thomas Skeat, the papyrologist from the British Museum, has argued, papyrus was affordable in the ancient world, as indicated by statements by the ancients and the bountiful evidence of discarded papyrus discovered throughout Egypt — very few of which were ever reused, even if they were blank on one side.[4] The cost of getting a book copied was not exorbitant, ranging from two to four drachmas, which is the equivalent of anywhere from one to six days' wages. Frederic Kenyon notes that as early as the fourth century B.C. there was a "considerable quantity" of "cheap and easily accessible" books to be found in Athens, which shows that a reading culture was growing even during that time.[5] In Hellenistic Egypt (300 B.C.–A.D. 300), as is indicated by the documentary and especially the literary finds, there were numerous books available, to the point that "Greek literature was widely current among the ordinary Graeco-Roman population," and this was a likely pattern throughout the Hellenistic world.[6]

That these books were accessible to a wide range of people is indicated by the fact that the most common literary author found in the papyri is the epic poet Homer, the major author read in the ancient Greek grammar school. Access to these books was gained through a variety of means. There was what amounts to what Loveday Alexander has called a commercial book trade. Alexander notes that the main motivation of authors to publish in ancient times — perhaps not too unlike modern times — was fame, not necessarily money. Hence there were not the same kinds of restrictions on access as we have created today. Authors themselves would probably have been involved in "publication" of their books.[7] Raymond Starr notes that the author would have written a rough draft, and then had it reviewed by others, such as slaves or friends. Once a final form of the text was formulated, it was circulated to a wider group of friends, before being more widely disseminated. As a result, perhaps the easiest way to secure a book was to borrow a copy from a friend and either have a slave or scribe copy it, or make one's own copy.[8] As Alexander notes, Aristotle, Cicero, Galen, and Marcus Cicero the younger all seem to have been part of this process.[9]

This transmission process is undoubtedly how many of the first cop-

---

4. T. C. Skeat, "Was Papyrus Regarded as 'Cheap' or 'Expensive' in the Ancient World?" *Aeg* 75 (1995): 75-93.

5. F. G. Kenyon, *Books and Readers in Ancient Greece and Rome* (Oxford: Clarendon, 1932), 24.

6. Ibid., 34, 36.

7. Loveday Alexander, "Ancient Book Production and the Circulation of the Gospels," in *The Gospel for All Christians: Rethinking the Gospel Audiences* (ed. Richard Bauckham; Grand Rapids: Eerdmans, 1998), 71-111.

8. Raymond J. Starr, "The Circulation of Literary Texts in the Roman World," *CQ* 37 (1989): 313-23.

9. Alexander, "Ancient Book Production," e.g., 88-89.

ies of the NT books would have been made, as churches loaned out and allowed copies to be made of early Christian letters or Gospels in their possession. Harry Gamble has shown that there were associations of people connected with book production, so that those who were interested in a particular type of literature would produce and share these types of books.[10] This perhaps accounts for an episode that the Jewish historian Josephus records, in which a rebel in Galilee confronted him with "a copy of the law of Moses in his hands" as he tried to work the crowd (Josephus, *Life* 134). This sharing of books would have included those who were interested in not only the Greek text of the Bible (i.e., the Old Greek or LXX) but also Gospel texts and Christian letters, for example, early Christian congregations. Thus, as the Christian community expanded, more copies of NT books were demanded by individual local congregations and so copies were borrowed from other churches and reproduced. The rapid spread of Christianity in the ancient world, therefore, accounts for the rapid production of NT books represented by the abundant number of manuscripts currently available (at least when compared to other literary and historical works in antiquity — see below on Statistics for New Testament Manuscripts).

As Christianity became more and more popular, a large part of the production of NT books was eventually turned over to professional scribes so that by the fourth century the NT had begun to be copied primarily in various **scriptoria** (plural of **scriptorium**), places of professional book manufacture. In a scriptorium, an original or **exemplar** (but not necessarily the original written by the author) was read aloud and copied down by scribes. Later, during the Byzantine period (roughly A.D. 867-1204), the NT was copied by individual monks in monasteries, where the documents were copied instead of being written down on the basis of verbal dictation.

Finally, we return to the issue of literacy. The classicist William Harris's well-known monograph on this topic was not the first to address the issue, but it was the first to study systematically the historical, documentary, and literary evidence, and then to attempt to quantify the literacy of the ancient world.[11] His work distanced him from those who had emphasized the oral culture of the ancient Greeks. Some rejected his findings by claiming

---

10. Harry Y. Gamble, *Books and Readers in the Early Church: A History of Early Christian Texts* (New Haven: Yale University Press, 1995), 8-10.

11. William V. Harris, *Ancient Literacy* (Cambridge: Harvard University Press, 1991), 267.

that he had overestimated the influence and capability of writing, but the majority found that he had *underestimated* the impact of literary culture, at least in the Greco-Roman context. Even if his statistics are accurate and are not underestimated — that overall 20-30 percent of men in the Roman Empire were literate, and that 10-15 percent of women were, for an overall literacy rate of no more than 15 percent — he seems to have neglected the fact that even those who were illiterate came into regular and widespread contact with literate culture. For example, a person illiterate in Greek might need to have a contract written out, and so would of necessity be a part of literate culture by virtue of needing to have this document prepared, and would need to deal with the consequences of it, such as a document sent in return. The classicist Alan Bowman goes so far as to state that a "large proportion" of the 80 percent who may have been formally illiterate were to some degree participants in literate culture.[12] Further, there are far more ancient documents still to be deciphered, as well as a number that were destroyed — all evidence of literacy that needs to be taken into account.[13] The classicist Keith Hopkins notes that, according to Harris's figures, there were over two million adult men in the Roman Empire who could read, and that this large number would have exerted a significant influence upon the society as a whole.[14] Finally, Catherine Hezser has shown that levels of literacy among Palestinians were far higher than the average of the Roman Empire,[15] evidence quite relevant to the study of early Christianity. This means that there would probably have been literate people in most early Christian churches, encouraging the circulation of early Christian literature. Nevertheless, since there was assuredly a large contingent of illiterate people among the congregations as well, letters and narratives were probably still most often read aloud.

12. A. K. Bowman, "Literacy in the Roman Empire: Mass and Mode," in *Literacy in the Roman World* (ed. Mary Beard; JRASup 3; Ann Arbor: Journal of Roman Archaeology, 1991), 119-31.

13. Ibid., 122; see also 121.

14. Keith Hopkins, "Conquest by Book," in *Literacy in the Roman World*, ed. Beard, 133-58.

15. Catherine Hezser, *Jewish Literacy in Roman Palestine* (TSAJ 81; Tübingen: Mohr Siebeck, 2010).

2. Writing Materials and the Forms of Ancient Books

Prior to the discovery and widespread utilization of the stalk of the papyrus plant as a writing material in the ancient Mediterranean world, wax tablets were used for the purposes of writing, in which a thin pointed stick called a stylus was used to impress letters upon the wax surface. By the time of the early Christian era, however, records and documents were written primarily on **papyrus** (an ancient form of paper made from the stalk of the papyrus plant) or, somewhat later, **parchment** (an ancient form of writing material made from prepared animal skins). Papyrus or parchment was usually used in the form of a **scroll** (in which individual pieces were connected together sequentially to form a roll upon which written material was placed on one side) or a **codex** (plural = *codices* or *codexes*) (an ancient book or leaf-bound form on which writing was done on both sides). The ink that was used depended upon the type of material in use. While a carbon-based solution, composed of charcoal and lampblack or water, was most often used to write on papyrus, Bruce Metzger and Bart Ehrman note that since "carbon inks do not stick well to parchment, another kind was developed, using oak galls and ferrous sulfate, known also as 'copperas.'"[16] Similarly, due to texture and firmness, pens made out of reed were best suited for writing upon papyrus, whereas quill or feather pens were better for writing on parchment.

a. Papyrus

The papyrus plant (see Fig. 3.1 on p. 40) was most abundant in the Nile Delta and therefore was produced primarily in Egypt, although it was known to grow in many other places in the Mediterranean world as well. In ancient times, the plant grew to between six and twelve feet tall, with a thin stem and a grassy blossom at the top. To convert the plant into flattened papyrus sheets that would accommodate writing required a number of steps. The first step was to remove the outer layer of skin. The stem was then divided into a number of vertical sections and cut into thin strips. In the first century, during the time of the naturalist Pliny the Elder, who wrote about papyrus, the strips were pressed together and

---

16. Bruce M. Metzger, *The Text of the New Testament: Its Transmission, Corruption, and Restoration* (4th ed. rev. Bart D. Ehrmann; Oxford: Oxford University Press, 2005), 10.

Figure 3.1 A papyrus plant (Wikimedia Commons)

held in place by the natural sap of the plant (*Nat.* 13.20-26). By at least the third century, during the reign of the Roman emperor Aurelian, glue began to be used in the manufacturing process (*Nat.* 13.26). However, the older process using the sap of the papyrus plant as adhesive turned out to be superior in terms of producing a more durable, longer lasting material. The result of the procedure was a textured, often brittle paper-like material that could be used as a surface for writing with ink. The John Rylands papyrus fragment of John's Gospel ($\mathfrak{P}^{52}$), the earliest NT fragment, provides an excellent example of what an early NT papyrus looked like (see Fig. 3.2). The oldest witnesses to the NT are written on papyrus since parchment was not heavily utilized in writing until shortly

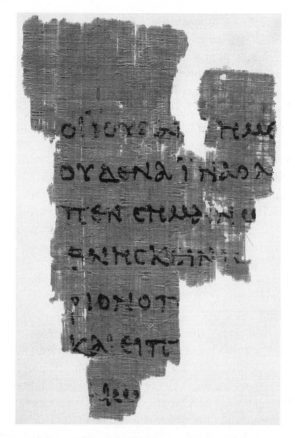

Figure 3.2 P⁵², a papyrus fragment from the Gospel of John
(The John Rylands University Library, The University of Manchester, Manchester, England.
Reproduced by courtesy of the University Librarian and Director)

after the NT period. Papyrus sheets would have been the writing material that the NT authors used to write their letters, compose their Gospels, and record their visions. This is confirmed by 2 John 12, where the word usually translated "paper" (χάρτης) refers to a piece of papyrus. Most of the NT papyri come from Egypt, with a few from Palestine, since the dry climate conditions especially of Egypt have allowed for their preservation — papyri quickly deteriorate in more humid climates, such as the northern Mediterranean.

Even in Egypt, little is known regarding the geographical origin of NT papyri, but we do know that a number of papyri were discarded in the rubbish heaps of the Fayum region and of the ancient city of Oxyrhynchus. **Oxyrhynchus** is a particularly important site where a number of NT and other early Christian papyri have been identified — papyri found at this site are indicated by the abbreviation **P.** (which stands for papyrus) **Oxy.** (which stands for Oxyrhynchus) prior to the papyrus number (e.g., P.Oxy. 3523 in the Oxyrhynchus collection, but within the NT papyri designated as 𝔓⁹⁰). Oxyrhynchus was known for having a vibrant Christian community and book culture, as the papyri found there clearly attest. Therefore, papyri from Oxyrhynchus have been useful not only in textual criticism but also in understanding contemporary Greek language and literature and various historical contexts for the transmission of the NT. Publication of the huge number of Oxyrhynchus papyri is an ongoing process, so unfortunately a large number of these papyri remain unpublished and have not yet been subjected to scrutiny by the academic community.

b. Parchment

The limited availability of the papyrus plant in other areas of the ancient Mediterranean world — being mostly, but not entirely, restricted to Egypt — meant other writing materials had to be used in the process of serious book production in locations where the papyrus plant did not grow. This led to the production of **parchment** or **vellum**, which employed treated animal skins rather than the papyrus plant (see Fig. 3.3). Pliny accredits the rise of the use of parchment outside Egypt to the decision of King Eumenes II (197-159 B.C.) of Pergamum (a city in western Asia Minor, now Turkey) to build a library comparable to the one in Alexandria. Ptolemy I, the king of Egypt at the time, was not happy with this plan and so he put an embargo on the export of papyrus in order to discourage Eumenes' efforts, forcing Eumenes to develop a leather-based writing material now known as parchment (Pliny, *Nat.* 13.21).[17] Regardless of the historical merits of the story, Pergamum was certainly famous for its parchment production, which became the most significant writing material in the ancient world by the third century — and for obvious reasons. In addition to being able to be produced anywhere where there were animals, parchment was more durable, longer lasting, and easier to bind than papyrus and could withstand various climate conditions. The texture was soft, and, in some cases,

---

17. For another ancient account, see *Let. Aris.* 9-12.

Figure 3.3 A fragment of a leaf of a parchment codex showing Psalm 3:4-8
(P.Mich.inv. 1573, recto; courtesy of the Papyrology Collection, University of Michigan Library)

traces of animal hair can still be found on the external side. The majority of significant NT manuscripts are recorded on parchment. The two most significant codices, Codex Sinaiticus and Codex Vaticanus (both from the fourth century A.D.), are written on parchment pages bound in book form. Although parchment is found in the scroll form also (e.g., some of the Dead Sea Scrolls), the codex gained popularity around the same time that parchment began to be the most common material used for writing in the ancient world. So the majority of the parchment NT manuscripts come in the form of codices.

c. Scroll

The NT authors and earliest Christian churches would have used the papyrus **scroll** to write and read their sacred literature in its earliest form.

Figure 3.4 A portion of the Great Isaiah Scroll
(Google Art Project / Wikimedia Commons)

This was the typical format for the publication of literary works in the Greco-Roman world of the turn of the millennia. One side of the papyrus was used for writing, and the other side was left blank (but cf. Rev 5:1). Scrolls had a number of disadvantages, however. They were inconvenient for referencing passages within a particular work because readers would have to keep unrolling the scroll until they found the desired place in the work. It was difficult to handle these rolls, especially if a literary text was particularly long. This limitation of length also discouraged authors from writing longer works; but, if they did, they usually had to compose the work in two or more volumes (e.g., Luke-Acts). This limitation on length may have led NT authors to compose anthologies or readers on a single scroll, containing a number of key passages on selected topics from a number of different literary works, instead of only a single continuous literary work (these are sometimes called *testimonia*). The production and use of testimonia was a common practice in the Greco-Roman schools as well as at Qumran. Such testimonia may have been used by someone like Paul who, in his travels, could not afford to carry around a bag full of cumbersome scrolls (no single scroll could contain the entire Bible or OT), but needed to have quick and easy access to Scripture as he composed his letters on the go. The Dead Sea scroll pictured in Figure 3.4 gives an idea of how an ancient scroll would have looked.

d. Codex

Due to the inconvenience of the scroll format, early Christians pioneered the invention of the **codex**, the first step toward the production of the modern book. The codex facilitated greater ease in referencing passages, allowed for writing on both sides, and allowed for various groups of books (e.g., the Gospels, Paul's Letters) to be collected in one volume. The codex was formed by laying numerous pieces of papyrus or parchment on top of one another, folding them in the center, and then sewing them together on the fold. This, then, formed a quire, and as many quires as were desired to make the book were then created and sewn together. The picture of Codex Sinaiticus (Fig. 3.5) shows what an ancient codex

Figure 3.5 A folio from Codex Sinaiticus showing a portion of Jeremiah
(Q49, fol. 5r; Jer. 48:9–49:15. Universitätsbibliothek Leipzig, Cod.gr.1)

looked like. There are four columns on each page — although the number of columns may vary — with a fold down the middle of the volume, where the quires have been made and sewn together. Although we know that the earliest NT documents were written on scrolls, the earliest manuscript we currently have ($\mathfrak{P}^{52}$, the John Rylands papyrus, Fig. 3.2 on p. 41) is a page from a codex.

3. Writing Styles

Philip Comfort and David Barrett conveniently list four types of hand-writing typically identified by **paleographers** (those who study ancient writing and inscriptions):

1. *Common:* the work of a semiliterate writer who is untrained in making documents. This handwriting usually displays an inelegant cursive.
2. *Documentary:* the work of a literate writer who has had experience in preparing documents. This has also been called "chancery handwriting" (prominent in the period A.D. 200–225). It was used by official scribes in public administration.
3. *Reformed documentary:* the work of a literate writer who had experience in preparing documents *and* in copying works of literature. Often, this hand attempts to imitate the work of a professional but does not fully achieve the professional look.
4. *Professional:* the work of a professional scribe. These writings display the craftsmanship of what is commonly called a "book hand" or "literary hand" and leave telltale marks of professionalism — such as stichoi markings (the tallying of the number of lines, according to which a professional scribe would be paid), as are found in $\mathfrak{P}^{46}$.[18]

The most important indicator of the date of ancient NT manuscripts is the kind of hand or script that the scribe used. The styles mentioned by Comfort and Barrett are found in varying degrees among early majuscule and later minuscule Greek hands. The earliest and most significant NT manuscripts are written in the majuscule hand. **Majuscule** (meaning "large") is a square hand with large letters that employs no spacing between the words

18. Philip W. Comfort and David P. Barrett, *The Text of the Earliest New Testament Greek Manuscripts* (Wheaton, IL: Tyndale House, 2001), 24.

and is only found in the earliest codices (usually not after the seventh century). Parker defines the majuscule hand as "a formal bookhand of a fair size in which almost all of the letters are written between two imaginary lines"[19] — all of the Greek manuscripts pictured above employ a majuscule hand, but the styles vary. This hand and the relevant manuscripts are sometimes referred to as **uncials**. Recent scholarly consensus, however, rejects this designation as referring only to a particular Latin majuscule and having little relevance to the Greek hand relevant to NT textual criticism. Paleographers typically discuss a number of other types of majuscule hand. The majority of NT manuscripts are written in what is referred to as a *biblical majuscule hand* — which is not, incidentally, limited to biblical manuscripts — characterized by straight upright letters, clearly distinct from one another, not running together as with a cursive hand. The *Roman majuscule* is an earlier hand distinguished by an alternation between thick and thin pen strokes as we see in $\mathfrak{P}^{46}$, for example (cited above). There is also a more decorative, rounded majuscule, most popular from 100 B.C. to A.D. 100, but represented among some biblical papyri (e.g., $\mathfrak{P}^{32}$, $\mathfrak{P}^{66}$, and $\mathfrak{P}^{90}$). Other distinct majuscule hands arose based upon the tendencies of the individual scribes. The hand employed in Codex Bezae, for example, seems to suggest that the scribe had a greater familiarity with Latin characters than Greek characters.[20] While Greek accents are attested as early as the third century B.C., they are only employed sporadically in manuscripts written in a majuscule hand. NT authors would have used something very close to the majuscule hand that we find in the earliest NT manuscripts, although handwriting styles would have varied — depending on whether a scribe was employed and the level of the scribe's competency.

Later manuscripts are written in a **minuscule** (meaning "small") hand (arising during the seventh and eighth centuries), characterized by smaller, clearer letters with the consistent use of spaces, breathing marks, various combined letters, and accents. This style is much more comparable to the modern Greek fonts used in printed editions, such as Nestle-Aland[27/28] or *UBSGNT*[4/5]. The minuscule tradition is distinctively characterized by its close relationship to the Byzantine textual tradition (see ch. 4). The earliest minuscule manuscript, the Uspenski Gospels (A.D. 835), is in a fully

---

19. David C. Parker, "The Majuscule Manuscripts of the New Testament," in *The Text of the New Testament in Contemporary Research: Essays on the Status Quaestionis* (2nd ed.; ed. Bart D. Ehrman and Michael W. Holmes; NTTSD 42; Leiden: Brill, 2013), 41.

20. Ibid., 53.

developed book hand in the standardized Koine of the Byzantine period. The minuscule tradition of NT manuscripts, though late, does provide important confirmatory material for textual criticism when it supports or contradicts certain isolated readings. There are also far more minuscule manuscripts than there are majuscules (only about 10 percent of extant manuscripts are written in the majuscule hand), making it much easier to trace the (geographical) origin of differences within various traditions that go back to the earlier majuscule manuscript tradition.

4. Scribal Additions, Alterations, and Aids

Early manuscripts of the NT contain a number of scribal additions, alterations, and aids for readers. These range from notes in the margins for various purposes to additions/changes for clarity to abbreviated sacred words. Scribes viewed these changes as helps for future scribes and readers of the text.

In addition to pioneering the codex, the early Christian community also introduced a set of abbreviations for sacred words known as the *nomina sacra*. Larry Hurtado states, "The *nomina sacra* are so familiar a feature of Christian manuscripts that papyrologists [scholars who study papyri] often take the presence of these forms as sufficient to identify even a fragment of a manuscript as indicating its probable Christian provenance."[21] For example, instead of writing out the Greek word for "Lord" (κύριος) in full, Christian scribes would use the contracted form ΚΣ. Similarly, for θεός ("God"), ΘΣ was used, and for Ἰερουσαλήμ ("Jerusalem"), ΙΛΗΜ or ΙΜ was employed. The use of these distinctively Christian forms has aided scholars in locating Christian or Jewish manuscripts when sorting through previously unclassified Greek materials.

A form of annotations found in a number of manuscripts is the result of corrections made by a διορθωτής, a specially trained scribe in the scriptorium who would check individual manuscripts for accuracy, typically noting his changes by a distinct form of handwriting or by using a different shade of ink.

The scribes that copied Codex Sinaiticus apparently had a conception of paragraph divisions, often initiating what they perceived to be the be-

---

21. Larry W. Hurtado, *The Earliest Christian Artifacts: Manuscripts and Christian Origins* (Grand Rapids: Eerdmans, 2006), 96.

ginning of a unit with a larger letter, often the Κ in καί ("and") or another conjunction. In Mark's Gospel, for example, 310 units are marked by a large initial letter and/or a shorter preceding line.

A number of aids were also introduced by scribes to assist in the public reading of Scripture. These include the insertion of chapter divisions and titles, scholia (brief commentary, usually in the side margin), references to parallel Gospel passages, various forms of introduction to particular books (e.g., information about the author), explanations of difficult words or phrases (usually in the side margins), additional punctuation, superscriptions indicating the title or author of a book, decorative ornamentation (especially in later manuscripts), and various liturgical aids (e.g., musical notes, marking of units for reading in worship service, usually in the side margins).

Not all changes introduced by scribes were intentional, however. The tedious nature of the scribal process coupled with the challenge of recording oral dictation (if the manuscript was produced in a scriptorium) or even of accurately copying a manuscript often resulted in a number of unintentional changes from the text being copied. These will be taken up in some detail in chapter 9, dealing with internal evidence.

5. Methods of Classifying Materials

Unfortunately, the current method of classifying NT manuscripts is fairly inconsistent — a price that came with the slow development of the discipline, the gradual discovery of new materials that needed to be classified, and the lack of standardization early on. Some manuscripts are classified according to script. Others are classified according to the material they are written on. Still others are classified according to content. Manuscripts written in the majuscule or minuscule hand are referred to as majuscule and minuscule manuscripts, as long as they are written on parchment (although this is not an issue for minuscule manuscripts, which are not written on papyrus). Manuscripts written on papyri, however, are classified as papyri manuscripts rather than according to the hand they are written in. A final, later group of sources for NT textual criticism not previously discussed are lectionaries. These are classified according to content (thus they are not treated above under "Writing Materials"). **Lectionaries** are collections of selected passages designed for use in Christian worship services, dating from ancient times up through the Reformation period. Passages are arranged in a distinct order and frequently introduced by liturgical notes, and various modifications are often made to the text in order to account for the occurrence of the passage in isolation from its original context.

6. Statistics for New Testament Manuscripts

An official list of Greek manuscripts, classified according to the categories defined above, includes the following numbers (although this does not indicate that all of the manuscripts are separate or even now in existence, and this number will have increased by the time of publication, as new manuscripts are constantly being discovered and catalogued):[22]

> Papyri: 128
> Majuscule Manuscripts: 2,911
> Minuscule Manuscripts: 1,807
> Lectionaries: 2,381
> Total: 7,227

When compared with other works of antiquity, the NT has far greater (numerical) and earlier documentation than any other book. Most of the available works of antiquity have only a few manuscripts that attest to their existence, and these are typically much later than their original date of composition, so that it is not uncommon for the earliest manuscript to be dated over nine hundred years after the original composition. The classicist and biblical scholar F. F. Bruce has conveniently catalogued this data.[23] The chart below is based upon his calculations.

Book	Date	Number of MSS	Oldest Copy
Caesar's *Gallic Wars*	58-50 B.C.	8-9	A.D. 800-808
Livy's *Roman History*	59 B.C.–A.D. 17	20 fragments	1 from the 4th century
Tacitus's *Histories/Annals*	A.D. 100	2	9th century A.D.
Tacitus's Minor Works	A.D. 100	1	10th century A.D.
Thucydides' *History*	460-400 B.C.	8	A.D. 900
Herodotus's *History*	488-428 B.C.	8	A.D. 900

22. An up-to-date "official" listing is kept at the University of Münster Institute for New Testament Textual Research (http://www.uni-muenster.de/INTF).

23. F. F. Bruce, *The New Testament Documents: Are They Reliable?* (6th ed.; 1981; repr. Grand Rapids: Eerdmans, 1988), 11.

Therefore, as Helmut Koester observes,

> Classical authors are often represented by but one surviving manuscript; if there are half a dozen or more, one can speak of a rather advantageous situation for reconstructing the text. But there are nearly five thousand [!] manuscripts of the NT in Greek. . . . The only surviving manuscripts of classical authors often come from the Middle Ages, but the manuscript tradition of the NT begins as early as the end of II CE; it is therefore separated by only a century or so from the time at which the autographs were written. Thus it seems that NT textual criticism possesses a base which is far more advantageous than that for the textual criticism of classical authors.[24]

Fortunately, the NT textual critic has the unique privilege of such a rich documentation of the textual transmission of the NT, but this also results in certain complexities since there are so many documents to compare. It then becomes the duty of the textual critic to assess the available manuscripts and weigh the variant readings in order to determine which reading most likely reflects the original.

7. Summary

In this chapter we have examined the material for writing in the first century, literacy, various writing styles, scribal editorial tendencies, methods for classifying NT manuscripts, and the statistics for NT manuscripts and other works from classical antiquity. Now that we have briefly examined the materials for textual criticism, it is appropriate to turn to consider more specifically the significant witnesses to the text of the NT.

KEY TERMINOLOGY
scriptorium/scriptoria
exemplar
papyrus
parchment
scroll

24. Helmut Koester, *Introduction to the New Testament,* vol. 2: *History and Literature of Early Christianity* (Philadelphia: Fortress, 1982), 16-17.

codex
Oxyrhynchus (P.Oxy.)
vellum
paleographers
majuscule
uncial
minuscule
nomina sacra
lectionaries

BIBLIOGRAPHY

Aland, Barbara, and Klaus Wachtel. "The Greek Minuscule Manuscripts of the New Testament." Pages 69-91 in *The Text of the New Testament in Contemporary Research: Essays on the Status Quaestionis.* 2nd ed. Ed. Bart D. Ehrman and Michael W. Holmes. NTTSD 42. Leiden: Brill, 2013.

Alexander, Loveday. "Ancient Book Production and the Circulation of the Gospels." Pages 71-111 in *The Gospel for All Christians: Rethinking the Gospel Audiences.* Ed. Richard Bauckham. Grand Rapids: Eerdmans, 1998.

Beard, Mary, ed. *Literacy in the Roman World.* JRASup 3. Ann Arbor: Journal of Roman Archaeology, 1991.

Bowman, A. K. "Literacy in the Roman Empire: Mass and Mode." Pages 119-31 in *Literacy in the Roman World.* Ed. Mary Beard. JRASup 3. Ann Arbor: Journal of Roman Archaeology, 1991.

Easterling, P. E., and B. M. W. Knox. "Books and Readers in the Greek World." Pages 1-41 in *Greek Literature.* Vol. 1 of *The Cambridge History of Classical Literature.* Ed. P. E. Easterling and B. M. W. Knox. Cambridge: Cambridge University Press, 1989.

Ehrman, Bart D., and Michael W. Holmes, eds. *The Text of the New Testament in Contemporary Research: Essays on the Status Quaestionis.* NTTSD 42. 2nd ed. Ed. Bart D. Ehrman and Michael W. Holmes. Leiden: Brill, 2013.

Ellis, E. Earle. *The Making of the New Testament Documents.* Leiden: Brill, 1999.

Epp, Eldon Jay. "The Papyrus Manuscripts of the New Testament." Pages 3-21 in *The Text of the New Testament in Contemporary Research: Essays on the Status Quaestionis.* 2nd ed. Ed. Bart D. Ehrman and Michael W. Holmes. NTTSD 42. Leiden: Brill, 2013.

Gamble, Harry Y. *Books and Readers in the Early Church: A History of Early Christian Texts.* New Haven: Yale University Press, 1995.

Harris, William V. *Ancient Literacy.* Cambridge: Harvard University Press, 1989.

Havelock, Eric. *The Literate Revolution in Greece and Its Cultural Consequences.* Princeton: Princeton University Press, 1982.

————. *The Muse Learns to Write: Reflection on Orality and Literacy.* New Haven: Yale University Press, 1986.

Hezser, Catherine. *Jewish Literacy in Roman Palestine.* TSAJ 81. Tübingen: Mohr Siebeck, 2001.

Hopkins, Keith. "Conquest by Book." Pages 133-58 in *Literacy in the Roman World.* Ed. Mary Beard. JRASup 3. Ann Arbor: Journal of Roman Archaeology, 1991.

Hurtado, Larry W. *The Earliest Christian Artifacts: Manuscripts and Christian Origins.* Grand Rapids: Eerdmans, 2006.

Kenyon, Frederic G. *Books and Readers in Ancient Greece and Rome.* Oxford: Clarendon, 1932.

Metzger, Bruce M. "Literary Forgeries and Canonical Pseudepigrapha." *JBL* 91 (1972): 3-24.

————. *The Text of the New Testament: Its Transmission, Corruption, and Restoration.* 4th ed. Rev. Bart D. Ehrman. Oxford: Oxford University Press, 2005.

Millard, Alan. *Reading and Writing in the Time of Jesus.* Biblical Seminar 69. Sheffield: Sheffield Academic Press, 2000.

Osburn, Carroll D. "The Greek Lectionaries of the New Testament." Pages 93-113 in *The Text of the New Testament in Contemporary Research: Essays on the Status Quaestionis.* 2nd ed. Ed. Bart D. Ehrman and Michael W. Holmes. NTTSD 42. Leiden: Brill, 2013.

Porter, Stanley E. "Textual Criticism." Pages 1210-14 in *Dictionary of New Testament Background.* Ed. Craig A. Evans and Stanley E. Porter. Downers Grove, IL: InterVarsity Press, 2000.

Porter, Stanley E., and Andrew W. Pitts. "Paul and His Bible: His Education and Access to the Scriptures of Israel." *JGRChJ* 4 (2008): 9-41.

Rappoport, S. *History of Egypt: From 330 B.C. to the Present Time.* Vol. 11. London: Grolier Society, 1904.

Skeat, T. C. "Was Papyrus Regarded as 'Cheap' or 'Expensive' in the Ancient World?" *Aeg* 75 (1995): 75-93.

Starr, Raymond J. "The Circulation of Literary Texts in the Roman World." *CQ* 37 (1989): 313-23.

Thomas, Rosalind. *Oral Tradition and Written Record in Classical Athens.* Cambridge: Cambridge University Press, 1989.

————. *Literacy and Orality in Ancient Greece.* Cambridge: Cambridge University Press, 1992.

CHAPTER 4

The Major Witnesses to the
Text of the New Testament

In addition to manuscripts (and lectionaries), discussed generally in the previous chapter, **patristic quotations** (quotations of the NT by the early church fathers) and early **versions** (translations) provide important data to aid in the task of reconstructing the text of the NT. This chapter surveys these major witnesses and the value that they have for textual criticism and understanding of the textual history and transmission of the text of the NT. Because of the voluminous data, this chapter is only intended to provide a brief introduction to a few of the more important witnesses (i.e., manuscripts that witness to the earliest form of the Greek text of the NT).

1. Introducing the Gregory-Aland Numbering System

The manuscripts and other witnesses to the text of the NT are located at a wide variety of sites worldwide. These sites include major national libraries, university libraries, public and private museums, and private collections. As a result, with such a wealth of evidence, it is difficult to keep track of all of the available manuscript sources of the NT, with each piece of evidence having its own physical location and identification within that place, without reference to any of the other evidence.

As the abundance of new manuscript evidence for the Greek NT — including the papyri, majuscules, minuscules, and lectionaries, besides the evidence from the church fathers and versions — came to be known, there were a number of efforts to organize the materials. The problem became acute during the second half of the nineteenth century, when the manuscripts increased at a faster rate than ever before. This major organizing effort was orchestrated by **Caspar René Gregory**, an American who became a well-known German NT scholar who specialized in textual criticism. He authored a number of major scholarly books, including the *Prolegomena* to **Constantine Tischendorf**'s 8th edition of the Greek NT (which we will mention again below), a major work on textual criticism, and a major work on canon. He is also the one who inaugurated the consolidated list of NT manuscripts, which he first published in 1908. The volume contains sections on the majuscules (of which Gregory listed 161), papyri (with 14, several of them having earlier been classified as other types of documents, such as lectionaries, before there was a category for papyri), minuscules (with 2,292), and lectionaries (with 1,540, and a few incomplete ones). In this volume, Gregory established the categories and enumeration system used to this day: the Gothic 𝔓 for papyri followed by an Arabic numeral (e.g., $\mathfrak{P}^{56}$), an Arabic numeral preceded by 0 and/or a capital letter up to Z and a capital Greek letter up to omega for majuscules (e.g., A 02, or 071), an Arabic number for minuscules (e.g., 1, 1924), and an Arabic number preceded by a small cursive *l* for lectionaries (e.g., *l*1043). One notices, however, that even though the categories are the same, not all of the numbers are used, and some manuscripts, even at this early stage, have been placed in various categories. These inconsistencies have continued in the list. After Gregory was killed in the First World War, the list was continued by **Ernst von Dobschütz** and then by **Kurt Aland**, whose Institute for New Testament Textual Research now maintains the list, even with its inconsistencies.[1]

2. Greek Manuscripts of the New Testament

The discovery and identification of NT manuscripts continues to this day, with numerous manuscripts being identified around the world. Many, if not most, of these manuscripts were discovered a long time ago and are now housed in various museums or libraries, especially church libraries of various sorts. Many of them have just recently been rediscovered and identified due to the changing political situation around the world, in which libraries that were previously inaccessible are now potentially

---

1. See Kurt Aland and Barbara Aland, *The Text of the New Testament: An Introduction to the Critical Editions and to the Theory and Practice of Modern Textual Criticism* (trans. Erroll F. Rhodes; 2nd ed.; Grand Rapids: Eerdmans, 1989), 73-75.

open to scholars. Most of these manuscripts are of late date, and often are lectionaries or minuscules. A few are majuscules, and even fewer are of earlier date. A few papyri are still regularly published, some with fairly early dates.

Arguably the most important person to discover, identify, and publish NT manuscripts is the German scholar from Leipzig, Constantine Tischendorf. Living in the nineteenth century, Tischendorf devoted his career as a scholar to discovering and publishing as many Greek NT (as well as other biblical and other language) manuscripts as he could find, so that he could establish the early reliability of the NT text. He undertook this task in direct opposition to the rise of German higher criticism, which was increasingly skeptical of the reliability of the NT. In the course of his travels to various places around Europe and the Middle East, Tischendorf discovered, identified, and published more manuscripts than any other scholar in history before or since. Among his many textual exploits were the decipherment of a majuscule manuscript that had been written in the fifth century but that then had been erased so that selections from a later Syriac church father's work could be written over it (Codex Ephraemi Rescriptus; C 04). This manuscript is a palimpsest, a document in which the original writing has been erased and written over. Many previous scholars had tried to decipher this manuscript, but Tischendorf accomplished the task and published an edition that is still highly reliable today. Tischendorf also published the first reliable edition of Codex Vaticanus (B 03), a very reliable early (fourth century) NT manuscript that had been in the Vatican Library since the fifteenth century and had been consulted by Erasmus for his edition of the Greek NT, published in 1516. These are just two of Tischendorf's many accomplishments.

The most important of them all, however, was his discovery of Codex Sinaiticus (‎א 01), which he identified in St. Catherine's Monastery at the base of Mount Sinai in the Sinai Peninsula. Tischendorf visited St. Catherine's Monastery three times. On the first trip, in 1844, he found the monks burning what he identified as the earliest manuscript he had ever seen — apparently they were cold and needed fodder for their fire! He was able to save the manuscript and was given a number of pages of the OT in Greek, which he took back to Leipzig and published. After a second trip, in 1853, during which it appeared that the manuscript had been forgotten or had disappeared, Tischendorf revisited the monastery one last time in 1859, and was shown the remains of the manuscript first seen in 1844. Through a process of negotiation, Tischendorf was able to borrow the manuscript so that it could first be copied, and then published, in 1862 in a beautiful facsimile edition sponsored by the czar of Russia. For this beautiful edition, of which only three hundred twenty-seven copies of the four-volume edition were printed, Tischendorf found special paper and designed a unique font, which included several different types of various characters so as to capture the original as realistically as possible. There is some controversy over how the manuscript came to be given to the czar, but the evidence is that the monks at the time bequeathed the manuscript to the czar in return for a number of considerations. This manuscript was later sold by the Soviet government in 1933 to the British people for £100,000, and it can be viewed today in the British Library.[2]

a. Papyri

The papyri today occupy pride of place in textual criticism, even though they are the most recent addition to the set of manuscripts available. Tischendorf was the first to refer to a NT papyrus ($\mathfrak{P}^{11}$) in 1855, and only 128 have been identified and published. There are some scholars who claim that much more use should be made of the papyri in establishing the text of the NT. However, they have entered into the establishment of the current eclectic text fairly minimally. The standard eclectic text is based upon the two major majuscule manuscripts (Sinaiticus and Vaticanus). There is some justification for this, as the two majuscule manuscripts are the earliest complete (or nearly complete) manuscripts we have. The papyri are all fragmentary, and only a few have more than a portion of a single book represented. Furthermore, there are also a number of majuscule manuscripts that are as old as some of the papyri.

The following chart organizes the papyri, not according to their Gregory/Aland number, which tends to reflect when they were entered into the list, but their estimated date of transcription. The list gives the Gregory/Aland number, the inventory number of the manuscript according to the collection to which it belongs, its proposed date (there are often differences of opinion regarding these dates, as the papyri are dated by handwriting), their NT content, and their textual character.

2. On the history of this manuscript and Tischendorf himself, see Stanley E. Porter, *Constantine Tischendorf: The Life and Work of a 19th Century Bible Hunter* (London: Bloomsbury, 2015).

Gregory-Aland Numbers	Publication Name/Numbers	Date	NT Books Contained	Textual Character
$\mathfrak{P}^{52}$	P.Rylands G. 457	A.D. 100-125	John 8:31-33, 37-38	Alexandrian
$\mathfrak{P}^{104}$	P.Oxy. 4404	beginning of second century	Matt 21:34-37, 43, 45(?)	Alexandrian
$\mathfrak{P}^{46}$	Chester Beatty II/P.Mich.Inv. 6238	mid-second century	Hebrews and all of Paul's Letters, except for 2 Thessalonians, the Pastorals, and Philemon	Affinities with the Alexandrian and Western text, but closer to the Alexandrian
$\mathfrak{P}^{66}$	P.Bodmer II/Inv. Nr. 4274/4298	mid-second century	Most of John	Western and Alexandrian
$\mathfrak{P}^{87}$	Cologne University Institut für Altertums Kunde Inv. Nr. 12	mid-second century	Philem 13-15, 24-25	Alexandrian
$\mathfrak{P}^{4} = \mathfrak{P}^{64}/\mathfrak{P}^{67}$	Chester Beatty II	mid- to late second century	Portions of Luke 1–6 ($\mathfrak{P}^{4}$) and Matt 3, 5, and 26 ($\mathfrak{P}^{64}/\mathfrak{P}^{67}$)	Strong affinities with Sinaiticus ($\aleph$) and Vaticanus (B)
$\mathfrak{P}^{98}$	P.IFAO Inv. 237[+a]	mid- to late second century	Rev 1:13–2:1	Unable to determine
$\mathfrak{P}^{90}$	P.Oxy. 3523	mid- to late second century	John 18:36–19:37	Most significant affinities with $\mathfrak{P}^{66}$
$\mathfrak{P}^{77}$	P.Oxy. 2683 + 4405	mid- to late second century	Matt 23:30-39	proto-Alexandrian, probably from the same codex as $\mathfrak{P}^{103}$
$\mathfrak{P}^{103}$	P.Oxy. 4403	mid- to late second century	Matt 13:55-57; 14:3-5	proto-Alexandrian, probably from the same codex as $\mathfrak{P}^{77}$
$\mathfrak{P}^{32}$	P.Rylands G. 5	mid- to late second century	Titus 1:11-15; 2:3-8	Sinaiticus ($\aleph$), Augiensis (F), and Boernerianus (G)

Gregory-Aland Numbers	Publication Name/Numbers	Date	NT Books Contained	Textual Character
𝔓¹⁰⁹	P.Oxy. 4448	mid- to late second century	John 21:18-20, 23-25	Too small to assess
𝔓¹⁰⁸	P.Oxy. 4447	late second century	John 17:23-24; 18:1-5	Agrees with Sinaiticus (א)
𝔓¹	P.Oxy. 2	mid-third century	Matt 1:1-9, 12, 14-20	Alexandrian, especially Vaticanus (B)
𝔓⁵	P.Oxy. 208+1781	early third century	portions of John 1, 16, and 20	Alexandrian, especially Sinaiticus (א)
𝔓¹³	P.Oxy. 657 + PSI 1292	first half of third century	portions of Heb 2–5 and 10–12	Usually agrees with Vaticanus (B)
𝔓²³	P.Oxy. 1229	early third century	Jas 1:10-12, 15-18	Affinities with Rescriptus (C), Sinaiticus (א) and Alexandrinus (A)
𝔓²²	P.Oxy. 1228	mid-third century	John 15:25–16:2, 21-32	eclectic

b. Majuscules

The two major majuscule manuscripts from the fourth century, Codex Sinaiticus and Codex Vaticanus, are the basis of the modern Greek NT. As discussed elsewhere, Westcott and Hort described these two manuscripts as the Neutral text. Even though textual critics reject this label today, many of them still use these two majuscule codices as the basis of their text and judge variants against these two manuscripts. Besides its use in the edition of Westcott and Hort (1881), Tischendorf used Codex Sinaiticus as the basis of his 8th edition (1869-72; see ch. 11), as well as providing an exemplary critical apparatus that is still valuable for consultation today. The Nestle text of the NT was based upon comparison of three published editions, including the Westcott and Hort edition and Tischendorf's 8th edition (see ch. 12).

The following chart provides a list of the major majuscule manuscripts that are commonly used in NT textual criticism.

Gregory-Aland Numbers	Publication Name/Numbers	Date	NT Books Contained	Textual Character
ℵ (01)	Aleph or Sinaiticus	4th century	The entire NT	Alexandrian
B (03)	Vaticanus	4th century	Includes all of the NT except Heb 9:14ff., 1-2 Timothy, Titus, Philemon, and Revelation	Alexandrian
W (032)	Washingtonianus	early 5th century	Gospels	Mixed; earliest representation of Byzantine text-type. Alexandrian in John 5:12–21:25.
A (02)	Alexandrinus	5th century	Most of the NT	Important in the Epistles and Revelation
C (04)	Ephraemi Rescriptus	5th century	Includes parts of every book except 2 Thessalonians and 2 John	mixed
D^{ea} (05)	Bezae/ Cantabrigiensis	5th century	Gospels and Acts	Western
D^{P} (06)	Claromontanus	6th century	All of Paul's Letters and Hebrews	Western
E^{2} or E^{a} (08)	Laudianus 35	6th or 7th century	Acts	Often agrees with Western or Byzantine
E (07)	Basilensis	8th century	Acts	Byzantine
L (019)	Regius	8th century	Gospels	Typically agrees with Vaticanus (B)
Ψ (044)	Athous Laurae	8th/9th century	Gospels, Acts, Paul's Letters and the General Letters	Agrees with Alexandrian, Western, and Byzantine in various places
F (010)	Augiensis	9th century	Paul's Letters	Western
G (012)	Boernerianus	9th century	Paul's Letters	Western

Gregory-Aland Numbers	Publication Name/Numbers	Date	NT Books Contained	Textual Character
Θ (038)	Koridethi	9th century	Gospels	Has affinities with Origen's and Eusebius's text in Caesarea

c. Minuscules

Minuscules, for the most part, are late in date, usually contain one or more major portion of the NT, and reflect the Byzantine text, that is, the text that came to be widely used throughout the Byzantine world (from the sixth century A.D. onward). Minuscules formed the basis of the first printed Greek NTs (by Erasmus in 1516; see ch. 5) and the translational base for many early translations, such as the KJV. Minuscules are the most common Greek NT manuscripts in existence, and hence they reflect what is sometimes called the Majority text, because of their sheer numbers. Some believe that the Byzantine text, because of its history and significance and numerical superiority, or the Majority text, because of its sheer numbers (the two are not identical terms, but similar in many ways), should still constitute the basis of the Greek NT used today. Some even argue that the Byzantine text reflects a textual tradition more reliable than any other. Most textual critics of the NT do not hold to this view, arguing that the Byzantine text's textual evidence tends to be significantly later (the majority of the texts are late, so they are not the majority at the earlier period), and that the earlier manuscripts such as the papyri and majuscules are more reliable.

Nevertheless, a number of minuscule manuscripts are important in textual criticism. Some of these are among the manuscripts that Erasmus used in establishing his Greek NT.

Gregory-Aland Numbers	Publication Name/Numbers	Date	NT Books Contained	Textual Character
33	Colbertinus 2844	9th century	Gospels, Acts, Paul, Catholic Epistles	Alexandrian with Byzantine readings

Gregory-Aland Numbers	Publication Name/Numbers	Date	NT Books Contained	Textual Character
81	———	A.D. 1044	Acts, Paul, Catholic Epistles	Typically agrees with Alexandrian, but with Byzantine readings
1739	Goltz	10th century, but may be a copy of a late-4th-century manuscript	Acts, Paul, Catholic Epistles	Alexandrian
1	Basilensis	12th-13th centuries	Gospels	Caesarean
Family 1 (¹)	The Lake Group	12th-14th centuries	Gospels	Caesarean. Note this group of manuscripts' role in the discussion of the *pericope adulterae* (John 7:53–8:11)
Family 13 (¹³)	The Ferrar Group	11th-15th centuries	Gospels	Caesarean. Note this group of manuscripts' role in the discussion of the *pericope adulterae* (John 7:53–8:11)

d. Lectionaries

The definition of a NT manuscript is that it provides continuous text of the Greek NT. Lectionaries are manuscripts that provide not continuous text but excerpts of various types that were created for liturgical use. Most lectionaries are relatively late in date and reflect the period after the development of relatively fixed lectional readings for the various days of the week. These lectionaries then isolate and include this portion of text, often with a suitable, brief introduction. The notion of a lectionary is highly problematic, however, for two major reasons. One of these is that it is difficult to establish that many of the papyri, and a good number of the majuscule texts, were in fact continuous text and not themselves excerpts.

The major example of the difficulty is that many papyri of John's Gospel include a portion of text of the Gospel and then the word "interpretation" written under the text (ἑρμηνεία), under which are various nonscriptural statements, with language redolent of the Gospel text in some ways. These papyri are clearly not continuous text, but what they are has been highly debated. They appear to include some kind of biblical interpretation or inspired statement. In any case, they are not continuous text. In other cases, fragments of papyrus or parchment are so small that it is difficult to know how much text was included. Some of these appear to be miniature codices with a small excerpt of a biblical text upon them. Finally, some NT manuscripts were later provided with notation to indicate how they were to be read and intoned in church services. Because of their use, even though they are NT manuscripts, these seem to be lectionary texts in the truest sense of the word — manuscripts that were used as the readings for the day, complete with instructions on their use. As a result, it is surprising that, besides causing confusion for the listing of manuscripts, lectionaries have been neglected in NT criticism, even though some are early and do attest to the text of the NT, as well as its early liturgical use.

A few of the more important lectionaries are one from the fourth century (*l*1604), one from the fifth century (*l*1043), and a few from the sixth century (*l*1276, *l*1347, *l*1354) but the vast majority of these are later.

3. Early Versions of the New Testament

Another significant set of sources for reconstructing the NT text is ancient versions or translations of the NT. These translations are the result of the efforts of early Christian missionaries to bring the NT to those who spoke other languages. Bruce Metzger summarizes the importance of the early versions:

> The church historian . . . can learn not a little from them concerning the spread of Christianity in the ancient world, and by identifying the parent text-type from which a given version was made it is possible to ascertain the headquarters and direction of missionary activity. Furthermore, since every translation is in some measure a commentary, one can trace the history of the exegesis of disputed passages as disclosed in successive modifications of a given version. Moreover, the additions and omissions in the transmitted text can tell us something about the

doctrinal, liturgical, or ascetical interests of those who made and used such translations.[3]

The oldest and most significant versions for textual criticism are written in Syriac, Latin, and Coptic, but we also have Ethiopic and Armenian versions of the NT.

a. Tatian's Diatessaron

The oldest version of the NT is **Tatian's *Diatessaron*** (most likely written ca. A.D. 172), from the Greek διὰ τεσσάρων, meaning "through four" (i.e., through the four Gospels). It is also the earliest widely used harmony of the Gospels. The *Diatessaron*, therefore, is an important source for textual criticism of the Gospels since it provides a window into the texts available to Tatian in the second century when he composed his harmony. This version — if it were to still be extant — actually predates most of the extant manuscripts of the NT that we have today. As William Petersen observes, "In raw chronological terms, the Diatessaron antedates all MSS [manuscripts] of the NT, save that tiny fragment of the Gospel of John known as 𝔓[52]."[4]

There is some disagreement as to whether the *Diatessaron* was originally composed in Greek or Syriac, but the latter option is generally regarded to be more likely. In any case, the original is now lost. What we know of the *Diatessaron* is transmitted to us in a variety of languages (esp. Syriac) and quotations from the early fathers. The text we now have is reconstructed from these various witnesses (totaling over 170 readings, including various fragments and quotations). We know the *Diatessaron*, in other words, through its various translations. And since the Gospels were translated into Syriac, Armenian, Georgian, Arabic, and (possibly) Latin

---

3. Bruce M. Metzger, *The Early Versions of the New Testament: Their Origin, Transmission, and Limitations* (Oxford: Clarendon, 1977), vii.

4. William L. Petersen, "The Diatessaron of Tatian," in *The Text of the New Testament in Contemporary Research: Essays on the Status Quaestionis: A Volume in Honor of Bruce M. Metzger* (ed. Bart D. Ehrman and Michael W. Holmes; SD 46; Grand Rapids: Eerdmans, 1995), 77. This discussion is brought up to date in Ulrich Schmid, "The Diatessaron of Tatian," in *The Text of the New Testament in Contemporary Research: Essays on the Status Quaestionis* (2nd ed.; ed. Bart D. Ehrman and Michael W. Holmes; NTTSD 42; Leiden: Brill, 2013), 115-42.

in the form of the *Diatessaron,* its significance among the early versions cannot be minimized — at least for Gospels textual criticism.

b. Syriac Versions

A number of early Syriac versions are important for reconstructing the text of the NT. The most important of these are the Old Syriac Version, the Syriac Peshitta, and the Philoxenian and/or Harclean Version(s).

(1) Old Syriac Version

The Old Syriac Version of the four Gospels is preserved in only two manuscripts, whose texts may date from the end of the second or beginning of the third century — although the manuscripts themselves were probably copied in the fourth or fifth century. There was also an Old Syriac Version of Acts and the Pauline Letters, but we know of it only through citations from the church fathers.

(2) Syriac Peshitta

The Syriac Peshitta or Peshitto (meaning "simple") was translated in the fourth or early fifth century and includes the entire NT, with the exception of 2 Peter, 2 and 3 John, Jude, and Revelation — these were not considered to be part of the **canon** (collection of books considered to be authoritative) in the Syriac church when the translation was created. The textual tradition for the Syriac Peshitta is both abundant and stable, meaning that we have over 350 manuscripts (many from the fifth and sixth centuries) with very little variation among them. This translation is still recognized and used today by the Syrian church.

(3) Philoxenian/Harclean Version(s)

A sixth/seventh-century Syriac translation that has been quite confusing for scholars is known as the Philoxenian and/or Harclean version(s), depending on whether one sees them as two different versions. The importance of this version(s) for our purposes, however, is that it provides an early Syriac translation of the Catholic Letters and Revelation, which were not translated in the Syriac Peshitta.

c. Latin Versions

Latin became a major linguistic force in the Roman Empire, eventually replacing Greek as the lingua franca or common language in the ancient world. Latin influence was especially prominent in the western empire, including North Africa, Italy, and Gaul, where some of the first Latin versions are attested. There are two major traditions of Latin versions: various Old Latin versions and the Latin Vulgate.

(1) Old Latin Versions

The church father Tertullian (ca. 160-225) is sometimes said to show awareness of a Latin translation of (at least) some of Paul's letters, various Catholic letters, and Acts that was available in the second century, but the oldest versions currently available from this tradition are from the fourth and fifth centuries. A distinction is typically made between African and European Old Latin versions. The **African Old Latin Version** (though some think it was produced in Italy) was probably translated around the early third century and is characterized by distinct (i.e., ancient) vocabulary that makes it recognizable.[5] The **European Old Latin Version** is a revision of the African Old Latin Version, probably in the late third century, but only attested during and after the fourth century throughout Europe.

(2) Latin Vulgate

Although the OT Vulgate appears to be a new translation of the Hebrew text, the NT seems to be a revision of the European Old Latin version. The revision was probably done in the late fourth century. The Gospels are generally believed to have been revised by Jerome, but the person responsible

---

5. J. H. Petzer, "The Latin Version of the New Testament," in *Text of the New Testament,* 2nd ed., ed. Ehrman and Holmes, 78.

for the revision of the rest of the NT is not known, although some have suggested Rufinus the Syrian and Pelagius. While the purpose of this new revision was to bring greater consistency among the Latin translations, it actually further complicated matters by causing more diversity among the Latin versions as the **Latin Vulgate** was copied throughout the history of the church and changes were introduced in the transmission process.

d. Coptic Versions

Although during the Hellenistic period (300 B.C.–A.D. 300) of Egypt Greek was the dominant language due to the large number of Greeks that had settled there, Copts or native Egyptian Christians (the term originally referred simply to Egyptian natives) spoke a form of Demotic Egyptian using Greek-type letters, beginning in the first century A.D. or so. Coptic was their first language, even though they probably also functioned in Greek. The dominant Greek influence in Hellenistic Egypt resulted in borrowed Greek vocabulary and syntax. Frederik Wisse calculates that "On the average about 15 percent of the words in early Coptic texts are Greek."[6] This Greek influence makes Coptic versions especially useful in ascertaining the Greek texts that were in use when the translation was made. We have no single continuous Coptic versions of the NT. They are unfortunately preserved only in fragmentary form. The significant Coptic versions include the Sahidic, Achmimic, Lycopolitan, Middle Egyptian, and Bohairic versions. These refer to various dialects of Coptic into which the NT was translated.

e. Ethiopic Version

The Ethiopic (Ge'ez) Version is restricted to a small portion of Africa and, although the oldest manuscript dates from around the tenth century, most come from during or after the fifteenth century. The prevailing opinion is that this version was translated book by book during the fourth and fifth centuries. There is some debate about whether the Ethiopic Version was

---

6. Frederik Wisse, "The Coptic Versions of the New Testament," in *Text of the New Testament*, 1st ed., ed. Ehrman and Holmes, 132. This discussion is brought up to date in Christian Askeland, "The Coptic Versions of the New Testament," in *Text of the New Testament*, 2nd ed., ed. Ehrman and Holmes, 201-29.

translated from Greek or Syriac, but it may turn out that some portions were translated from a Greek text whereas others used a Syriac text. While this version is considerably late, it has been useful in particular areas of textual criticism, especially in assessing the disputed ending of Mark's Gospel.

f. Armenian Version

According to Joseph Alexanian, "The Bible was translated into Armenian in the early fifth century as part of an historic struggle to unify the Armenian people and preserve their religion and culture in the battles between the Persian Empire on the east and the Byzantine Empire on the west."[7] The Armenian Bible was then thoroughly revised later in the fifth century. All of the NT manuscripts we currently have of the Armenian Version come from this revision, but a few OT manuscripts reflect the earlier, initial translation. The Armenian Version provides an important Caesarean witness (see ch. 5) to the text of the NT.

We are fortunate to have such an abundance of versional evidence for the Greek NT, not all of which can be dealt with here. We have had to pass over a number of other versions, such as the Georgian and Gothic. However, when one deals with translations, one must always keep in mind that no two languages match up perfectly, as mirrors of each other; and as a result, there are difficulties in using one to reconstruct the other. For example, Latin does not have an article, whereas Greek has an article. Therefore it is difficult to use the Latin evidence to establish whether an article was used, for example, before an instance of a given noun. Thus caution is necessary when using the versions.

4. Patristic Quotations

Quotations of the NT from the early church fathers — referred to as **patristic quotations** — also play an important role in reconstructing

---

7. Joseph M. Alexanian, "The Armenian Version of the New Testament," in *Text of the New Testament,* 1st ed., ed. Ehrman and Holmes, 157. This discussion is brought up to date in S. Peter Cowe, "The Armenian Version of the New Testament," in *Text of the New Testament,* 2nd ed., ed. Ehrman and Holmes, 253-92.

the NT text in that they give us insight into what text types (see ch. 5) were available and in use *when* and *where* they wrote. In some cases, this makes the church fathers a more certain source than Greek manuscripts since the date and geographical location of the church fathers are usually easy to ascertain. Despite their importance for textual criticism, the early church fathers remain one of the most understudied witnesses to the NT text.

A number of difficulties in using the church fathers in reconstructing the NT text are often noted, such as whether individual fathers cited the NT from memory or from a written source, whether the quotation was intended to be a paraphrase or a direct citation, and the occurrence of inconsistencies in the transmission of the patristic texts themselves. Other problems arise from the fact that in some instances a church father may attest to two or more versions of the same text, making it difficult to determine which is earlier or original. A further difficulty is that many of the church fathers do not have the same extant manuscript evidence and their writings have not been critically edited to the same standard as the NT text. Sometimes an additional stage of textual criticism must be performed upon the patristic source before its value for NT textual criticism can be determined. Bruce Metzger and Bart Ehrman have conveniently listed some of the more important church fathers who frequently cite the NT and whose names are sometimes found in the critical apparatus:[8]

> Ambrose of Milan, d. 397
> Ambrosiaster (= pseudo-Ambrose) of Rome, second half of fourth
>   century
> Athanasius, bishop of Alexandria, d. 373
> Augustine, bishop of Hippo, d. 430
> Chrysostom, bishop of Constantinople, d. 407
> Clement of Alexandria, d. ca. 212
> Cyprian, bishop of Carthage, d. 258
> Cyril of Alexandria, d. 444
> Didymus of Alexandria, d. ca. 398
> Ephraem the Syrian, d. 373
> Epiphanius, bishop of Salamis, d. 403

---

8. Bruce M. Metzger, *The Text of the New Testament: Its Transmission, Corruption, and Restoration* (4th ed. rev. Bart D. Ehrman; Oxford: Oxford University Press, 2005), 131.

Eusebius, bishop of Caesarea, d. 339 or 340
Gregory of Nazianzus in Cappadocia, d. 389 or 390
Gregory of Nyssa in Cappadocia, d. 394
Hilary of Poitiers, d. 367
Hippolytus of Rome, d. 235
Irenaeus, bishop of Lyons, d. ca. 202
Isidore of Pelusium, d. ca. 435
Jerome (= Hieronymus), d. 419 or 420
Justin Martyr, d. ca. 165
Lucifer of Calaris (Cagliari), d. 370 or 371
Marcion, flourished at Rome, d. 150–60
Origen of Alexandria and Caesarea, d. 253 or 254
Pelagius, fourth-fifth century
Primasius, bishop of Hadrumentum, d. soon after 525
Pseudo-Hieronymus, fifth–sixth century
Rufinus of Aquileia, d. 410
Tatian, flourished ca. 170
Tertullian of Carthage, d. after 220
Theodore of Mopsuestia in Cilicia, d. 428

Other important patristic writings that frequently cite the NT include the *Didache* (A.D. 50-160), an early Christian worship manual that relies heavily upon Gospel material; the writings of Polycarp (A.D. 59-155), the disciple of the apostle John; the writings of Ignatius of Antioch (A.D. 35-107); and the *Letter to Diognetus* (A.D. 100-150).

5. Summary

The manuscript evidence of the Greek NT is abundant and falls into at least two categories. The first category comprises the manuscripts themselves, which are categorized as papyri, majuscules, minuscules, or lectionaries. Even though these are not clearly separated categories, they are useful starting points for distinguishing the major sources for the Greek NT, especially the papyri and majuscules, the latter of which constitute the basis of the contemporary Greek NT. The second category includes the early versions and church fathers. Although these are not primary sources, they can, with the proper handling, provide insights into the NT text.

BIBLIOGRAPHY

Aland, Kurt, and Barbara Aland. *The Text of the New Testament: An Introduction to the Critical Editions and to the Theory and Practice of Modern Textual Criticism.* Trans. Erroll F. Rhodes. 2nd ed. Grand Rapids: Eerdmans, 1989.

Alexanian, Joseph M. "The Armenian Version of the New Testament." Pages 157-72 in *The Text of the New Testament in Contemporary Research: Essays on the Status Quaestionis: A Volume in Honor of Bruce M. Metzger.* Ed. Bart D. Ehrman and Michael W. Holmes. SD 46. Grand Rapids: Eerdmans, 1995.

Askeland, Christian. "The Coptic Versions of the New Testament." Pages 201-29 in *The Text of the New Testament in Contemporary Research: Essays on the Status Quaestionis.* 2nd ed. Ed. Bart D. Ehrman and Michael W. Holmes. NTTSD 42. Leiden: Brill, 2013.

Baarda, Tjitze. "The Syriac Versions of the New Testament." Pages 97-112 in *The Text of the New Testament in Contemporary Research: Essays on the Status Quaestionis: A Volume in Honor of Bruce M. Metzger.* Ed. Bart D. Ehrman and Michael W. Holmes. SD 46. Grand Rapids: Eerdmans, 1995.

Birdsall, J. Neville. "The Georgian Version of the New Testament." Pages 173-87 in *The Text of the New Testament in Contemporary Research: Essays on the Status Quaestionis: A Volume in Honor of Bruce M. Metzger.* Ed. Bart D. Ehrman and Michael W. Holmes. SD 46. Grand Rapids: Eerdmans, 1995.

Burton, Philip. "The Latin Version of the New Testament." Pages 167-200 in *The Text of the New Testament in Contemporary Research: Essays on the Status Quaestionis.* 2nd ed. Ed. Bart D. Ehrman and Michael W. Holmes. NTTSD 42. Leiden: Brill, 2013.

Childers, Jeff W. "The Georgian Version of the New Testament." Pages 293-327 in *The Text of the New Testament in Contemporary Research: Essays on the Status Quaestionis*. 2nd ed. Ed. Bart D. Ehrman and Michael W. Holmes. NTTSD 42. Leiden: Brill, 2013.

Cowe, S. Peter. "The Armenian Version of the New Testament." Pages 253-92 in *The Text of the New Testament in Contemporary Research: Essays on the Status Quaestionis*. 2nd ed. Ed. Bart D. Ehrman and Michael W. Holmes. NTTSD 42. Leiden: Brill, 2013.

Ehrman, Bart D., and Michael W. Holmes, eds. *The Text of the New Testament in Contemporary Research: Essays on the Status Quaestionis*. 2nd ed. NTTSD 42. Leiden: Brill, 2013.

Fee, Gordon D., rev. Roderick L. Mullen. "The Greek Fathers for New Testament Textual Criticism." Pages 1351-63 in *The Text of the New Testament in Contemporary Research: Essays on the Status Quaestionis*. 2nd ed. Ed. Bart D. Ehrman and Michael W. Holmes. NTTSD 42. Leiden: Brill, 2013.

Metzger, Bruce M. *The Early Versions of the New Testament: Their Origin, Transmission, and Limitations*. Oxford: Clarendon, 1977.

Metzger, Bruce M. *The Text of the New Testament: Its Transmission, Corruption, and Restoration*. 4th ed. Rev. Bart D. Ehrman. Oxford: Oxford University Press, 2005.

Porter, Stanley E. *How We Got the New Testament: Text, Transmission, Translation*. Grand Rapids: Baker, 2013.

Schmid, Ulrich B. "The Diatessaron of Tatian." Pages 115-42 in *The Text of the New Testament in Contemporary Research: Essays on the Status Quaestionis*. 2nd ed. Ed. Bart D. Ehrman and Michael W. Holmes. NTTSD 42. Leiden: Brill, 2013.

Williams, Peter J. "The Syriac Versions of the New Testament." Pages 143-66 in *The Text of the New Testament in Contemporary Research: Essays on the Status Quaestionis*. 2nd ed. Ed. Bart D. Ehrman and Michael W. Holmes. NTTSD 42. Leiden: Brill, 2013.

Wisse, Frederik. "The Coptic Versions of the New Testament." Pages 131-41 in *The Text of the New Testament in Contemporary Research: Essays on the Status Quaestionis: A Volume in Honor of Bruce M. Metzger*. Ed. Bart D. Ehrman and Michael W. Holmes. SD 46. Grand Rapids: Eerdmans, 1995.

Zuurmond, Rochus, rev. Curt Niccum. "The Ethiopic Version of the New Testament." Pages 231-42 in *The Text of the New Testament in Contemporary Research: Essays on the Status Quaestionis*. 2nd ed. Ed. Bart D. Ehrman and Michael W. Holmes. NTTSD 42. Leiden: Brill, 2013.

CHAPTER 5

Text-Types

As the original autographs were copied and then these copies were further copied in early Christian communities, small changes or *variants* were introduced. As copies began to spread across the ancient world, the copies produced and circulated in various regions began to evidence similar variants or readings. The Alands compare the phenomenon to ripples in a pond:

> The circulation of a document began either from the place (or church province) of its origin, where the author wrote it, or from the place to which it was addressed. . . . Copies of the original would be made for use in neighboring churches. The circulation of a book would be like the ripples of a stone cast into a pond, spreading out in all directions at once. When the book was shared by repeated copying throughout a whole diocese or metropolitan area, the close ties between dioceses would carry it from one district to another, where the process would be repeated.[1]

We have evidence of this process of textual transmission in Col 4:16, where the recipients in Colossae are commanded to read the letter to the Laodiceans in their own church and to allow the letter written to them to be read in the church in Laodicea. As copies of the NT moved farther and farther from their origin, this process of circulation eventually resulted in a number of geographically based textual families or **text-types**.

---

1. Kurt Aland and Barbara Aland, *The Text of the New Testament: An Introduction to the Critical Editions and to the Theory and Practice of Modern Textual Criticism* (trans. Erroll F. Rhodes; 2nd ed.; Grand Rapids: Eerdmans, 1989), 55.

Text-types share a number of similar readings that are not typical in other families. At the time when many of these text-types were identified, they were often associated with actual physical locations. As a result, some believe the **Alexandrian text-type** was associated with Alexandria, Egypt (an ancient center of textual scholarship from before the time of the NT), and was the oldest and closest to the original autographs. But distinct textual families also are sometimes thought by scholars to have emerged in Caesarea in Palestine (the **Caesarean text-type**), Rome (the **Western text-type**) and Byzantium (the **Byzantine text-type**, also known as the Syrian or Koine text-type or sometimes loosely associated with the Majority text). After briefly reviewing the use of text-types in NT textual criticism, we consider each family and its value for textual criticism in this chapter.

1. The Use of Text-Types in New Testament Textual Criticism

For the most part, contemporary textual critics view the Alexandrian text-type as the superior witness to the text of the NT. This, however, has not always been the case. The first printed editions of the Greek NT were based on the Byzantine text-type. This trend continued for around three hundred years, until scholars such as J. J. Griesbach, Constantine Tischendorf, and B. F. Westcott and F. J. A. Hort came to recognize the superiority of the Alexandrian family of manuscripts.

Although the first printed edition of the NT is often accredited to one published in 1516 by the great Dutch scholar **Desiderius Erasmus**, a theologian well known for his debates with the Protestant reformer Martin Luther, his edition was preceded in printing by the 1514 edition of the (NT portion of the) **Complutensian Polyglot**, a Greek-Latin edition of the entire Bible. However, though printed earlier, the polyglot was not published until after Erasmus's due to ecclesiastical politics. While the manuscripts used to compile the Complutensian Polyglot remain unknown, it is certain that Erasmus relied mainly on a relatively small number of twelfth- and thirteenth-century manuscripts from the Byzantine family and did not consult earlier manuscripts, even when they were available. Because of its popularity, a later publisher referred to the text that resulted from Erasmus's efforts as the **Textus Receptus** (the "received text") since it was widely accepted as the Greek text of the NT. But as Kurt Aland and Barbara Aland note, Erasmus's edition(s) was far from uniform: "the text published by Colinaeus . . . in 1534, the first edition to follow Erasmus' five (constantly revised) editions, shows numerous differences from them, partly derived from the Complutensian text . . . and partly due to the use of additional manuscripts."[2] Nevertheless, the Textus Receptus was considered to be the best representation of the NT text for several centuries to come.

While several scholars had questioned the Textus Receptus in a number of places, especially **Johann Jakob Griesbach** (1745-1812), the major turning point away from the Textus Receptus was marked by the discovery of Codex Sinaiticus (see ch. 4) by Constantine Tischendorf (1815-1874) and the comprehensive editions of the NT that he diligently compiled, especially the 8th edition, which used Sinaiticus. Tischendorf understood this Alexandrian witness (see below) as the most important available witness to the early text of the NT and symbolized its priority in textual criticism by using the first letter of the Hebrew alphabet (א, *aleph*) as its symbol. But it was **Brooke Foss Westcott** (1825-1901) and **Fenton John Anthony Hort** (1828-1892) who really set the trajectory for the high priority placed upon the Alexandrian text in contemporary NT textual criticism. Along with Codex Sinaiticus, they emphasized Codex Vaticanus (see ch. 4) as important Alexandrian witnesses to the NT text. They were persuaded that when Codex Vaticanus and Codex Sinaiticus were in agreement this reading represented the **Neutral Text**, against which variations should be measured. While contemporary scholars claim not to hold the Alexandrian text in this high regard (though the most widely used text of the NT is based upon these two codices), most still consider it to be the oldest, most reliable witness to the NT text.

2. Individual Text-Types

a. Alexandrian Text

The two oldest and closest to complete copies of the NT, Codex Sinaiticus and Codex Vaticanus (see ch. 4), are representatives of the **Alexandrian text-type**.[3] It is not, as Westcott and Hort proposed, that Sinaiticus and

---

2. Ibid., 6.

3. Codex Sinaiticus is complete for the NT, whereas Codex Vaticanus breaks off in the book of Hebrews, the text from there to the end being replaced by a later minuscule hand.

Vaticanus together represent a separate, stronger witness, distinct from the Alexandrian text-type. While the dual testimony of these two important codices undoubtedly represents a very strong and reliable reading, it is now generally accepted that this reading simply testifies to the broader Alexandrian text-type. In practice, manuscripts from the Alexandrian tradition are now widely recognized to have greater weight than manuscripts from other traditions.

b. Western Text

Based on NT citations from the early church father Irenaeus that appeared to bear affinities with later manuscripts of the **Western text**, Westcott and Hort suggested that it could be dated back to as early as the second century. Nevertheless, they remained skeptical about the validity of the Western text-type as an independent witness to the text of the NT, except in cases of shorter readings. However, little further evidence exists that would support the sustained development of a Western text-type in the second century, and the citations from Irenaeus probably evidence something like a proto- or pre-Western text-type. The Western text as we know it probably fully emerged early in the fourth century under efforts in the East (many scholars question whether "Western" is even an appropriate label for this family) toward revising the available manuscripts in order to make them more useful for liturgical and theological purposes. Today the Western text-type is preserved in primarily three forms. The Gospels and Acts are represented in *Codex Bezae Cantabrigiensis* (symbolized by D), a bilingual Greek-Latin manuscript dating from the fifth century. The other two key representatives of the Western tradition are among the ancient versions: (1) manuscripts *k* and *e* from the Old Latin Version, and (2) the Old Syriac Version.

c. Caesarean Text

The **Caesarean text-type** is the most recently discovered of the textual families and has the fewest representatives. It was identified by W. H. Farrar in 1868 when he noticed affinities between three minuscule Gospel manuscripts, constituting what is now known as Family 13 or the Farrar family. Other manuscripts said to follow the Caesarean tradition are Codex Koridethi and Family 1. Origen's citations of the NT are often said to correspond to the Caesarean text, and the modern textual critic J. Harold Greenlee has suggested that Cyril of Jerusalem's Gospel citations depend upon a Caesarean text-type.[4] Recent scholarship has seriously questioned whether there is such a thing as the Caesarean text-type, especially as it is relatively restricted in manuscripts and late in date.

d. Byzantine Text

Until recently in modern textual criticism, the **Byzantine text** has been almost entirely dismissed as a reliable witness to the NT text. Many (a few serious academics seek to establish solid scholarly support for this theory) who continue to insist on its value for textual criticism today are driven by the theological a priori that God preserved his Word within the Byzantine tradition, the assumption that the number of manuscripts is superior to the age of the manuscripts in determining reliability (thus the Byzantine text is often referred to as the Majority Text), and/or by the assumptions driving more extreme KJV-only fundamentalism. None of these lines of reasoning proves to be convincing, however. Although a comprehensive analysis of this discussion is outside of the scope of this chapter, a brief response to a few of the more textually oriented lines of reasoning is warranted here.

The theological assumption that God would have preserved his word specifically in the Byzantine church is entirely unsubstantiated exegetically, historically, and rationally. There is just no way to prove or disprove this claim: it is unfalsifiable and explanatorily vacuous. The argument from numbers clearly breaks down when it is realized that most of the Byzantine manuscripts are dated after the ninth century. Mere late numerical copying of manuscripts by medieval scribes in no way entails that the manuscript tradition that was copied was in some way more accurate than those copied several centuries earlier, from even earlier texts. Otherwise, one could just copy numerous Alexandrian manuscripts today, providing the tradition with more validity each time a document is copied. Furthermore, the rhetoric of fundamentalists and KJV-only advocates is rarely based on the rigors of biblical scholarship and insists instead upon perpetuating a

---

4. J. Harold Greenlee, *Introduction to New Testament Textual Criticism* (Grand Rapids: Eerdmans, 1964), 90.

theory that is untenable in light of the textual and historical evidence (to say nothing of its often implicit argument that God preserved not only the text but its translation in the KJV).

There is no evidence of a Byzantine tradition prior to the fourth century, nor are there citations of the Byzantine text from the church fathers prior to the fourth century. As we have already discussed, the earliest manuscripts of the NT are found among the papyri, and, of the 128 currently available, none of them contains distinctively Byzantine readings. One likely conclusion to draw from this is that the Byzantine text was probably the result of efforts toward standardizing the Greek text (further confirmed by the fact that the Byzantine tradition consistently has longer readings in places where it disagrees with other traditions) and does not reflect an early tradition of the NT text.

3. Summary

As individual NT books were received and circulated in the early Christian church, various copies were made and deployed throughout the ancient world. As manuscripts were circulated within particular geographical regions they began to take on particular characteristics/readings, unique to their location, resulting in localized text-types or textual families. Four major textual families have been identified and studied by NT textual critics: (1) Alexandrian, (2) Western, (3) Caesarean, and (4) Byzantine. We suggest that the Western and Byzantine text-types, however, may have been the result of a standardized revision process.

KEY TERMINOLOGY
Alexandrian text-type
Caesarean text-type
Western text-type
Byzantine text-type
Desiderius Erasmus
Complutensian Polyglot
Textus Receptus
Johann Jakob Griesbach
Brooke Foss Westcott
Fenton John Anthony Hort
Neutral text

BIBLIOGRAPHY

Aland, Kurt, and Barbara Aland. *The Text of the New Testament: An Intro-duction to the Critical Editions and to the Theory and Practice of Modern Textual Criticism.* Trans. Erroll F. Rhodes. 2nd ed. Grand Rapids: Eerd-mans, 1989.

Fee, Gordon D. "The Majority Text and the Original Text of the New Testa-ment." Pages 183-208 in Eldon Jay Epp and Gordon D. Fee, *Studies in the Theory and Method of New Testament Textual Criticism.* SD 45. Grand Rapids: Eerdmans, 1993.

Greenlee, J. Harold. *Introduction to New Testament Textual Criticism.* Grand Rapids: Eerdmans, 1964.

Porter, Stanley E. *How We Got the New Testament: Text, Transmission, Trans-lation.* Grand Rapids: Baker, 2013.

Wallace, Daniel B. "The Majority Text Theory: History, Methods, and Cri-tique." Pages 711-44 in *The Text of the New Testament in Contemporary Research: Essays on the Status Quaestionis.* 2nd ed. Ed. Bart D. Ehrman and Michael W. Holmes. NTTSD 42. Leiden: Brill, 2013.

CHAPTER 6

What Is a Textual Variant?
Definitions and Boundaries

We have already introduced the idea of a textual discrepancy between manuscripts (see ch. 5). These discrepancies are called variants. Since no two ancient Greek manuscripts of the NT are identical, there are several hundred thousand variants found among the seven thousand plus manuscripts. In this chapter we clarify and expand upon this notion and explore the appropriate boundaries for a textual variant. Do we consider a variant a difference in spelling, morphology, or word choice, or are the larger units in which a variant occurs to be considered as a variant? And if variants do occur beyond the morphological and word levels, then how do we define the boundaries of the variant, or, in other words, where does the variant-unit begin and end? These definitional questions are both foundational and crucial to text-critical studies since the notion and existence of textual variants underlie the entire text-critical enterprise.

1. Readings and Variant-Units

The traditional tendency and common presumption among most textual critics is to understand textual variation in terms of a difference between manuscripts at any level. The variant may involve something as superficial as spelling or as significant as the use of different wording. These variations are rarely considered in light of the larger units in which they occur. As Eldon Epp notes, "The common or surface assumption is that any textual reading that differs in any way from any other reading in the same unit of text is a 'textual variant,' but this simplistic definition will not suffice."[1]

---

1. Eldon Jay Epp, "Toward the Classification of the Term 'Textual Variant,'" in Eldon

E. C. Colwell and E. W. Tune's programmatic article, "Variant Readings," helped scholars begin to see textual variants in light of their immediate linguistic contexts and broader textual traditions (e.g., Alexandrian, Western). Colwell and Tune begin by distinguishing a **reading** from a **variant-unit**. A variant-unit is a "passage or section of the Greek NT where our MSS [manuscripts] do not agree as to what the Greek text is."[2] Readings are the individual variant forms that make up variant-units. But a variant-unit must also have support from at least two Greek manuscripts in order to count as a reading that represents a particular text-type and to be considered in the text-critical process — it must not be a singular reading (see below). The variant-unit then becomes the basis for establishing the relationship of a specific manuscript or manuscripts to a particular text-type, since the individual readings are part of a larger group of variations (i.e., the variant-unit) and agree with a variant-unit in at least one other textual family. Manuscripts in textual families then are most convincingly aligned with one another when they show variation tendencies within variant units, rather than in individual readings. This distinction, therefore, moves the discussion away from (often arbitrarily) positing variation from some kind of norm (where some manuscript or group of manuscripts functions as the external standard according to which the reading in question is said to deviate) to focusing on the relationship between or among textual families.

2. Types of Textual Variation and Text-Critical Significance

Colwell and Tune also distinguish between several types of variation based upon their significance for the task of textual criticism. Their work in this area has been developed and refined by Eldon Epp and Gordon Fee. As stated above, a reading is a textual variation in any form between two or more Greek manuscripts. However, not every reading is to be considered a *variant* as well. There is an important distinction to make among the concepts of reading, variant, and variant-unit. Whether a reading is

Jay Epp and Gordon D. Fee, *Studies in the Theory and Method of New Testament Textual Criticism* (SD 45; Grand Rapids: Eerdmans, 1993), 48.

2. E. C. Colwell and E. W. Tune, "Variant Readings: Classification and Use," *JBL* 83 (1964): 254; repr. (with slight changes) as "Method in Classifying and Evaluating Variant Readings," in E. C. Colwell, *Studies in Methodology in Textual Criticism of the New Testament* (NTTS 9; Leiden: Brill, 1969), 97.

considered a variant is based upon whether it is significant or "useful for the broad tasks of NT textual criticism, including the determination of a [manuscript]'s relationship with all other [manuscripts], the location of a [manuscript] within the textual history and transmission of the NT, and the ultimate goal of establishing the original text."[3] Readings can be significant or insignificant in this sense and only **significant readings** should be considered variants. Colwell and Tune propose three types of **insignificant readings** or readings that are not necessarily useful to the major aim of textual criticism, the establishing of the original text (see ch. 1) (though they will undoubtedly be useful for other purposes, such as assessing the character of the manuscript itself, gaining information about the manuscript's social context, etc.): (1) **nonsense readings** (the reading does not make sense or is ungrammatical in some way, probably due to a scribal error), (2) **dislocated readings** (readings that can be shown, with a fair amount of certainty, to be the result of a scribal error), and (3) **singular readings** (readings found in only one NT manuscript). Epp and Fee also discuss **orthographic readings** under this heading, which are subtle differences in spelling or abbreviations. These insignificant readings are not to be considered in the text-critical procedure nor are they to be included in the standard text-critical apparatuses (see ch. 12, where we will discuss these). A textual variant, then, is defined as significant in contrast to what it is not. Readings that are significant will not fall into one of the four categories mentioned above. Positive criteria for identifying significant readings or variants still need to be developed.

3. Levels of Language and Variant-Unit Boundaries

One of the problems with the notion of variant-unit that Colwell and Tune rightly anticipated was the issue of defining the boundaries of the variant-unit or the appropriate procedure for determining *variant-unit segmentation*. The problem is, "One scholar may subdivide what another scholar regards as a single unit."[4] How do we determine at what point the variant-unit begins or ends? How do variant units segment into separate and individual variant-units? Colwell and Tune suggest that this question is answered "by noticing those elements of expression in

---

3. Epp, "Toward Classification," 57.
4. Colwell and Tune, "Variant Readings," 255 (= repr. 98).

the Greek text which regularly exist together."[5] But as both Epp and Fee recognize, this criterion is so underdeveloped as to be of very little practical use.

Epp seeks to solidify the initial Colwell-Tune proposal for delimiting variant-unit boundaries by building his criterion for determining variant-unit segmentation into his definition of a variant-unit: *"that segment of text, constituting a normal and proper grammatical combination, where our manuscripts present at least two 'variants.'"*[6] Epp clearly recognizes the subjectivity and lack of precision involved in this criterion, since there may be individual variants embedded in a larger variant-unit and the criterion is not clear as to what constitutes a "normal and proper" grammatical combination or how extensive the boundaries of such a combination can be pressed. As a result, Epp suggests that the "shortest" possible grammatical combination that encompasses all of the relevant variants be used as the definition of a variant-unit. This analysis still fails to provide the precision and formal criteria required for marking variant-unit boundaries.

Fee seeks to establish a more formally grounded proposal based upon three types of variation: (1) the addition or omission of textual data; (2) the substitution of textual data, from smaller units of meaning, such as morphemes, to larger units of meaning, such as clauses; and (3) word order.[7] These categories *may* (but we are clearly skeptical) help clarify some of the issues in the embedding of variants, but they still do not help in establishing solid criteria for detecting the boundaries of the larger variant-unit. Furthermore, word order, which functions for Fee as a key criterion, is used inconsistently by him. Sometimes he means the structure of noun phrases (e.g., the position of the article in relation to its noun) and at other times he means clause structure (e.g., the position of the adjunct within the clause). Rather than establishing formal criteria for variant-unit segmentation, Fee's model really just provides one way of grouping variant-units together and comparing them.

A more promising, formally grounded and methodologically simple way forward in determining variant-unit boundaries and dealing with the problem of the embedding of variants is found in an analysis that is

---

5. Ibid. (= repr. 99).

6. Epp, "Toward Classification," 61.

7. Gordon D. Fee, "On the Types, Classification, and Presentation of Textual Variation," in Epp and Fee, *Studies in Theory and Method,* 64.

grounded upon the structure of the Greek language. This analysis depends upon identifying individual linguistic levels and the components that make them up, beginning with the smallest meaningful unit and graduating to larger meaningful units of text. The morpheme is typically acknowledged to be the smallest unit of structure, followed by the word, phrase/ group, clause, and the sentence/clause complex levels (a clause complex is an independent clause with the other clauses that are dependent upon it). Each higher linguistic level is made up of elements from lower levels. Words are formed from morphemes, word groups or phrases from words, clauses from word groups, and so on. The identification and understanding of these levels of structure within the Greek language can enable us to identify syntactically defined variant-units. As a result, variant-unit segmentation can be understood according to precise boundaries based on Greek-language structure. A variant-unit is determined by its syntax or grammatical structure. For example, a word group level variant-unit would consist of the units of a word group, such as a head term (usually a noun) and its modifiers (adjectives, prepositional phrases, etc.). A clause level variant-unit would consist of a predicator (the main verb) and its associated complements (direct and indirect objects) and adjuncts (such as adverbial participles). And so on. Variations can then be categorized as differences within the structure of the individual level in question, which determines the boundaries of the variant-unit. A word group level variant-unit would consist of a variation between manuscripts that is identified as showing variety among the elements of the word group. This could consist of, for example, a variation in the head term and one of its modifiers. Instead of thinking of variations within variant-units in terms of embedding (as does Epp), it becomes more natural to speak of variant-units that operate at the respective levels of the language. So since a clause is made up of word group elements, we may speak of a **clause variant-unit** as a set of differences at the clause level (e.g., the position of the adjunct) or a **word group variant-unit** as a set of differences within the element(s) that make up the word group or a word variant-unit as differences in individual words or morphological variant-unit as differences of morphology (such as a verbal ending, alternating between first and third person). These variations may occur through (1) addition/omission, (2) substitution, and/or (3) order/structure. This model also has the distinct advantage of having been employed in the tagging of the entire NT through the OpenText.org project, so that a model for electronic encoding of computer readable texts along these lines has already been established.

To show the usefulness of this linguistically based approach, it will be helpful to compare it with Fee's analysis of a variant-unit found in John 7:1. Fee diagrams the unit consisting of five variations as follows:[8]

(a) μετὰ ταῦτα περιεπάτει ὁ Ἰησοῦς
(b) μετὰ ταῦτα περιεπάτει Ἰησοῦς
(c) περιεπάτει ὁ Ἰησοῦς μετὰ ταῦτα
(d) περιεπάτει μετ᾽ αὐτῶν ὁ Ἰησοῦς
(e) περιεπάτει ὁ Ἰησοῦς

Regarding this set of variations, he says, "whatever one may call the larger unit, there are two clear and basically unrelated sets of variants; and in a quantitative analysis one would want two sets of manuscript agreements: (1) add/omit/substitution/word order μετὰ ταῦτα/ὁ Ἰησοῦς, where the agreements in variants *a* and *b* are counted together, and *c, d,* and *e* separately; (2) add/omit the definite [*sic*] article, where the MSS in variant *b* would be in agreement against all the rest."[9]

The problem with Fee's analysis is that it does not really help us in understanding variant-unit segmentation or how smaller variant-units embed in larger ones. What it shows is one way of grouping variant-units together, not why they group together. According to the linguistically based model that we are presenting in this chapter, the variant-unit in question would be considered a clause variant-unit. This variant-unit is defined by the syntactic boundaries of the clause under consideration, and includes the subject and adjunct (in other words, where the units μετὰ ταῦτα/αὐτῶν and ὁ Ἰησοῦς/Ἰησοῦς are placed). But there are differences at the word group level as well (i.e., whether Ἰησοῦς appears with or without the article and whether the object of the preposition μετὰ is ταῦτα or αὐτῶν). This clause level analysis both delimits the boundaries and explains variant embedding. At the clause level, μετὰ ταῦτα/αὐτῶν functions as an adjunct, περιεπάτει as a predicator, and ὁ Ἰησοῦς/Ἰησοῦς as an explicit subject. The omission of the article is not relevant at this level because Ἰησοῦς functions as the subject either way. At the clause level (a) and (b) read together against (c)-(e), the two sets of which, as Fee notes, should be considered separately. But (e) also reads against (a)-(d) at the clause level since it omits the adjunct. This results in two sets of variants at the clause level. Further, at the word group

8. Ibid., 64.
9. Ibid., 64-65.

level, the omission/addition of the article must also be seen in relation to the contrast between (d) and the others regarding the object of the preposition. The omission/addition of the article is its own variant-unit because it is marked syntactically at the word group level, as is the change in object of the preposition. Thus there is the omission/addition of the article in relation to its head term in (b) against all of the others, and the substitution of the different head term with the preposition in (d) against (a)-(c). The first set of variations relates to word group elements in the subject component of the clause and the second relates to word group elements in the adjunct component of the clause so that nesting of variant-units can be understood as a natural phenomenon of the language and classified accordingly. So we have two variant-units — a clause variant-unit and a word group variant-unit — each with two sets of variations.

4. Summary

This chapter presents some key definitions and distinctions concerning *textual variant* and related terminology. We have also seen that the notion of a textual variant is more complex than simply identifying differences between manuscripts. It involves identifying readings, variants, and variant-units. Finally, various approaches to defining appropriate boundaries for a "variant-unit" are evaluated. In light of their inadequacy or lack of precision, we have offered a linguistically based approach, grounded in the levels of the Greek language.

KEY TERMINOLOGY
reading
variant-unit
variant
significant readings
insignificant readings
nonsense readings
dislocated readings
singular readings
orthographic readings
variant-unit segmentation
clause variant-unit
word group variant-unit

BIBLIOGRAPHY

Colwell, E. C., and E. W. Tune. "Variant Readings: Classification and Use." *JBL* 83 (1964): 253-61. Repr. (with slight changes) as "Method in Classifying and Evaluating Variant Readings." Pages 96-105 in E. C. Colwell, *Studies in Methodology in Textual Criticism of the New Testament*. NTTS 9. Leiden: Brill, 1969.

Epp, Eldon Jay. "Toward the Classification of the Term 'Textual Variant.'" Pages 47-61 in Eldon Jay Epp and Gordon D. Fee, *Studies in the Theory and Method of New Testament Textual Criticism*. SD 45. Grand Rapids: Eerdmans, 1993.

Fee, Gordon D. "On the Types, Classification, and Presentation of Textual Variation." Pages 62-79 in Eldon Jay Epp and Gordon D. Fee, *Studies in the Theory and Method of New Testament Textual Criticism*. SD 45. Grand Rapids: Eerdmans, 1993.

CHAPTER 7

Methodology (1):
Modern Text-Critical Methodologies

This chapter is the first of four methodological chapters. Before considering the methodology behind weighing different types of evidence when deciding which variant most likely reflects the original, it is necessary to explore the various approaches to the evidence itself. There are four distinct methodological frameworks for textual criticism in contemporary NT scholarship, each emphasizing a different dimension of the evidence: (1) stemmatic approach; (2) Majority text approach; (3) various eclectic methods; and (4) single text model. The student of textual criticism should have a very basic knowledge of each approach. We survey these various methods so that students might have an awareness of the different methods textual scholars use in weighing variants. In order to streamline this sometimes more technical methodological information, we have confined most criticisms we may have of these methods to the notes.

1. Stemmatic Approach

The **stemmatic** or **genealogical approach** is the dominant model for textual criticism in classical studies, but, due to advances in computer technology, has recently become much more important in NT textual criticism. In recent scholarship, the stemmatic approach has been promoted by Peter Maas and later refined by M. L. West. The goal of stemmatic textual criticism is to follow the manuscript tradition back to an extant or theoretical **archetype** through constructing a **stemma** or **family tree** that traces the relations of the relevant variants. This archetype then becomes the basis for the critical edition. When all of the variants within the stemma can be accounted for, then we have a **closed recension**. Problems arise, however, when there is an **open recension** (not all of the variants within the stemma can be accounted for). This situation may result in complexities that hinder the reconstruction of the stemma and force the textual critic to turn to other forms of tabulation in order to account for the variants.

It is not surprising that traditionally the stemmatic approach has found more use and success in classical studies than it has in NT studies, since the textual tradition for classical sources is typically very limited (especially for entire works; see ch. 3 for a comparison). Constructing a stemma is far more manageable for a classical text than it is for a document like the NT, for which the manuscript evidence is so abundant. Westcott and Hort originally gave a nod to this method when they developed their text-critical methodology in their 1881 edition, but they chose not to apply it or refine it for use in NT textual criticism, expressing skepticism regarding its value. A few NT scholars have been more optimistic, however. Eldon Epp, for example, has sought to formulate a stemmatic approach for examining the NT that "attempts to reconstruct the history of the NT text by tracing the lines of transmission back through our extant [manuscripts] to the very earliest stages and then choosing the reading that represents the earliest attainable level of the textual tradition." Therefore, "when faced with a variant-unit . . . the reading would be chosen that comes from the earliest cluster or stream of textual tradition."[1] Epp refers to this stemmatic-inspired approach to NT textual criticism as the **historical-documentary method** and sees its strength in the emphasis that it lays upon external evidence.

Until recently, most NT scholars have not been persuaded of the value of stemmatic approaches for recovering the NT text, even reformulated versions like Epp's. However, this has radically changed with the advent of computer technology. The Münster Institute for New Testament Textual Research has developed a form of stemmatic approach called the **coherence-based genealogical method** (CBGM). This approach takes all of the variants known to exist for a given passage, whether they are deemed significant or insignificant, and, through high-speed computer processing that tests various agreements and disagreements among the variants and possible genealogical relationships and how they might fit together to form

1. Eldon Jay Epp, "Decision Points in Past, Present, and Future New Testament Textual Criticism," in Eldon Jay Epp and Gordon D. Fee, *Studies in the Theory and Method of New Testament Textual Criticism* (SD 45; Grand Rapids: Eerdmans, 1993), 32-33.

connected variant chains, is able to reconstruct a stemmatic flow of the variants to what is called the *initial text*. The initial text is not necessarily the original text that was written by the author of the NT document, but is the reconstructed text that accounts best for the relationships among the variants. The CBGM has begun to be used in textual criticism of the NT, as it is the method used for the *Editio Critica Maior* project, which began with the reconstruction of the Catholic Epistles. There is great optimism in some circles regarding this approach.[2]

2. Byzantine/Majority Text Approach

We previously raised the issue of the **Byzantine/Majority text approach** in chapter 5. We turn now to consider in more detail the methodology that drives this understanding and those who have been associated with it. Many have equated these two. Technically, however, the Byzantine and the Majority text approaches cannot be conflated, since the one argues for a particular textual tradition (the Byzantine approach) found in a set of manuscripts and the other argues for determining the text based upon numerical calculation (the Majority text approach). Nevertheless, we will treat the two together here for the sake of convenience as methods concerned to defend in some way the idea that the best textual evidence comes from our later, more abundantly represented NT manuscripts. As their names imply, these theories emphasize the tradition with the most or "majority" manuscript representation, which is unquestionably the Byzantine textual tradition. Advocates of this model, in other words, insist that the superior textual tradition should be determined by the tradition that was

---

2. Gerd Mink, "Contamination, Coherence, and Coincidence in Textual Transmission," in *The Textual History of the Greek New Testament: Changing Views in Contemporary Research* (ed. Klaus Wachtel and Michael W. Holmes; SBLTCS 8; Atlanta: Society of Biblical Literature, 2011), 141-216. The coherence method has its limitations, however. These include the lack of an adequate definition of what is meant by *coherence*. Coherence becomes a mathematical calculation, rather than a literary concept that appreciates the possible means for variants within a given manuscript. Further, the individual traits of a manuscript are completely overlooked, because variants are studied in isolation apart from their original contexts. There is also a problem with relating the initial text to the original text. The goal of textual criticism should, we believe, be the reconstruction of the original text, not a later stage in textual transmission. Finally, the limits created by the need for technology restricted to those who have access to the materials required to develop and run this program make textual criticism into a task beyond the abilities of any but the few, thus hindering access.

in widespread use throughout Christendom from the end of the first millennium to the fall of Byzantium and that this textual tradition is reflected in numbers of manuscripts rather than date.

Daniel Wallace marks the rise of interest in the Majority text theory in the 1970s with the debate between Zane Hodges and Gordon Fee, although he also recognizes precursors to the discussion in the 1940s and 50s. In the 1980s, Wilbur Pickering (the first president of the Majority Text Society) published the influential edition, *The Greek New Testament According to the Majority Text,* and Hodges and his colleague Arthur Farstad continued to publish material in defense of the majority text. Harry Sturz also played a significant role in this discussion, with his publication of *The Byzantine Text-Type and New Testament Textual Criticism,* which argued that papyrological evidence supported an early date for the Byzantine tradition and that the argument from preservation perpetuated by other Majority text supporters was unconvincing. William Pierpont and Maurice Robinson's reconstructed Byzantine text, published in 1991, was also a pivotal advance in the discussion, especially in its denial of the validity of the stemmatic approaches incorporated by Hodges and Farstad in their Majority text.

Two significant schools of Byzantine/Majority text advocates can be identified in contemporary discussion. The first, represented by Hodges and Farstad, insists that majority readings will typically be the readings that most likely reflect the original, but each reading should nevertheless be considered in the context of its development within the manuscript tradition. The second approach, represented by Pickering, Pierpont, and Robinson, is rigidly committed to the validity of the majority reading, regardless of other factors. This second model dates back to the Majority text methodology of the Anglican scholar Dean J. W. Burgon in the late 1800s. Wallace also notes a third group represented by a few Dutch scholars that recognizes the validity of non-Byzantine traditions, but still places priority upon the Majority text.

A few criticisms of the Majority text theory have already been put forward in chapter 5 in dealing with various text-types. Others will be mentioned in chapter 13, in the context of English translations.[3]

---

3. Here we may also examine the major theoretical point that numerical representation is the most reliable guide to the original reading. Typically, when Majority text advocates are confronted with the fact that the numerous documents that make up the Byzantine tradition come mostly from the ninth century and following, they respond that this must be due to a recognition of their superiority by the church that resulted in continued use in light of deterioration of other manuscripts and their traditions. But if this is the case, as Daniel

3. Eclectic Methods

Eclectic methods emphasize the contribution and evaluation of various witnesses to the text of the NT, in terms of both **external evidence** (Greek manuscripts, church father citations, and early versions) and **internal evidence** (scribal tendencies). As Stanley Porter notes,

> The idea is that rather than confining oneself to a reconstructed stemma or relying on the reading found in the largest number of manuscripts, it is assumed that any given manuscript may or may not preserve a correct reading. Thus a process is needed to draw from all of the available resources to reconstruct what is thought to be the earliest reading and hence closest to the original text.[4]

The major modern editions of the NT, such as NA$^{27/28}$ and *UBSGNT*$^{4/5}$, are based on this methodology and are therefore often referred to as **eclectic texts**. Two types of eclectic methods have emerged in NT text-critical scholarship. **Thoroughgoing** or **rigorous eclecticism** (a few others have termed it *radical/impartial eclecticism* and *judicious criticism*) is characterized by its emphasis upon internal evidence (see ch. 10), whereas **reasoned** or **rational eclecticism** seeks to *consider* both internal and external criteria together (see ch. 8, on external criteria). Thus Epp helpfully refers to the former group of critics as eclectic specialists, since they specialize in one body of evidence (i.e., internal evidence) and the latter group as eclectic generalists, since they seek to consider all of the relevant evidence.[5]

Wallace asks, "what is to explain how they became the majority from the ninth century on?" ("The Majority Text: History, Methods, and Critique," in *The Text of the New Testament in Contemporary Research: Essays on the Status Quaestionis* [2nd ed., ed. Bart D. Ehrman and Michael W. Holmes; NTTSD 42; Leiden: Brill, 2013], 731). Several other questions are left unanswered by the Majority text approach as well. Statistical probability of documents simply cannot explain why no distinctively Byzantine readings are identifiable in the Greek manuscripts, church fathers, or versions from the first several centuries — certainly some remains would have been left, even if the manuscripts were in constant use. If the Majority text most accurately reflects the original, we would expect some traces of it chronologically close to the original. These significant obstacles for the Majority text approach still have not been convincingly overcome by its adherents.

4. Stanley E. Porter, "Textual Criticism," in *Dictionary of New Testament Background* (ed. Craig A. Evans and Stanley E. Porter; Downers Grove, IL: InterVarsity Press, 2000), 1212.

5. Eldon J. Epp, "The Eclectic Method in New Testament Textual Criticism: Solution or

a. Thoroughgoing Eclecticism

George D. Kilpatrick (who died in 1989) and J. Keith Elliott, two important British scholars, have played the most significant role in developing and advocating thoroughgoing eclecticism — although Epp rightly traces its origins back to 1920 with C. H. Turner's "Notes" on Markan usage. Elliott defines the method as one "that allows internal considerations for a reading's originality to be given priority over documentary considerations." He notes further that "the thoroughgoing eclectic critic feels [*sic*] able to select freely from among the available fund of variants and choose the one that best fits his or her internal criteria . . . [and] is skeptical about the high claims made for the reliability of some MSS [manuscripts] or about arguments favoring a particular group of MSS."[6] The principal criteria for determining the reading that most reflects the original, then, are for the most part internal, considering issues such as style, language use, theology, and scribal habits (specific internal criteria are listed and explained in ch. 10). Advocates of this method often insist that **conjectural emendation** (when it is believed that the original reading is not found in any extant manuscript, and the critic offers a hypothetical conjecture) is unnecessary since the model assumes that the original reading is present in some extant manuscript, even if it is a relatively late one. As Kilpatrick insists, "We may assume as a rule of thumb that at each point the true text has survived somewhere or other among our manuscripts."[7] The practical result of this method is that late Byzantine manuscripts, for example, are given just as much weight as early papyri and the fourth-century majuscules, and therefore — not surprisingly — many decisions made according to this methodology reflect late Byzantine readings.

Although thoroughgoing eclecticism *may* help in locating the original in instances where the internal evidence is unambiguously clear, this is not always the case. And while thoroughgoing eclectics insist on the objectivity of their criteria, issues of style, language use, theology, and other internal considerations are rarely as formally based as they propose or as clear-cut as they need to be. A wholesale diminishing of external

---

Symptom?" in *New Testament Textual Criticism: Its Significance for Exegesis: Essays in Honor of Bruce M. Metzger* (ed. Eldon Jay Epp and Gordon D. Fee; Oxford: Clarendon, 1981), 214.

6. J. Keith Elliott, "Thoroughgoing Eclecticism in New Testament Textual Criticism," in *Text of the New Testament,* ed. Ehrman and Holmes, 321.

7. George D. Kilpatrick, "Conjectural Emendation in the New Testament," in *New Testament Textual Criticism,* ed. Epp and Fee, 349.

evidence ends up placing the entirety of the decision upon the shoulders of the critic, without due consideration of the objective controls provided by external considerations.[8] This represents the primary reason why most NT textual critics have rejected thoroughgoing eclecticism in favor of some form of reasoned eclecticism.

b. Reasoned Eclecticism

During the time that Kilpatrick was insisting upon the superior role of internal evidence, French scholar M.-J. Lagrange and American E. C. Colwell were laying the foundations for what would later be referred to as reasoned eclecticism. In more recent years, Eldon Epp and J. H. Petzer have also played significant roles in developing the model. After briefly describing the battle over the last few centuries concerning the importance of internal versus external evidence, Epp notices that a "temporary 'cease-fire' that most — but certainly not all — textual critics have agreed upon [is] called 'moderate' or 'reasoned' eclecticism . . . , in which it is recognized that no single criterion or invariable combination of criteria will resolve all cases of textual variation and which, therefore, attempts to apply evenly and without prejudice any and all criteria — external and internal — appropriate to a given case, arriving then at an answer based on the relative probabilities among those applicable criteria."[9] In other words, reasoned eclecticism attempts to find a balance between internal and external evidence when weighing which readings most likely represent the original. Among reasoned eclectics, external and internal considerations are given more and less weight, but often external evidence is given priority unless good internal considerations are present to indicate otherwise or where external evidence is inconclusive (e.g., when the evidence is even or close to evenly divided). In such situations, internal criteria provide a useful tool for helping to discern among external factors.

---

8. Gordon Fee summarizes the difficulties with thoroughgoing eclecticism in terms of two fundamental problems that make it unviable as a model for NT textual criticism: "(1) It assumes a faulty theory of textual corruption and transmission, and therefore an unrealistic — and unhistorical — attitude toward the various textual witnesses. (2) Having abandoned the evidence of the witnesses, it leaves textual judgments to the whims of the individual practitioner. This problem is especially acute whenever variation can be shown to have two equally plausible explanations" ("Rigorous or Reasoned Eclecticism — Which?" in Epp and Fee, *Studies in Theory and Method*, 125-26).

9. Epp, "Decision Points," 40.

Despite the use of both internal and external evidence, the same criticisms are applicable to reasoned eclecticism as are lodged above against thoroughgoing eclecticism. There are not clear criteria regarding the balance between external and internal criteria. Even if one puts greater priority on external evidence, it is not clear how one decides, on the basis of the manuscript evidence alone, which manuscript to favor over another.

4. Single Text Model

Another approach that has not been significantly explored as a method for NT textual criticism is the **single text model**.[10] Instead of using an eclectic method to create a modern edition from a collection of diverse readings found in various textual traditions, the single text model proposes using a single ancient text. The oldest complete text of the NT is found in the significant fourth-century Codex Sinaiticus (see ch. 4). Therefore, a single text model would take Codex Sinaiticus and use it as the basis of a modern edition of the NT. What it means to use a singular manuscript like Codex Sinaiticus as the basis of a modern edition might vary in some people's minds (e.g., whether spelling was regularized or clear errors in the text were corrected), but the idea is that the edition reflects a text actually used by the ancient church. The appeal of this model is that it leaves the text-critical responsibilities with the ancients, since these ancient texts themselves were apparently eclectic texts (see below). Presumably, these ancient editors would have had access to much earlier and better manuscripts than modern editors and therefore would have probably been in a better position to make text-critical decisions.

The general quality of our two major fourth-century codices (Sinaiticus and Vaticanus, even though Vaticanus is not entirely complete), their (relative) completeness, and their early date have given them a position of priority in text-critical circles from the time of Tischendorf and Westcott and Hort to the present. Examination of subsequent editions that put emphasis upon the Alexandrian textual tradition, such as the NA or *UBSGNT* text, shows that Sinaiticus and Vaticanus still reign supreme in that the vast majority of these editions reflect one or both of these two manuscripts.

---

10. We note, however, that the single text model is the one practiced in OT textual criticism, where the Hebrew text used is based on a single manuscript. This is currently the Leningrad Codex, with an edition of the Aleppo Codex in preparation.

Despite much discussion of the NT Greek papyri, many of them fairly recently discovered and published, their importance for NT textual criticism has not eclipsed the significance of the two major codices. Indeed, the departures by modern so-called eclectic Greek texts from these major codices are often few in number in a given NT book, sometimes confined for the most part to variations in spelling.

In the light of this, it is worth considering whether there should not be a return to use of such a text as Codex Sinaiticus. Rather than being a scholarly construct of the twentieth century, Codex Sinaiticus, along with other ancient manuscripts, constituted an ancient manuscript actually used and revised by various early Christian communities (the various correcting hands of Sinaiticus attest to its use, but also raise a number of important critical issues). Therefore, it provides unparalleled access to an earlier form of the text as used by early Christians.

5. Summary

In this chapter we have briefly considered four approaches to NT textual criticism. The stemmatic approach, once confined to classical studies, has had a recent resurgence of interest in the form of the coherence-based genealogical method, but there still appear to be limitations based on the treatment of variants. The Majority text has been considered valuable by a few scholars, but most find its theoretical basis unconvincing. Although two forms of eclecticism have emerged in the last century, it is now generally recognized that only an eclectic model that gives due consideration to external evidence, as we find in reasoned eclecticism, can provide adequate objectivity for textual determinations. Although the single text model has not yet been fully explored by NT scholars, it may have some promising potential for text-critical studies.

KEY TERMINOLOGY
stemmatic/genealogical approach
archetype
stemma
family tree
closed recension
open recension
historical-documentary method

coherence-based genealogical method
Majority text approach
eclectic methods
external evidence
internal evidence
eclectic texts
thoroughgoing/rigorous eclecticism
reasoned/rational eclecticism
conjectural emendation
single text model

BIBLIOGRAPHY
Porter, Stanley E. "Textual Criticism." Pages 1210-14 in *Dictionary of New Testament Background*. Ed. Craig A. Evans and Stanley E. Porter. Downers Grove, IL: InterVarsity Press, 2000.

Stemmatic/Historical-Documentary Approach
Epp, Eldon Jay. "Decision Points in Past, Present, and Future New Testament Textual Criticism." Pages 17-44 in Eldon Jay Epp and Gordon D. Fee, *Studies in the Theory and Method of New Testament Textual Criticism*. SD 45. Grand Rapids: Eerdmans, 1993.
Wachtel, Klaus, and Michael W. Holmes, eds. *The Textual History of the Greek New Testament: Changing Views in Contemporary Research*. SBLTCS 8. Atlanta: Society of Biblical Literature, 2011.

The Majority Text
Fee, Gordon D. "The Majority Text and the Original Text of the New Testament." Pages 183-208 in Eldon Jay Epp and Gordon D. Fee, *Studies in the Theory and Method of New Testament Textual Criticism*. SD 45. Grand Rapids: Eerdmans, 1993.
Hodges, Zane C., and A. L. Farstad. *The Greek New Testament According to the Majority Text*. 2nd ed. Nashville: Nelson, 1985.
Pickering, Wilbur. *The Identity of the New Testament Text*. Rev. ed. Nashville: Nelson, 1980.
Pierpont, W. G., and Maurice A. Robinson. *The New Testament in the Original Greek According to the Byzantine/Majority Textform*. 2nd ed. Atlanta: Original Word, 2005.
Sturz, Harry A. *The Byzantine Text-Type and New Testament Textual Criticism*. Nashville: Nelson, 1984.

Wallace, Daniel B. "The Majority Text: History, Methods, and Critique." Pages 711-44 in *The Text of the New Testament in Contemporary Research: Essays on the Status Quaestionis.* 2nd ed. Ed. Bart D. Ehrman and Michael W. Holmes. NTTSD 42. Leiden: Brill, 2013.

Thoroughgoing Eclecticism

Elliott, James Keith. *New Testament Textual Criticism: The Application of Thoroughgoing Principles: Essays on Manuscripts and Textual Variation.* NovTSup 137. Leiden: Brill, 2010.

———. "Thoroughgoing Eclecticism in New Testament Textual Criticism." Pages 745-70 in *The Text of the New Testament in Contemporary Research: Essays on the Status Quaestionis.* 2nd ed. Ed. Bart D. Ehrman and Michael W. Holmes. NTTSD 42. Leiden: Brill, 2013.

Kilpatrick, George D. "Conjectural Emendation in the New Testament." Pages 349-60 in *New Testament Textual Criticism: Its Significance for Exegesis: Essays in Honour of Bruce M. Metzger.* Ed. Eldon Jay Epp and Gordon D. Fee. Oxford: Clarendon, 1981.

Turner, C. H. "Marcan Usage: Notes, Critical and Exegetical on the Second Gospel." *JTS* 25 (1923/24): 377-86.

Reasoned Eclecticism

Colwell, E. C. *Studies in Methodology in Textual Criticism of the New Testament.* NTTS 9. Leiden: Brill, 1969.

Epp, Eldon Jay. "The Eclectic Method in New Testament Textual Criticism: Solution or Symptom?" Pages 141-73 in *New Testament Textual Criticism: Its Significance for Exegesis: Essays in Honour of Bruce M. Metzger.* Ed. Eldon Jay Epp and Gordon D. Fee. Oxford: Clarendon, 1981.

Fee, Gordon D. "Rigorous or Reasoned Eclecticism — Which?" Pages 124-40 in *New Testament Textual Criticism: Its Significance for Exegesis: Essays in Honour of Bruce M. Metzger.* Ed. Eldon Jay Epp and Gordon D. Fee. Oxford: Clarendon, 1981.

Holmes, Michael W. "Reasoned Eclecticism in New Testament Textual Criticism." Pages 771-802 in *The Text of the New Testament in Contemporary Research: Essays on the Status Quaestionis.* 2nd ed. Ed. Bart D. Ehrman and Michael W. Holmes. NTTSD 42. Leiden: Brill, 2013.

Lagrange, M.-J. *Critique textuelle.* Vol. 2: *La critique rationelle.* 2nd ed. Ebib. Paris: Gabalda, 1935.

Petzer, J. H. "Eclecticism and the Text of the New Testament." Pages 47-62 in *Text and Interpretation: New Approaches in the Criticism of the New*

Testament. Ed. Patrick J. Hartin and J. H. Petzer. NTTS 15. Leiden: Brill, 1991.

Single Text Model

Porter, Stanley E. "Why So Many Holes in the Papyrological Evidence for the Greek New Testament?" Pages 167-86 in *The Bible as Book: The Transmission of the Greek Text.* Ed. Scot McKendrick and Orlaith O'Sullivan. London: British Library Publications and Oak Knoll, 2003.

————. "Textual Criticism in the Light of Diverse Textual Evidence for the Greek New Testament: An Expanded Proposal." Pages 305-37 in *New Testament Manuscripts: Their Texts and Their World.* Ed. Thomas J. Kraus and Tobias Nicklas. TENTS 2. Leiden: Brill, 2006.

————. *How We Got the New Testament: Text, Transmission, Translation.* Grand Rapids: Baker, 2013.

CHAPTER 8

Methodology (2):
Weighing External Evidence

When assessing variant readings, the textual critic is concerned with essentially two types of evidence: external and internal. We have discussed these in the previous chapter, but they bear review. **External evidence** deals with the manuscripts that support a given reading. It is external in the sense that it considers external witnesses to the text. **Internal evidence**, which we will examine in the next chapter, deals with both scribal and authorial tendencies. It is internal in the sense that it is limited to textual considerations such as language, style, and context; that is, phenomena internal to the text. Scholars have established a number of guidelines that help in the process of determining which variant is closer to the original text. In the next two chapters we will explore several guidelines of textual criticism related to weighing external and internal evidence. Many of these criteria tie back in some way or another to **Johann Jakob Griesbach**'s rules for textual criticism developed in the eighteenth century. Bruce Metzger goes so far as to state that "Griesbach (1745-1812) laid foundations for all subsequent work on the Greek text of the New Testament."[1] Many subsequent textual critics have repeated, refined, and modified these guidelines, until today textual critics agree on many of them — though not all. There is still much debate, as well as room for disagreement, over the guidelines for textual criticism. For the most part, these rules apply to eclectic critics, as opposed to those who endorse the Byzantine/Majority text or a single text method. However, even these approaches require some text-critical judgments to be made, and some of these guidelines can still be useful.

---

1. Bruce M. Metzger, *The Text of the New Testament: Its Transmission, Corruption, and Restoration* (4th ed., rev. Bart D. Ehrman; Oxford: Oxford University Press, 2005), 165.

In this and the following two chapters, we will outline *a* (not necessarily *the*) method for working through variant readings in an attempt to recover the original text of the NT based roughly on the reasoned eclecticism method laid out in the previous chapter. Several other methods were also discussed in that chapter and each has validity, so these steps should not be taken as a definitive text-critical method but instead as a suggestive approach to weighing variant readings in an attempt to recover the original text (one could also, for example, simply adopt Sinaiticus as an ancient eclectic text that likely reflects or closely resembles the original).

1. The Priority of External Evidence

External evidence, most textual critics agree, should take priority in making text-critical judgments, because it is the most objective tangible evidence that we have for the textual history of the NT. Too often in text-critical discussions — even among reasoned eclectics, and especially by thoroughgoing eclectics — internal evidence has overturned external considerations. The manuscripts themselves should not be allowed to be overruled by our judgments about what a scribe would have done in a particular situation. These internal considerations can be quite helpful when external evidence is not decisive, but substantial external support (i.e., where a reading is supported by the old, high quality, geographically and genetically diverse witnesses — see below) should typically rule out even the most powerful internal considerations. This primary view of the external evidence assumes a particular version of reasoned eclecticism (on this view see ch. 7). Internal evidence, then, is especially helpful when external considerations do not point decidedly in one direction or are only moderately in favor of a particular reading. Both the Byzantine/Majority text and single text models almost exclusively rely upon the external evidence.

2. External Criteria

When evaluating external evidence, we must remember that not all evidence bears the same weight. A reading that has numerous manuscripts supporting it, for example, might not bear the same weight as a reading that is supported by fewer but older manuscripts, since these older manuscripts may well be closer to the original. As Metzger, a reasoned eclectic, once insisted, "Witnesses are to be weighed rather than counted."[2] Therefore, it is important to have good criteria in place for evaluating the significance of particular manuscripts and their relative weight in assessing textual variants. Three such **external criteria** are discussed below: (a) date and text-type, (b) geographical distribution, and (c) genealogical relationship.

a. Date and Text-Type

The process of dating a manuscript is very difficult. Philip Comfort and David Barrett go so far as to call it "educated guesswork."[3] But as they note, a number of external and circumstantial factors aid the paleographer in getting general ideas as to the date of a manuscript. For example, we will sometimes know the latest date at which a manuscript could have been copied. This is often based in some way upon the location where it was found. This might involve the known history of the site, such as with Qumran. The latest possible date for the manuscripts found there is A.D. 68, since that is the date that the Qumran caves were abandoned. The date might also be established on the basis of documentary manuscripts (manuscripts that contain documentary information, such as letters, receipts, wills, etc.) found with the biblical manuscripts that contain information concerning the date of the manuscript finds, possibly even having dates indicated by the documents. As explained in chapter 3, handwriting and the materials being used also factor into the dating of a manuscript. Manuscripts written in majuscule hands are generally earlier than those written in minuscule hands. Manuscripts written on papyrus are also typically earlier than those written on parchment. This is not always the case, however. Some have complained that papyri have been given too prominent a place in recent textual criticism of the Greek NT simply on the basis of the material on which they are written, which does not guarantee that the manuscript is early. We have parchment manuscripts, for example, that date earlier than some papyri. That undue emphasis is often placed upon the importance of the papyri emerges from the confusion of inconsistent classification of materials discussed in chapter 3. The significance of the manuscript especially relies upon its date (and other considerations dis-

---

2. Metzger, *Text of the New Testament,* 3rd ed. (New York: Oxford, 1992), 209.

3. Philip W. Comfort and David P. Barrett, *The Text of the Earliest New Testament Greek Manuscripts* (Wheaton, IL: Tyndale House, 2001), 20.

cussed below) when it is being weighed against other evidence, not the material it was written on.

Only a few manuscripts have been dated during the second century. Most are papyri, but also an important fragment of Acts 5 from the late second century recorded on parchment (0189) written in a majuscule hand. See chapter 4 above for lists of these manuscripts.

Besides the biblical manuscripts, we also have other Greek manuscript evidence that does not play a direct role in textual criticism but that we should at least recognize and take into account as appropriate. The most important of this evidence is some of the quotations found in some of the early church fathers and early church writings, such as Justin Martyr, the *Didache,* the *Shepherd of Hermas,* the *Letters of Ignatius,* and *1 and 2 Clement.*[4] A number of apocryphal Gospels (Jesus stories written in the second century and beyond, especially among the papyri Gospel fragments, e.g., P.Egerton 2 and P.Köln 255, P.Oxy. 4009, PSI XI.1200bis, and perhaps P.Oxy. 1) can be dated roughly within the second century and can be used in efforts to reconstruct the NT text as well, since they contain a number of canonical Gospel parallels. However, because they are not continuous text manuscripts of the NT, they must be used cautiously. Stanley Porter suggests four stages for using this (and to a lesser degree later apocryphal Gospel) evidence in textual criticism: (1) establish the text of these manuscripts, with as little influence from canonical works as possible; (2) compare these texts with the canonical text at every point; (3) attempt to establish textual characteristics of the apocryphal Gospels in light of the range of available evidence for the text of the NT; and (4) use the apocryphal Gospels, especially the early ones, as a form of evidence for the readings found in the NT.[5]

The third-century manuscript evidence of the Greek NT is more abundant. Here we have a larger number of papyri and a few more parchment manuscripts written in a majuscule hand. See chapter 4 for lists of such manuscripts.

By the fourth century, parchment as a writing surface and the codex as a document form had begun to be more widely used. The most significant

---

4. Some early versions, such as Coptic, Old Syriac, and Old Latin, may date to the second century, but their manuscript evidence is later. Tatian's *Diatessaron* was created in the second century from the four Gospels, but it is now available only through much later versions.

5. Stanley E. Porter, "Apocryphal Gospels and the Text of the New Testament before A.D. 200," in *The New Testament in Early Christianity: Proceedings of the Lille Colloquium, July 2000* (ed. Christian-B. Amphoux and J. Keith Elliott; HTB 6; Lausanne: Zèbre, 2003), 242.

documents from this period are the two major fourth-century Alexandrian codices (for detailed information on these and other manuscripts, see ch. 4), Sinaiticus and Vaticanus. There are papyri from this period as well, but they are no more significant than the parchment manuscripts dating from the same era, although this reality is often not conveyed in discussions of the papyri. In the fifth century, several important codices were written as well, including Alexandrinus, Ephraemi Rescriptus, Bezae, and Washingtonianus. From the sixth century we have Claromontanus. Codices from the eighth and ninth centuries include Regius (8th), Athous Laurae (8th-9th), Augiensis (9th), Boernerianus (9th), and Koridethi (9th). From the tenth to the fifteenth century, large numbers of minuscule manuscripts emerged reflecting the Byzantine or Majority text tradition.

The date of a manuscript, however, must always be considered in conjunction with its text-type. For example, a manuscript may be from the sixth century but evidences the standardizing practices of the Byzantine tradition, drastically minimizing its significance. Yet a sixth-century Alexandrian majuscule manuscript, as a representative of a tradition attested much earlier, may bear great significance. According to the Alands, "In terms of age, only [majuscule] manuscripts from the third/fourth century or earlier have an inherent significance, i.e., those of the period before the development of the great text types."[6] The reason for this is the alien influences upon later texts, especially influences from the Byzantine tradition. Therefore, when weighing external evidence, the most weight should be placed upon manuscripts — regardless of the material they are composed on — that date from the fourth century and before. Later manuscripts can have some measure of importance in determining an original reading or supporting a reading found in earlier manuscripts, depending upon whether the text-type represented goes back to an earlier period. This is true up until around the tenth century, when the minuscule manuscripts represent an almost exclusively Byzantine tradition.

On the basis of this discussion, **step #1** in weighing external evidence can be summarized as follows:

Step 1: *Check the date of the witness and the date of the type of text that it embodies.*

6. Kurt Aland and Barbara Aland, *The Text of the New Testament: An Introduction to the Critical Editions and to the Theory and Practice of Modern Textual Criticism* (trans. Erroll F. Rhodes; 2nd ed.; Grand Rapids: Eerdmans, 1989), 104.

b. Geographical Distribution

A second consideration related to weighing external evidence involves the geographical distribution of the witnesses involved. The identification of text-types, which has been recognized since before the time of Griesbach, has gone hand in hand with linking these text-types to geographical regions of origin (even though they are sometimes indicated by major cities representative of these regions). This geographical theory of textual criticism was most rigorously developed and propounded by the NT scholar B. H. Streeter in his study of the Gospels.[7] In this study, Streeter categorized both NT manuscripts and other texts, such as versions, in terms of what he called local texts, that is, associating these texts with a number of particular locations. One does not need to go to the extremes of Streeter in recognizing that manuscripts, even if they do not originate in a particular location, can be grouped together on the basis of common patterns of variants and that such manuscripts may well have been associated with certain areas of early Christianity.

As a result, we can see the importance of appreciating the relationship between text-types and geographical locations. Certain readings may be found within manuscripts that are associated with particular locations, and not with others. This leads to the recognition that readings supported by witnesses from a wide range of geographical locations are to be favored over those that are only supported by manuscripts from one geographical region. For example, all other things being equal, a reading supported by an Alexandrian manuscript and a Western manuscript is theoretically stronger than two or even three Alexandrian manuscripts and no Western manuscripts. This is because wide geographical attestation for a reading indicates more likelihood that it reflects an earlier common tradition and is closer to the original and less of a likelihood that the reading originated due to a copyist's error that circulated in a given region as peculiar to that region. Consistency across a broad range of locales increases the probability that the agreement among manuscripts goes back to the original. Therefore, **step #2** in weighing external evidence can be summarized as follows:

Step 2: *Check the geographical distribution of the witnesses that endorse a particular variant.*

---

7. B. H. Streeter, *The Four Gospels: A Study of Origins Treating of the Manuscript Tradition, Sources, Authorship, and Dates* (London: Macmillan, 1924).

c. Genealogical Relationship

This criterion is similar to that of geographical distribution; but, instead of focusing upon geographical locations, it draws attention to genealogical relationships. In textual criticism, **genealogical** or **genetic relationships** refer to a definable relationship between two or more documents that share a common origin. These relationships are typically characteristic of larger text-types or **groups** or **families** with common variants and similarities that help identify various genetic relationships that in turn help locate documents in the context of a larger family or text-type. These common traits among groups/families are sometimes called **family characteristics**. Recent scholarship has devoted substantial attention to questions revolving around how to identify and classify genetic relationships among NT manuscripts.

The **traditional method** for assessing these relationships operated off the now superseded assumption (though not yet entirely abandoned) that the Textus Receptus was the standard text against which all others should be assessed. This method, common up through the middle of the twentieth century, simply involved noting textual variation from the printed text of the Greek NT found in the Textus Receptus. A number of earlier textual critics observed the significant flaws inherent in this method, including Westcott and Hort and Hermann von Soden. But it was not until 1945, with Metzger's devastating criticism of this method (prompted especially by appreciation of the potential of the discovery of the papyri for textual criticism) that marking variation from the Textus Receptus was recognized to be an inadequate approach.

The first positive alternative to this approach has come to be known as the **quantitative method** of textual classification. Instead of using the Textus Receptus as a singular standard text against which all variation is measured, this method seeks to compare witnesses to one another, focusing on variations and similarities that are considered significant for determining genetic relationships, that is, relationships that show common origins. E. C. Colwell was the first to propose a model that was a practical and reasonable alternative to comparing witnesses one by one to all other manuscripts. He suggested the identification of three types of readings designed to facilitate ease of characterization and accuracy: (1) multiple readings, (2) distinctive readings, and (3) quantitative analysis. For Colwell, multiple readings were found in three or more distinct traditions, established manuscript groups, or versions. Distinctive readings, the second point of identification, is aimed at demonstrating the relationship, as suggested by step 1. This confirmatory step involves locating **distinctive readings** (readings particular to a specific tradition or family) of that group or tradition within the manuscripts themselves. If distinctive readings were located within step 2, this led to the third and final step: a thorough quantitative analysis, in which the manuscript under consideration is compared with the other manuscripts in the family that it has been associated with via steps 1 and 2 to ensure that it agrees with that family in the majority of cases (for Colwell, this meant a minimum of 60-65 percent agreement).[8]

Colwell's quantitative analysis met with widespread support, though the first two steps of his method were not as well received. But quantitative analysis on its own did not prove ultimately to be accepted either. This has led to a second method, known as the **group profile method. Group profiles** are patterns of attestation, that is, collections of characteristic readings for groups. (This should not be confused with Colwell's distinctive readings: readings may be characteristic of but not distinctive to a group.) Group profiles are then used in combination with quantitative analysis as the basis for determining genetic relationships. The **Claremont Profile Method** is the best-known version of group profiling. Developed by Frederik Wisse and Paul McReynolds while they were graduate students at Claremont Graduate School working (originally under Colwell) on collecting manuscripts for the International Greek New Testament Project (an initiative aimed at providing an exhaustive critical apparatus for the Gospels), this method is based upon tracking where manuscripts agree with particular family profiles. When manuscripts agree in two-thirds of the readings in question, they are said to be of the same group.

Although there has been a great deal of scholarly discussion about how to discover and classify genealogical relationships among text-types, it is helpful simply to remember that the driving idea behind this principle is that the strongest variants will have a wide range of text-types supporting them rather than being limited to, say, an Alexandrian or Western body of witnesses. The reason is that genetic relationships between manuscripts supporting a particular reading may mean that the two witnesses are actually only one. For example, a Syriac version may appear to provide a

---

8. See E. C. Colwell, *Studies in Methodology in Textual Criticism of the New Testament* (NTTS 9; Leiden: Brill, 1969). It should be noted, however, that this cross-referencing of manuscripts was not to be done against the (sometimes) thousands of manuscripts in a particular family, but was to be compared instead to what were considered to be representative samples from each group.

separate witness to the *Diatessaron,* but it may be shown that they have a genetic relationship indicating a single testimony rather than two genetically separate witnesses.

Step 3: *Check the genealogical relationship of texts and families. If the number of texts supporting a reading is large but they all originate in the same type (or even the same earlier text), the evidence is weaker than if there were fewer manuscripts from several text-types or locations.*

One notices, then, that the **strongest readings** will be the ones *supported by the oldest manuscripts representing the widest geographical spread and having no evident genealogical relationship.* In other words, readings supported by manuscripts of an early date from a variety of locations will have an initial presumption of being strongest, especially when no genetic relationship can be demonstrated among the witnesses.

3. Summary

In this chapter we have insisted upon the priority of external evidence in making text-critical decisions and pointed to three criteria that textual critics often use in weighing external evidence: (1) date and text-type, (2) geographical distribution, and (3) genealogical relationship.

KEY TERMINOLOGY
external evidence
internal evidence
Johann Jakob Griesbach
external criteria
genealogical/genetic relationships
groups/families
family characteristics
traditional method
quantitative method
distinctive readings
group profile method
group profiles
Claremont Profile Method
strongest readings

BIBLIOGRAPHY

Aland, Kurt, and Barbara Aland. *The Text of the New Testament: An Introduction to the Critical Editions and to the Theory and Practice of Modern Textual Criticism.* Trans. Erroll F. Rhodes. 2nd ed. Grand Rapids: Eerdmans, 1989.

Colwell, E. C. *Studies in Methodology in Textual Criticism of the New Testament.* NTTS 9. Leiden: Brill, 1969.

Comfort, Philip W., and David P. Barrett. *The Text of the Earliest New Testament Greek Manuscripts.* Wheaton, IL: Tyndale House, 2001.

Ehrman, Bart D. *Studies in the Textual Criticism of the New Testament.* NTTS 33. Leiden: Brill, 2006.

Epp, Eldon Jay. "The Claremont Profile Method for Grouping New Testament Minuscule Manuscripts." Pages 211-20 in Eldon Jay Epp and Gordon D. Fee, *Studies in the Theory and Method of New Testament Textual Criticism.* SD 45. Grand Rapids: Eerdmans, 1993.

Metzger, Bruce M. *The Text of the New Testament: Its Transmission, Corruption, and Restoration.* 4th ed. Rev. Bart D. Ehrman. Oxford: Oxford University Press, 2005.

Porter, Stanley E. "Apocryphal Gospels and the Text of the New Testament before A.D. 200." Pages 235-59 in *The New Testament in Early Christianity: Proceedings of the Lille Colloquium, July 2000.* Ed. Christian-B. Amphoux and J. Keith Elliott. HTB 6. Lausanne: Zèbre, 2003.

CHAPTER 9

Methodology (3):
Weighing Internal Evidence (1):
Transcriptional Probabilities

Internal evidence is concerned with the actual wording of manuscripts in relation to their language, style, and context (as opposed to the manuscripts and their text-types and locations), and is typically weighed according to two sets of criteria: transcriptional probabilities and intrinsic probabilities. **Transcriptional probabilities** involve determining the probability of a variant-unit being due to established scribal tendencies. **Intrinsic probabilities** involve determinations of how likely a given variant-unit is in light of what an author is more likely to have written. These two major considerations in weighing internal evidence will be the focus of the next two chapters. This chapter will deal with transcriptional probabilities and chapter 10 will address intrinsic probabilities. That each of these sets of criteria is identified by an emphasis on probability is significant. There is no way to weigh internal evidence with absolute certainty, since by definition this evidence is founded upon a set of predictions about how the author or scribe would have behaved in particular circumstances based upon our limited knowledge of scribal habits or tendencies and patterns of authorial usage (difficulties are greatly multiplied here when dealing with authors for whom we only have a very small body of literature, e.g., Jude). *Consideration of internal criteria is extremely valuable when external evidence is not decisive or when it only moderately favors a particular reading.*

1. The Genetic Principle

The **genetic principle** or **principle of origin** is the name we have given to what many textual critics consider to be the most basic and fundamental principle for weighing internal evidence. This principle states that *the reading that best explains the origin of the others is most likely the original.* In other words, if it is clear that the variants under consideration could all have plausibly arisen from one of the particular variants, then the variant from which the others could have arisen is the variant that is most likely to represent the original reading. Sometimes this reading is obvious, while other times the reading that best explains the others begins to emerge as the transcriptional and intrinsic probabilities are considered.

For example, in Gal 2:20 there is the question of whether Paul wrote that he lives in faith that is τοῦ υἱοῦ τοῦ θεοῦ ("of the son of God") or τοῦ θεοῦ καὶ τοῦ Χριστοῦ ("of God and Christ"). In NA²⁷/²⁸ the second reading, listed in the apparatus, is supported by several important early manuscripts. There is fairly strong textual support for this reading, then, since there are old (esp. 𝔓⁴⁶ and B), as well as geographically and textually diverse (Alexandrian and Western), witnesses supporting it (see chs. 4, 5, and esp. 8 on external evidence). But the external evidence is also strong in favor of the first reading, printed within the NA²⁷/²⁸ text: notably, ℵ and A. This is a great instance, then, to consider internal criteria to see which reading we should favor. The genetic principle is particularly useful in this case. This principle was in fact the major motivation for the editors of NA²⁷ choosing the reading υἱοῦ τοῦ θεοῦ instead of θεοῦ καὶ τοῦ Χριστοῦ. In *A Textual Commentary on the Greek New Testament,* reflecting the text-critical rationale behind why the UBS committee made the choices that they did in preparing the text of NA²⁷ and *UBSGNT*⁴ (on these editions, see ch. 12), Bruce Metzger states: "The reading that best explains the origin of the others is the customary Pauline expression τοῦ υἱοῦ τοῦ θεοῦ, which is widely attested by a broad spectrum of Greek, versional, and patristic witnesses. It is probable that in copying, the eye of the scribe passed immediately from the first to the second τοῦ, so that only τοῦ θεοῦ was written (as in ms. 330); since what followed was now incongruous, copyists either added τοῦ υἱοῦ or inserted καὶ Χριστοῦ."[1] In other words, the first reading can explain the second one. A few other principles, which will be discussed

---

1. Bruce M. Metzger, *A Textual Commentary on the Greek New Testament* (2nd ed.; London: United Bible Societies, 1994), 524. Note that the logic of the committee is often followed in the examples below in order to provide insight for the student as to how textual critics think through various text-critical problems as they compile an eclectic text.

below, are at work here in tandem with the genetic principle, but it should be clear from this example how the principle is intended to work when evaluating variant readings.

2. Transcriptional Probabilities

The goal of assessing transcriptional probabilities is to discover whether scribal errors have been introduced into the text (accounting for a particular reading) or to notice whether particular scribal habits or tendencies have created certain readings. The major focus at this level of analysis then is upon how the text may have been altered during its transmission by a scribe who reflected these transcriptional probabilities. Of course, all internal considerations have the focus on scribal changes as their aim, in the sense that all variations from the original are due to copyists' alterations of some sort. But transcriptional probabilities focus specifically on the negative question of how a scribe might have (consciously or unconsciously) altered the text, whereas intrinsic probabilities focus on the more positive question of what the author is most likely to have originally written. The processes of investigating transcriptional probabilities can be summarized as the first step in weighing internal evidence:

Key Principle: *Determine which variant is most likely to have been introduced as a result of common scribal practices in copying the text.*

Several text-critical canons have been designated to encompass what are called scribal tendencies.

a. Scribal Errors

The first type of transcriptional data that is important to consider is common scribal errors. These errors were introduced by ancient scribes for a variety of reasons, including errors resulting from misreading a text, mishearing a text (if the text was being copied in a scriptorium while the exemplar was being read aloud), mental mistakes, and misjudgments. Scribes also, from time to time, would attempt to correct what they perceived to be errors in the text that had resulted from previous textual transmission. In this sense, the scribes were themselves some of the earliest textual critics of the NT. When weighing text-critical evidence, therefore, it is important to examine which readings are most likely the result of a scribal error. There are a number of types of scribal errors.

1. Parablepsis

Parablepsis (or overlooking) is an error that occurs whenever a scribe skips over any portion of text. This can occur for a variety of reasons, but is often introduced into the text due to lines of text ending in similar letters (referred to as **homoeoteleuton**, Greek for "similar ending"). Examples of parablepsis always involve skipping over portions of text, often because of similar wording that seems to have confused the scribe into believing that he has already written a passage, when he has not. Sometimes this skipping may involve only a word similar to one already written, while in other instances a scribe may skip a longer section of material, including an entire line. An instance of the first type of parablepsis is found in Jude 1, where τετηρημένοις is omitted in 630 and 1505 among others, according to the NA[27] apparatus (the NA[28] apparatus is different because it follows the *Editio Critica Maior* — see chapter 12). This omission can be accounted for by parablesis due to the use of ἠγαπημένοις and τετηρημένοις, creating homoeoteleuton. The exemplar may have originally looked something like this:

Line 1: ΤΟΙΣ ΕΝ ΘΕΩ ΠΑΤΡΙ ΗΓΑΠΗΜΕΝΟΙΣ
Line 2: ΚΑΙ ΙΗΣΟΥ ΧΡΙΣΤΟΥ ΤΕΤΗΡΗΜΕΝΟΙΣ

When the scribe was copying the text, instead of writing τετηρημένοις (ΤΕΤΗΡΗΜΕΝΟΙΣ) when he got to the end of line 2, thinking that he had already recorded this word, he copied the next word in the text instead, κλητοῖς (ΚΛΗΤΟΙΣ) (see line 2 below) so that the copied text looked like this:

Line 1: ΤΟΙΣ ΕΝ ΘΕΩ ΠΑΤΡΙ ΗΓΑΠΗΜΕΝΟΙΣ
Line 2: ΚΑΙ ΙΗΣΟΥ ΧΡΙΣΤΟΥ ΚΛΗΤΟΙΣ . . .

An example of the second type of parablepsis, involving an entire line of text, is also easy to envisage. A scenario could be easily imagined in which an entire line could be omitted if there was an intervening line between lines 1 and 2 above. For example, let us say the text read as follows (imagining that there is Greek text on lines 2 and 4 below):

Line 1: ΤΟΙΣ ΕΝ ΘΕΩ ΠΑΤΡΙ ΗΓΑΠΗΜΕΝΟΙΣ
Line 2: . . .
Line 3: ΚΑΙ ΙΗΣΟΥ ΧΡΙΣΤΟΥ ΤΕΤΗΡΗΜΕΝΟΙΣ
Line 4: . . .

It is easy to see how, after copying line 1, a scribe's eye could skip down to line 3, therefore omitting line 2, and moving on to copy line 3 rather than correctly copying line 2 from the exemplar.

2. Homoeoarkton

A scribe may also make an omission due to similar beginnings of a line. This is sometimes referred to as **homoeoarkton** (or homoeoarcton). This can be seen in the omission of οὐδὲ ἐκ θελήματος ἀνδρὸς ("not of the will of man") in John 1:13 from B* (the * indicates the original hand of Vaticanus [B] where a change has been made by a later scribe). Notice the similarities with the beginning of two lines of text in John 1, in which the second is not found in B*:

Line 1: ΟΥΔΕ ΕΚ ΘΕΛΗΜΑΤΟΣ ΣΑΡΚΟΣ
Line 2: ΟΥΔΕ ΕΚ ΘΕΛΗΜΑΤΟΣ ΑΝΔΡΟΣ

The omission is easily accounted for by the likelihood that the scribe skipped over line 2 due to its similarities with line 1 and began copying line 3: ἀλλ' ἐκ θεοῦ ἐγεννήθησαν. It does not help matters that the endings of lines 1 and 2 are similar as well!

3. Haplography

Haplography occurs when a word, syllable, or letter is only written once when it should have been written twice. For example, in Acts 13:19 we find καὶ καθελὼν, supported by several important early manuscripts (e.g., ℵ, 𝔓⁷⁴). But other important manuscripts like B delete the initial καὶ. This likely happened due to haplography since καθελὼν and καὶ begin in the same way, with κα, leading the scribe to delete καὶ.

4. Simple Omission

Other omissions, especially of a word or letter — we shall call them **simple omissions** — may be unrelated to similarities within the context and may simply be the result of careless oversight. For instance, Codex Laudianus (E) omits παρεκάλουν from Acts 13:42, probably due to the fact that the manuscript has very short lines (sometimes only a word), which make deletion of a word/line very easy if the scribe is not careful.

5. Dittography

The reverse error of haplography is **dittography**, a case of writing a word, syllable, or letter twice when it should have been written only once. A similar example to the one from John above can be observed in Acts 10:40: ὁ θεὸς ἤγειρεν [ἐν] τῇ τρίτῃ ἡμέρᾳ. Notice the ending of ἤγειρεν. A more certain instance of this phenomenon can be observed in Rom 5:2, where the NA[27/28] apparatus lists ℵ and A, among others, in support of the reading ἐσχήκαμεν ἐν τῇ πίστει instead of ἐσχήκαμεν τῇ πίστει. There is some decent external support for the variant reading, but it is easy to see how the variant reading likely arose due to dittography.

6. Metathesis

When letters or words are reversed from their proper positions, this is referred to as **metathesis**. An interesting example of this type of scribal error may have occurred in the copying of Heb 12:15 with the use of ἐνοχλῇ (present subjunctive of ἐνοχλέω, "to trouble"). A number of scholars are convinced that this reading arose from metathesis of ἐν χολῇ ("in gall") (probably confirmed in 𝔓[46]), which reverses οχ in ἐνοχλῇ to χο in ἐν χολῇ.

7. Fusion and Fission

The error of combining two words into a single word is known as **fusion**. One could imagine a similar error in which a single word may be divided into two words (sometimes called **fission**). Paul Wegner notices a clear example of fusion in Mark 10:40: some manuscripts (ℵ, B*, D) have ἀλλ' οἷς ("but for whom") rather than ἄλλοις ("for others").[2] Fusion may also occur between parallel passages, especially in the Synoptics, for example, where the wording from one passage may be fused into another.

8. Substitution

A wide range of factors accounts for **substitutions** of a letter, syllable, word, phrase, or even passage for other wording in the original. Substitutions may be intentional or unintentional. Sometimes referred to as homophony, an error in copying the text may result from mishearing or misreading words, where a word with a similar sound or spelling to the word in the original is substituted for the original. An example is Acts 17:27, where the *nomen sacrum* KN replaced ΘN, leading to the variant τὸν κύριον in some later manuscripts against τὸν θεόν (reflected in NA$^{27/28}$/*UBSGNT*$^{4/5}$) in several early manuscripts (most notably $\mathfrak{P}^{74}$ ℵ A B). The substitution was not of a word but of a single letter. This error is also sometimes the result of a confusion of letters of a similar shape. A substitution of synonyms may occur as in Acts 18:26, where the noun phrase τὸν λόγον τοῦ κυρίου is substituted for τὴν ὁδὸν τοῦ θεοῦ in several later manuscripts. This is probably an intentional substitution. Deliberate substitutions of various kinds will be dealt with more below.

b. Difficult Readings

It is typically acknowledged that *the most **difficult reading** that still makes sense is to be regarded as closest to the original.* That is, the reading that appears initially to be difficult to grasp, but when studied in greater detail makes good sense, is probably closer to the original. The logic behind this principle is that scribes tended to correct/change what was difficult to them. There is also a connection between this principle and the genetic principle, since the most difficult reading can often explain the other variants as clarifications of the most difficult reading. The qualification that the most difficult reading must "make sense" is intended to account for readings that are most difficult because an error makes the

---

2. Paul D. Wegner, *A Student's Guide to Textual Criticism of the Bible: Its History, Methods, and Results* (Downers Grove, IL: InterVarsity Press, 2006), 49.

text unintelligible. So if a reading is most difficult because it makes no sense, that reading is not likely original even though it may be the most difficult reading.

The criterion of difficulty can be illustrated in weighing the evidence supporting the reading in Acts 20:28. The NA[27] text reads: ποιμαίνειν τὴν ἐκκλησίαν τοῦ θεοῦ, ἣν περιεποιήσατο διὰ τοῦ αἵματος τοῦ ἰδίου ("to shepherd the church of God which he purchased through his own blood"). Some of the early manuscripts (notably ℵ and B) have κυρίου ("Lord") instead of θεοῦ ("God"). One of the most substantial reasons that θεοῦ is preferred to κυρίου here is that it is the more difficult reading and therefore can explain the origin of the variant κυρίου. It is plausible that a scribe would correct the text from "God" to "Lord" since it may have raised questions in certain scribes' minds how God has blood. It would seem much more natural to talk about the church being purchased with the Lord's own blood rather than God's blood. The question may be considered negatively as well. Why would a scribe change the text from what would seem very natural (Lord) to the more (seemingly) unnatural (God)? Therefore, reading "God" here would be more difficult for the scribe and, therefore, is more likely to be original.

c. Shorter and Longer Readings

Since the pioneering text-critical work of Johann Griesbach, another canon used in weighing transcriptional probabilities is the priority of the shorter reading. Traditionally, *the priority of the shorter reading* (**Griesbach's canon**) has been preferred because, it is suggested, scribes were more likely to add text for the purpose of clarification than to omit it. When in doubt, the tendency among scribes was to retain and add rather than to remove and omit. The shorter reading can also often provide an explanation of the other readings, which can be viewed as likely expansions of the original. Recently, however, James Royse has called this principle into question, demonstrating that scribes tend to omit more often than they add material.[3] Therefore, he shows that the longer reading is to be preferred unless (1) it seems late on genealogical grounds (see above); (2) it seems to arise as a result of a scribe attempting to harmonize the

---

3. James R. Royse, *Scribal Habits in Early Greek New Testament Papyri* (NTTS 36; Leiden: Brill, 2008), 593-608.

reading with the immediate context, parallel, or OT passages; or (3) the longer reading seems to be the result of a scribe's attempt to improve the grammar of the original (see below).[4]

At the end of Mark 6:51 the NA[27/28] text reads ἑαυτοῖς ἐξίσταντο ("they were completely amazed"). This reading is supported by significant older manuscripts, including ℵ and B. However, καὶ ἐθαύμαζον is added in a number of good manuscripts (notably A D W) — though the external evidence clearly leans in the direction of omitting καὶ ἐθαύμαζον since ℵ and B are older than A D and W. So do we prefer the longer, slightly less well attested reading here? Probably not. Since harmonization appears to account for the longer reading, the shorter reading is preferred.

d. Less Harmonized Readings

Scribal practices in the ancient world also tended toward harmonization with other passages, in which a scribe might intentionally or unintentionally bring his text into conformity with another passage. Therefore, *less harmonized readings most likely reflect the original.* This tendency is most common in Gospel criticism, but can be observed in other parts of the NT as well. For example, Colossians and Ephesians have a number of parallel passages, and we find evidence among ancient scribes of harmonizing between them.

We also observe harmonizations with the OT, especially with the LXX. We can see this tendency, for example, among the variant readings for Matt 19:4, which reads in NA[27/28]: ὁ κτίσας ("the one who created"). This reading is supported most significantly by B. However, the alternative reading, ὁ ποιήσας ("the one who made") instead of ὁ κτίσας, also has good external support, from ℵ among others. Through internal considerations related to harmonization, we can assess this case where the external evidence is roughly equal. It is likely that the reading arose from scribal tendencies to harmonize this text with the LXX version of Gen 1:27, which uses the Greek verb ποιέω. Therefore, the less harmonized reading is ὁ κτίσας.

---

4. See, however, Dirk Jongkind, *Scribal Habits of Codex Sinaiticus* (Texts and Studies 3/5; Piscataway, NJ: Gorgias, 2007), 138-39, who argues that Royse has overstated his case through misrepresenting Griesbach's canon, which was nuanced in ways that Royse overlooks.

e. Less Grammatically Refined Readings

Scribes also tended toward improving and clarifying grammar rather than making it less grammatical or awkward. This principle often supports the more difficult reading since grammatically unrefined readings tend to be more difficult. Thus *less grammatically refined readings* more likely reflect the original.

In Mark 6:2 NA²⁷/²⁸ reads καὶ αἱ δυνάμεις τοιαῦται διὰ τῶν χειρῶν αὐτοῦ γινόμεναι, supported by ℵ* (the * indicates the original scribe of Sinaiticus when a correction has been made) and B, among others. A number of witnesses offer readings that clarify the grammar, including ℵ¹ (the superscripted ¹ on the ℵ indicates the first corrector of Sinaiticus). Even though these later readings tend to be grammatically superior, they are inferior readings from a text-critical perspective since a scribe is more likely to smooth the grammar than worsen it.

f. Doctrinal Alterations?

In his book *The Orthodox Corruption of Scripture* and its popular counterpart, *Misquoting Jesus,* Bart Ehrman argues that, in addition to accidental alterations and making changes in order to clarify the text in certain cases, ancient scribes also changed the text to suit particular doctrinal agendas, often rendering our hopes of reconstructing the original text uncertain. Our position is that while we must allow that certain scribes may have had doctrinal agendas that impacted their transmission of the text from time to time, this was the exception rather than the rule. Figures in the ancient world like Marcion, who made significant doctrinally motivated changes to the text, were not scribes but teachers. Ancient scribes generally considered it their duty to copy rather than interpret or alter the text to suit their or others' doctrinal beliefs. This is not to say doctrinal alterations did not happen from time to time, but it certainly was not part of regular scribal practice. As Ehrman acknowledges,

> It is probably safe to say that the copying of early Christian texts was by and large a "conservative" process. The scribes — whether non-professional scribes in the early centuries or professional scribes of the Middle Ages — were intent on "conserving" the text they were passing on. Their ultimate concern was not to modify the tradition, but to

preserve it for themselves and for those who would follow them. Most scribes, no doubt, tried to do a faithful job in making sure that the text they reproduced was the same text they inherited.[5]

Since theological tampering with the text was not typical, where doctrinally motivated alterations do occur they rarely affect the reconstruction of the text in a substantial way, since the majority of witnesses will not evidence theological revisionist tendencies. The major conclusion in terms of text-critical practice to be drawn into a simple principle:

Key Principle: *Variants should be explained as doctrinally motivated alterations only when more standard (and common) canons for accounting for textual variation fail.*

The logic is simple: the typical scribal practices are more likely to account for variation than nontypical or obscure or supposed doctrinal practices. This is where Ehrman is himself inconsistent. He admits that **doctrinally motivated alteration** was the exception, not the rule, but builds his entire case upon variants that are often easily explained using the standard transcriptional probabilities outlined above. *He seeks to explain variations by exceptional (i.e., uncommon) scribal practice when they are easily accounted for by more standard (i.e., common) scribal practices.* And when changes are clearly doctrinally motivated, the external attestation is usually so slim and/or geographically and genetically isolated that these variants warrant little attention. *Misquoting Jesus* provides us with a convenient collection of what are (apparently, at least in Ehrman's mind) the most persuasive examples of doctrinally motivated alterations that bring uncertainty to the hopes of accurately recovering the original text (in Ehrman's opinion).

1. Antiadoptionistic Alterations

The first set of changes that he mentions along these lines are changes supposedly introduced by anitadoptionists. **Adoptionists** were a group of theologians who believed that Jesus was not God's eternal Son but was

---

5. Bart D. Ehrman, *Misquoting Jesus: The Story Behind Who Changed the Bible and Why* (San Francisco: HarperSanFrancisco, 2005), 178. In this section we interact with Ehrman, *Misquoting Jesus,* 153-75.

adopted as his Son, usually at his baptism. Ehrman notes three examples of these antiadoptionist alterations. The first text he points to is 1 Tim 3:16, where he notes that some manuscripts support the reading θεὸς ("God") (e.g., ℵᶜ Aᶜ) (the superscript ᶜ indicates a change to the manuscript by a later scribe) instead of ὅς ("who") (e.g., ℵ* A*) (the * indicates the original hand when a later scribe has added a correction). First, this is not really an adoptionist alteration — it is not treated under this heading in *Orthodox Corruption of Scripture*. If anything, it seems to reflect a tendency toward high Christology by use of "God" rather than the relative pronoun with reference to Jesus. Second, the evidence that it was an intentional alteration in order to strengthen the christological orientation of the passage is weak at best and is easily explained in light of a simple letter substitution, an extremely common scribal error. It was probably the case that ος was substituted for the *nomen sacrum* θς accidentally — the change of a single letter, theta for omicron. This is a simpler explanation than Ehrman's proposal and accounts for the variant within the context of common scribal practice.

A second example of a supposed antiadoptionist change that Ehrman highlights is from Luke 3:22,[6] where the text reads: σὺ εἶ ὁ υἱός μου ὁ ἀγαπητός, ἐν σοὶ εὐδόκησα ("you are my beloved son, in you I am well pleased"). Ehrman argues that the Western reading, which inserts "today I have begotten you," is the result of adoptionist revisions. Even if this is the case, the external evidence is weak (only being found in Western witnesses) and should not warrant major consideration in reconstructing the text. As a result, it does not have substantial bearing on the NT being "changed" in such a way that it inhibits our ability to reconstruct the text. But the variant seems to be explained more plausibly in light of the common scribal tendency toward harmonization. The scribes were probably harmonizing the passage with Ps 2:7, which apparently had a significant place in oral tradition regarding Jesus, since the author of Hebrews cites it in connection with Jesus (Heb 1:5), apparently referring to Jesus' baptism. (And shouldn't we expect similar antiadoptionistic tendencies in Heb 1:5? There are apparently none.) Depending upon when Hebrews and Luke are dated, there could also be a tendency toward harmonizing Luke with

---

6. Ehrman wrongly cites 3:23 as the passage under consideration (*Misquoting Jesus*, 159; though it is correct in his earlier discussion in *The Orthodox Corruption of Scripture: The Effect of Early Christological Controversies on the Text of the New Testament* [New York: Oxford University Press, 1993], 62-67).

Hebrews. Even more convincing is the parallel with Acts 13:33, which also cites the psalm in connection with Jesus. It is very likely that the D text and its Western relatives were bringing the passage into harmony with Luke's other volume. The D text also exhibits tendencies to harmonize with the LXX, which provides further evidence for a harmonization in the Western tradition. Ehrman's entire case here is built upon the plausibility of the Western reading being original and is therefore based almost entirely on internal considerations (though some church fathers do cite this weaker reading). Yet the internal evidence also seems to be in favor of the reading represented in the NA²⁷/²⁸/*UBSGNT*⁴/⁵ text. When this is combined with the strong external support for this reading, it becomes clear that Ehrman's case is not sturdy enough to support his conclusions. At the very best, the evidence is inconclusive, which in no way provides a clear example of the phenomenon that Ehrman is attempting to note.

The third adoptionistic reading put forward by Ehrman is found in John 1:18. In NA²⁷/²⁸/*UBSGNT*⁴/⁵, the text reads μονογενὴς θεὸς, with the following manuscripts in support of it: 𝔓⁶⁶ ℵ* B C* L, among others. A number of manuscripts have an article modifying θεὸς before μονογενὴς, including ℵ¹ 𝔓⁷⁵ 33, among others. There are manuscripts, however, that read υἱὸς instead of θεὸς, some with various subtle differences between them (e.g., A C Θ). Ehrman has concern here that the witnesses supporting the reading found in the NA²⁷/²⁸/*UBSGNT*⁴/⁵ text are limited to the Alexandrian text-type. He suggests that a scribe in Alexandria may have introduced this change early on in order to propagate a high Christology. But this fails to take into consideration the support from 𝔓⁶⁶, which seems to have been in circulation at a date before the emergence of clear text-types. This reality is reflected by the fact that it does not clearly align with a particular textual family, but does have some Western and Alexandrian tendencies. The text is from an early period marked by irregularities when compared with the major textual traditions and is characterized by the Alands as a "free text."[7] In any case, it seems hard to tell how changing υἱὸς to θεὸς would have added anything to the high Christology already conveyed in John 1:1-3. Nevertheless, the possibility of a doctrinal revision cannot be ruled out, but it seems unclear how this would add or take away from the theology of John's Gospel as a whole. If "Son" is read here, then

---

7. Kurt Aland and Barbara Aland, *The Text of the New Testament: An Introduction to the Critical Editions and to the Theory and Practice of Modern Textual Criticism* (trans. Erroll F. Rhodes; 2nd ed.; Grand Rapids: Eerdmans, 1989), 100.

God still became flesh since the Son of God is God according to 1:1-3. And if "God" is read here, the Son remains in view as God incarnated in human flesh since the Son had already been described as God in 1:1-3.

2. Antidocetic Alterations

Docetists (from δοκέω, "to seem" or "to appear") believed that Jesus only *appeared* to be flesh and blood. In reality, he was a spirit being. Ehrman suggests that scribes intentionally altered the text to guard against this tendency.

The first passage he mentions is Luke 22:43-44. Ehrman argues that since the text is not likely original — and we grant this point — it must have been added by antidocetists in order to strengthen the affirmation of Jesus' humanity. There is simply no way to prove this. It is mere conjecture. It is just as likely (indeed, we think more likely) that it circulated as part of early oral and extracanonical tradition about Jesus and was inserted by a scribe who considered it to be a legitimate part of the tradition — and it very well may have been, even if Luke did not originally record it. Furthermore, sweating blood seems to be an odd way of affirming Jesus' humanity since this is a very rare human experience. Ehrman's case here for doctrinal revision, then, is at best weakly supported.

Next, Ehrman turns his attention to the account of the Lord's Supper in the same chapter of Luke, just a few verses earlier (22:17-19). Ehrman argues that the clause that appears at the end of verse 19 and all of verse 20 in NA$^{27/28}$/*UBSGNT*$^{4/5}$ were added to combat docetist heresy rather than accidentally deleted: 19 τὸ ὑπὲρ ὑμῶν διδόμενον· τοῦτο ποιεῖτε εἰς τὴν ἐμὴν ἀνάμνησιν. 20 καὶ τὸ ποτήριον ὡσαύτως μετὰ τὸ δειπνῆσαι, λέγων· τοῦτο τὸ ποτήριον ἡ καινὴ διαθήκη ἐν τῷ αἵματί μου τὸ ὑπὲρ ὑμῶν ἐκχυννόμενον ("which is given for you. Do this in remembrance of me. In the same way he took the cup after they had eaten and said, 'This cup, which is poured out for you, is the new covenant in my blood'"). Ehrman suggests the possibility that these words were not original; however, almost all of our best manuscripts contain them. They are omitted only in D.[8] So Ehrman has to argue his case almost exclusively on internal grounds. And even if the likelihood of the omission in the Western tradition being original is granted, Ehrman still appeals to a very unusual practice (doctrinal alter-

---

8. sy^c omits only 22:20.

ation) when the variant could easily be explained by reference to standard scribal habits of harmonization. The addition could easily be explained by a scribal attempt to harmonize the text with the Pauline passage with very similar wording, 1 Cor 11:23-25. So even if Ehrman's internal arguments are considered persuasive, there is no need to understand the alteration to be doctrinally driven.

The final so-called antidocetic tendency suggested by Ehrman is found in Luke 24:51-52. The final clause of 24:51, καὶ ἀνεφέρετο εἰς τὸν οὐρανόν, is omitted in ℵ* and D (among others), a substantial array of external evidence. Nevertheless, the rest of the manuscript tradition supports the longer reading — one might say that the external evidence is close to evenly balanced here, with slightly more support for the longer reading. Ehrman disagrees with NA$^{27/28}$/$UBSGNT^{4/5}$ and argues that the shorter reading is original, which makes sense since he assumes that the change was intentional. In addition to being the more difficult reading (due to the tension it creates with the chronology in Acts where the ascension happens after forty days), however, the omission can be accounted for by scribal error of homoeoarkton:

Line 1: ΚΑΙ ΑΝΕΦΕΡΕΤΟ ΕΙΣ ΤΟΝ ΟΥΡΑΝΟΝ
Line 2: ΚΑΙ ΑΥΤΟΙ ΠΡΟΣΚΥΝΗΣΑΝΤΕΣ ΑΥΤΟΝ

Notice the similarity in line beginnings (without the separation between the first two words, as in the exemplars, the similarity would be even more apparent) that may have caused this omission. Since the longer reading can be accounted for by accidental omission, it is to be preferred. So again, Ehrman appeals to very rare scribal tendencies (doctrinal alteration) when typical patterns of scribal errors may easily explain the variation within the tradition.

3. Antiseparationist Alterations

Another group of heretics in the earliest centuries of Christianity are known as **separationists**. Separationists affirm that Jesus' human and divine natures were separate. Jesus embodied two distinct beings, one human and the other divine. Separationist Christology came to be advocated by a group of teachers known as **gnostics**, who were characterized by their emphasis upon apprehending a mysterious knowledge of divine things. Ehrman contends that several passages evidence scribal changes to the text intended to help avoid wording that could allow for separationist Christology.

The first text Ehrman discusses is Heb 2:9. A few manuscripts, mostly quite late (e.g., the minuscule 1739* and a few church fathers) replace χάριτι θεοῦ ("by the grace of God") with χωρὶ θεοῦ ("without God"). Ehrman claims that χωρὶ θεοῦ must have been original, but that scribes early on changed it so that separationists could not use the text to suggest that Jesus' divine person left him at death. There is just no way to substantiate this claim. There is not substantial external evidence in favor of χωρὶ θεοῦ being original — it is supported only in later sources. Even if internal considerations were significant enough to overturn external support, this still would not establish a doctrinally motivated change since the words are close enough in spelling to be accounted for by a scribal mental or visual error.

Ehrman also contends that in a few Western witnesses (e.g., D) a scribal change from τί ἐγκατέλιπές με ("Why have you forsaken me?") to τί ὠνείδισάς με ("Why have you taunted me?") in Mark 15:34 was motivated by scribes who feared that gnostics would use the text to promote separationist tendencies. Ehrman is correct to notice that this Western variant most likely reflects an intentional change by a scribe. Whether this was to guard against separationism is less obvious. The doctrine of Jesus being forsaken by the Father may have seemed incomprehensible. In any case, this is probably a legitimate instance where the most likely explanation is a doctrinal alteration. Yet it should also be noticed that this change is isolated to a few obscure (aside from D) Western witnesses. In other words, the change was not pervasive in the manuscript tradition. This illustrates two important points. First, it shows that scribes were not that prone to protect the text from misinterpretations; and second, it demonstrates that when these alterations do take place it does not have an impact upon our ability to reconstruct the text because these changes show up in only a few witnesses.

Finally, Ehrman points to a marginal note for 1 John 4:2-3 in the tenth-century manuscript 1739 (which was likely copied from a fourth-century document) that reads "looses (λύει) Jesus" instead of "does not confess (μὴ ὁμολογεῖ) Jesus." According to Ehrman, the reading is clearly not original, but a scribe must have made the alteration in order to strengthen John's critique of separationism, which "loosened" from Jesus the Christ. Yet again, this is probably a legitimate doctrinal alteration (that never even made it into the main text!), but it is so obscure and late as to not warrant much attention or have any bearing on the reconstruction of the text.

4. Concluding Remarks

Ehrman concludes that once scribes doctrinally "altered their texts, the words of the texts quite literally became different words, and these altered words necessarily affected the interpretations of words by later readers."[9] Is this a legitimate conclusion to draw from the evidence Ehrman has presented? It seems doubtful. In the only places in which intentional doctrinal observations can be convincingly established, there is no significant bearing on the reconstruction of the text (with John 1:18 being the only possible exception). In other instances, Ehrman has to attempt to explain variants that are easily accounted for within standard scribal practice (usually, scribal errors of various sorts or attempts at harmonization) by appeals to a more obscure phenomenon (doctrinal alteration). Theological variants are useful for helping determine the doctrine of a particular scribe or community precisely because they do not dominate the manuscript tradition. Their rarity makes them useful for studying the theological context and beliefs of early Christian scribes and communities, but not for reconstructing the NT text. We may conclude, then, that doctrinal alterations should not be a significant factor in weighing internal evidence and they certainly are not pervasive enough to undermine the textual critic's ability to reasonably reconstruct the text.

3. Summary

In this chapter we have highlighted the secondary role of internal evidence as a productive tool when external evidence is not decisive. We also introduced the genetic principle and pointed to one of two major sets of criteria that textual critics often use when weighing internal evidence: transcriptional probabilities. Transcriptional probabilities assess the probability that particular variants arose as a result of scribal errors and/or practices. This first step in weighing internal evidence deals, in particular, with assessing which variants conform to known scribal tendencies through a

9. Ehrman, *Misquoting Jesus*, 175.

number of established canons, which include the treatment of scribal errors, difficult readings, shorter readings, less harmonized readings, less grammatically refined readings, while challenging Ehrman's speculative conclusions regarding the question of doctrinally motivated alterations.

KEY TERMINOLOGY

transcriptional probabilities
intrinsic probabilities
genetic principle/principle of origin
A Textual Commentary on the Greek New Testament
parablepsis
homoeoteleuton
homoeoarkton
haplography
simple omissions
dittography
metathesis
fusion
fission
substitutions
difficult reading
shorter and longer readings
Griesbach's canon
less harmonized readings
less grammatically refined readings
doctrinally motivated alterations
adoptionists
docetists
separationists
gnostics

BIBLIOGRAPHY

Aland, Kurt, and Barbara Aland. *The Text of the New Testament: An Introduction to the Critical Editions and to the Theory and Practice of Modern Textual Criticism.* Trans. Erroll F. Rhodes. 2nd ed. Grand Rapids: Eerdmans, 1989.

Ehrman, Bart D. *The Orthodox Corruption of Scripture: The Effect of Early Christological Controversies on the Text of the New Testament.* New York: Oxford University Press, 1993.

————. *Misquoting Jesus: The Story Behind Who Changed the Bible and Why*. San Francisco: HarperSanFrancisco, 2005.

Epp, Eldon Jay, and Gordon D. Fee. *Studies in the Theory and Method of New Testament Textual Criticism*. SD 45. Grand Rapids: Eerdmans, 1993.

Greenlee, J. Harold. *Scribes, Scrolls, and Scripture: A Student's Guide to New Testament Textual Criticism*. Grand Rapids: Eerdmans, 1985.

————. *The Text of the New Testament: From Manuscript to Modern Edition*. Peabody, MA: Hendrickson, 2008. [A revision of *Scribes, Scrolls, and Scripture*.]

Jongkind, Dirk. *Scribal Habits of Codex Sinaiticus*. Texts and Studies 3/5. Piscataway, NJ: Gorgias, 2007.

Landon, Charles. *A Text-Critical Study of the Epistle of Jude*. JSNTSup 135. Sheffield: Sheffield Academic Press, 1996.

Metzger, Bruce M. *The Text of the New Testament: Its Transmission, Corruption, and Restoration*. 4h ed. rev. Bart D. Ehrman. Oxford: Oxford University Press, 2005.

Royse, James R. *Scribal Habits in Early Greek New Testament Papyri*. NTTS 36. Leiden: Brill, 2008.

CHAPTER 10

Methodology (4):
Weighing Internal Evidence (2):
Intrinsic Probabilities

In this chapter we deal with the second step in weighing internal evidence — evaluating intrinsic probabilities. The goal of assessing intrinsic probabilities is to discover which variant the author is most likely to have written based upon what we know about his style. The major focus at this level of analysis is upon the author rather than the scribe. Of course, all internal considerations have this focus as their aim in the sense that all variations are variations from the original. But intrinsic probabilities focus specifically on the positive question of what an author is most likely to have written, whereas transcriptional probabilities focus on the more negative question of what a scribe is most likely to have introduced (intentionally or accidentally) into the text. The processes of investigating intrinsic probabilities can be summarized as the second step of weighing internal evidence:

Key Principle: *The variant that has the most continuity with the author's style is likely the original.*

The numerous text-critical principles designed to support this step will be discussed below.

1. Stylistic Continuity

Style is a vague term in NT studies, and this is unfortunate as it leads to imprecision. For example, textual critics usually discuss style under the heading "style and vocabulary," but this confuses the issue since vocabulary is one way in which an author's style is expressed. They are not two distinct categories — as the definition below makes clear. Andrew Pitts has provided a thorough linguistic treatment of the issue. According to Pitts, a study of an author's **style** pertains to the variation in language that occurs as a response to social situations.[1] This highlights in some ways how difficult it may be to use style as a criterion since it can vary so dramatically, depending upon the social situation the author is addressing. However, evidence for a variant reflecting an author's style can be increased if one is assessing an author's style based on writings that share a similar social setting (thus 1 Timothy will have a much different style than Romans since the social settings radically differ). Therefore, when examining an author's style in order to determine the intrinsic probability of a variant, the textual critic is concerned with discovering the variant that has the most cohesion with the immediate context, has the most coherence with the author's theological emphases (though this too may vary with social situations, so we must be careful here), and reflects the author's use of language and sources. All other things being equal, *the variant that most conforms to the author's style at all of these levels (contextual cohesion, theological coherence, linguistic conformity, and source consistency) is most likely to be the original.* This is the major governing principle when weighing intrinsic probabilities and may be referred to as the principle of **stylistic continuity**. Put negatively, variants that do not conform to patterns of style that can be observed in an author, especially in the immediate context of the discourse, are least likely to be original. For example, liturgical forms (standardized forms of expression common in worship practices, e.g., a potential ancient creed such as we find in Phil 2:6-11) and harmonizations will tend to cause patterns of discontinuity, indicating possible scribal interference in the transmission of the text.

2. Cohesion

Cohesion is the textual phenomenon that describes the linguistic features and functions that enable texts to "hang together" as texts: it refers to the unity of a text created through the use of syntax and lexis. It provides

---

1. Andrew W. Pitts, "Style and Pseudonymity in Pauline Scholarship: A Register Based Configuration," in *Paul and Pseudepigraphy* (ed. Stanley E. Porter and Gregory P. Fewster; PAST 6; Leiden: Brill, 2013), 113-52.

the foundation for the unity (continuity) and intelligibility (coherence) of a text. Contextual cohesion creates an interpretive framework in which "some element in the discourse is dependent on that of another. The one PRESUPPOSES the other in the sense that it cannot be effectively decoded except by recourse to it."[2] For example, a phrase like "that man" assumes that a particular man has already been introduced in the previous context. This phrase then is cohesive with and dependent upon the surrounding context for its meaning. M. A. K. Halliday and Ruqaiya Hasan discuss four types of cohesion in English: (1) conjunctions and continuity, (2) referential cohesion, (3) substitution and ellipsis, and (4) lexical cohesion.[3] We can observe these and other types of cohesion in the Greek of the NT. Indeed, any device or form can be used to create a cohesive pattern, and often this will aid in textual criticism.

For example, in Col 3:5-12 we have three imperatives (νεκρώσατε, "put to death," 3:5; ἀπόθεσθε, "put off," 3:8; ἐνδύσασθε, "put on," 3:12), each followed by a string of indicatives. This is a passage that illustrates the use of many different cohesive devices in this relatively small unit of the NT. This creates a kind of grammatical cohesion through syntactic patterning. How does this help us with textual criticism? We have some important evidence (most significantly 𝔓⁴⁶, and some internal considerations) for reading the subjunctive (ψεύδησθε) in 3:9 — even though neither the NA nor the *UBSGNT* apparatus recognizes or includes this evidence.[4] This is where the concept of cohesion comes in. Since there is an established pattern of contextual cohesion that is used to structure this text (imperatives in primary clauses, followed by indicatives in secondary clauses), the subjunctive conforms with the author's style better than the imperative, since using an imperative here would confuse the structure. Therefore, the subjunctive is more intrinsically probable by virtue of contextual cohesion.

Traditionally, considerations of cohesion in biblical studies have involved the consideration of more limited syntactic tendencies (i.e., much smaller units of text) of an author and especially the use of vocabulary. For example, many scholars have rejected the long ending of Mark (16:9-20) because the vocabulary used there is so different from the words he uses elsewhere in the Gospel. The following words occur in the long ending,

2. M. A. K. Halliday and Ruqaiya Hasan, *Cohesion in English* (English Language Series 9; London: Longman, 1976), 2, 4.

3. M. A. K. Halliday, *Halliday's Introduction to Functional Grammar* (rev. C. M. I. M. Matthiessen; 4th ed.; London: Routledge, 2014), 603-7; cf. Halliday and Hasan, *Cohesion,* 13.

4. See Stanley E. Porter, "P.Oxy. 744.4 and Colossians 3:9," *Bib* 73 (1992): 565-67.

for instance, but nowhere else in the Gospel: ἀπιστέω ("to disbelieve"), βλάπτω ("to harm"), βεβαιόω ("to confirm"), ἐπακολουθέω ("to follow"), θεάομαι ("to see"), μετὰ ταῦτα ("after these things"), πορεύομαι ("to go"), συνεργέω ("to work together"), ὕστερον ("later"). In other words, there is no cohesion between the lexical items in the long ending of Mark and the Gospel of Mark as a whole.

3. Theological and Literary Coherence

Theological and literary coherence has to do with the meaning of a text: it is the feature that provides the text with intelligibility and therefore relates to which themes, motifs, and characters are emphasized by an author throughout the text. Authors and books of the NT tend to have particular themes (whether theological, literary, or linguistic) that provide coherence to their discourses. Therefore, one way of assessing the intrinsic probability of a variant is by determining whether it is theologically coherent with the author's broader theological framework or whether it coheres with their use of literary devices, such as characterization (e.g., characterizing a particular participant [e.g., Peter] in a certain context) or particular linguistic ways of describing certain phenomena. In other words, all other factors being equal, the variant that most coheres with the theology and literary and linguistic structure that is developed by a book or author will be the one that is most likely original. In John 12:32, for example, some good witnesses read πάντα ("all" [neuter]) ($\mathfrak{P}^{66}$ ℵ et al.) instead of πάντας ("all" [masculine]). There are no examples in John's Gospel of the neuter being used to refer to people. Therefore, reading the neuter here would seem to suggest the idea of universal or cosmic redemption (Christ will redeem all of creation to himself). John's theological emphasis in his Gospel, however, is upon the universal availability of the atonement to Jews and Greeks (not as much the redemption of creation), and so the masculine (which is used to refer to people) coheres better with John's theological framework than the neuter. Of course, this principle must be used with discretion and in tandem with other more formally grounded criteria, especially the weight of the external evidence, since it may be that a scribe harmonized the text to fit John's theology or that lack of theological or literary coherence constitutes a more difficult reading. Thus this principle serves more of a confirmatory function.

4. Linguistic Conformity

In order to highlight the confusion over style in textual criticism and NT studies more broadly, we may cite here G. D. Kilpatrick's definition of stylistic correction: there are essentially "three kinds of stylistic correction of the text: (1) the elimination of the traces of Semitic idiom, (2) the correction from a non-literary Greek to a literary Koine, (3) the correction to standards of Attic Greek."[5] From our perspective, Kilpatrick's definition is only one very restricted type of style, known as **language formality** since it deals with the form of the language that is being used. Therefore, we may speak of whether the language used in a possible variant conforms to the language form used by the author. It is this category of style and its relevance to textual criticism that we want to consider in this section. In practice, the principles of **linguistic conformity** affirm that, all other things being equal, *the reading that most closely conforms to the form of language (e.g., Semitizing, vulgar, nonliterary, literary) used by the author is the most likely to be original.*

Some scholars, such as Kilpatrick, believe that scribes Atticized the NT language between A.D. 100 and 200. (This theory is often put forward as evidence for the need of thoroughgoing eclecticism; see ch. 7.) **Attic Greek** was a literary style of Greek popularized in ancient Athens, representing a high, literary form of Greek. Therefore, to **Atticize** the NT means that scribes attempted to bring the language of the NT into conformity with the high literary standards found in a select few ancient Athenian authors. However, the theory of Atticizing the early texts does not provide a consistent framework since much of the NT does not reflect Atticizing tendencies.[6] Some scribes, for example, may have used Attic word order instead of nonliterary Greek word order, in which case nonliterary word order likely represents the original. For example, in Attic Greek verbs tend to occur at the end of their clauses whereas in nonliterary (esp. NT) Greek they tend to occur at the beginning. Much of this too will depend upon the author. Luke-Acts is composed in a more literary style, whereas John's writing comes closer to

---

5. George D. Kilpatrick, "Style and Text in the Greek New Testament," in *Studies in the History and Text of the New Testament in Honor of Kenneth Willis Clark* (ed. Boyd L. Daniel and M. Jack Suggs; SD 29; Salt Lake City: University of Utah, 1967), 153. On stylistic correction, see also, e.g., J. Keith Elliott, *The Greek Text of the Epistles to Timothy and Titus* (Salt Lake City: University of Utah Press, 1968), passim.

6. See J. A. L. Lee, "The Atticist Grammarians," in *The Language of the New Testament: Context, History, and Development* (ed. Stanley E. Porter and Andrew W. Pitts; ECHC 3; LBS 6; Leiden: Brill, 2013), 283-308.

vulgar nonliterary Greek in places. We would expect less Atticizing (if this does rarely exist in the NT) in John than in Luke-Acts, in other words.

Another significant element of linguistic conformity involves **Semitic influence**, which may take the form of Hebrew or (esp.) Aramaic interference with syntax or vocabulary. The scribal tendency was to smooth out Semitized language. Put positively, Semitic forms of expression can often be taken to indicate the originality of a reading. This is especially important in Gospel analysis, where John and Matthew write from a Semitic background. But since we also have good evidence for some of Jesus' teaching in Greek, the Greek style may be original too if the passage was likely originally transmitted in Greek (e.g., the Sermon on the Mount or Jesus' dialogue with Pilate, which cannot have transpired in Aramaic).[7] Therefore, it will be important to assess whether a text was likely originally produced in Aramaic or Greek. If a teaching of Jesus, for example, was originally delivered in Aramaic, the possibility that the original author retained Semitic elements is more likely than the hypothesis that a later scribe added them.

That being said, we must note that there is a great deal of debate among scholars concerning what counts as a Semitism. For example, Mark's Gospel has a tendency to begin its clauses with καί ("and"). At one point, many scholars said this reflected the common Semitic tendency of using the equivalent Semitic conjunction at the beginning of its clauses in order to carry the narrative forward. But now numerous examples have been illustrated from Greek papyri (which have no reason to be influenced by Semitic languages!) in which narratives are carried forward by καί in a way that is similar to what is found in Mark. So while continuity of linguistic form can be factored into the discussion at times, not all scholars will find this body of evidence equally compelling.

5. Source Consistency

A final canon that is especially relevant in Synoptic Gospel studies — and could factor in at other places where sources might be involved (e.g., 2 Peter/Jude) — is source consistency. Most scholars believe that Mark was written first and was used as a source by Matthew and Luke when they

---

7. See Stanley E. Porter, "Jesus and the Use of Greek in Galilee," in *Studying the Historical Jesus: Evaluations of the State of Current Research* (ed. Bruce Chilton and Craig A. Evans; NTTS 19; Leiden: Brill, 1994), 123-54.

composed their Gospels (the view known as **Markan priority**). Some have viewed Matthew as the first Gospel, with Luke and Mark using Matthew as a source. Still other (mostly) more recent scholars have sought to explain Gospel similarities and differences primarily by reference to the fact that they all draw upon the same body of oral tradition. So depending upon one's theory of Gospel relationships, the issue of sources will factor into the text-critical discussion. For example, assuming Markan priority for now, at Mark 1:40 NA$^{27/28}$/*UBSGNT*$^{4/5}$ has καὶ γονυπετῶν ("and kneeling down") in brackets. Several manuscripts (e.g., D W) omit it, but it is present in others (e.g., א). In addition to the weight of the external evidence being on the side of retaining it, similar readings (i.e., words for kneeling) are found in the parallel passages in Matt 8:2 and Luke 5:12, indicating that it was probably original in Mark since Mark functioned as Matthew and Luke's source — or, at least, so the theory goes.

6. Summary

In this chapter we have highlighted the role of internal evidence as a productive secondary tool when external evidence is not decisive and have pointed to another set of criteria that textual critics often use when weighing internal evidence: intrinsic probabilities. Whereas transcriptional probabilities assess the probability that particular variants arose as a result of scribal errors and/or practices, intrinsic probabilities deal with the level of probability that a particular variant was written by the author. Transcriptional probabilities, the first step in weighing internal evidence (covered in ch. 9), deal with assessing which variants conform to known scribal tendencies. Intrinsic probabilities, the second step in weighing internal evidence, deal with assessing which variants conform to what is known of an author's style. A number of principles of textual criticism have been discussed that support step 2 when weighing internal evidence, including stylistic continuity, contextual cohesion, theological coherence, linguistic conformity, and source consistency.

KEY TERMINOLOGY
style
stylistic continuity
cohesion
theological and literary coherence

language formality
linguistic conformity
Attic Greek
Atticize
Semitic influence
Markan priority

BIBLIOGRAPHY

Aland, Kurt, and Barbara Aland. *The Text of the New Testament: An Intro-duction to the Critical Editions and to the Theory and Practice of Modern Textual Criticism.* Trans. Erroll F. Rhodes. 2nd ed. Grand Rapids: Eerd-mans, 1989.

Epp, Eldon Jay, and Gordon D. Fee. *Studies in the Theory and Method of New Testament Textual Criticism.* SD 45. Grand Rapids: Eerdmans, 1993.

Greenlee, J. Harold. *Scribes, Scrolls, and Scripture: A Student's Guide to New Testament Textual Criticism.* Grand Rapids: Eerdmans, 1985.

———. *The Text of the New Testament: From Manuscript to Modern Edition.* Peabody, MA: Hendrickson, 2008. [Revision of *Scribes, Scrolls, and Scripture.*]

Halliday, M. A. K. *Halliday's Introduction to Functional Grammar.* Rev. C. M. I. M. Matthiessen. 4th ed. London: Routledge, 2014.

Halliday, M. A. K., and Ruqaiya Hasan. *Cohesion in English.* English Language Series 9. London: Longman, 1976.

Kilpatrick, George D. "Style and Text in the Greek New Testament." Pages 153-60 in *Studies in the History and Text of the New Testament in Honor of Kenneth Willis Clark.* Ed. Boyd L. Daniel and M. Jack Suggs. SD 29. Salt Lake City: University of Utah, 1967.

———. "Atticism and the Future of ZHN." *NovT* 25 (1983): 146-51.

Landon, Charles. *A Text-Critical Study of the Epistle of Jude.* JSNTSup 135. Sheffield: Sheffield Academic Press, 1996.

Metzger, Bruce M. *The Text of the New Testament: Its Transmission, Corruption, and Restoration.* 4th ed. Rev. Bart D. Ehrman. Oxford: Oxford University Press, 2005.

Moulton, James Hope, Wilbert Francis Howard, and Nigel Turner. *A Grammar of New Testament Greek.* 4 vols. Edinburgh: T&T Clark, 1906-1976.

Pitts, Andrew W. "Style and Pseudonymity in Pauline Scholarship: A Regis-ter Based Configuration." Pages 113-52 in *Paul and Pseudepigraphy.* Ed. Stanley E. Porter and Gregory P. Fewster. PAST 6. Leiden: Brill, 2013.

Porter, Stanley E. "P.Oxy. 744.4 and Colossians 3:9." *Bib* 73 (1992): 565-67.

CHAPTER 11

Modern Critical Editions: A Brief History

This chapter serves as a prelude to chapters 12–13, which discuss the use of critical editions (ch. 12) and the role they have played in biblical translation (ch. 13). It will be helpful before moving on to those topics to get a good idea of the history behind the printed critical editions of the Greek NT. Two major phases of the history are traced below in two sections. We start with the edition by Cardinal Francisco Ximénes and follow the history up to Nestle, where the heritage of our modern $NA^{27/28}$ and $UBSGNT^{4/5}$ begins. The second phase is marked by the rise of the manual edition, and the section on this phase gives particular attention to plotting out the historical development from the old Nestle edition to the most recent editions of NA and *UBSGNT*. There are other ways to track the history (the rise and fall of the Textus Receptus is another common framework), but this way of presenting the data is particularly useful in understanding the history behind the standard Greek editions we use today.

1. Critical Editions from Ximénes to Nestle

The history of the printed Greek text begins with the invention of printing in the 1450s made possible by the **Gutenberg Press**. The first printed Bible was a Latin Bible that came to be known as the **Gutenberg Bible** — only a few remain today, each worth millions of dollars because of their unique status as the first printed Western book. Cardinal **Francisco Ximénes de Cisneros** (1437-1517) printed the first completed portion of his **Complutensian Polyglot** (a polyglot is an edition with several languages, including Greek, in this case) on January 10, 1514; and **Desiderius**

Erasmus, the renowned humanist from Rotterdam, published an edition of the Greek NT on March 1, 1516. Although the polyglot was printed first, Erasmus's publisher, **Johann Froben**, marketed Erasmus's edition as the first published Greek edition (the *editio princeps*).

Erasmus's text met with mixed reviews initially. One of the most substantial criticisms, made by **Diego Lopez de Zuñiga** (**Jacobus Stunica**, an editor of Ximenes's polyglot), was that Erasmus had removed a significant portion of 1 John 5, known as the *Comma Johanneum:* "For there are three that bear record in heaven, the Father, the Word, and the Holy Ghost: and these three are one. And there are three that bear witness in earth, the Spirit, and the water, and the blood: and these three agree in one" (1 John 5:7-8, KJV). Erasmus's reply was that none of the Greek manuscripts that he had access to contained these words — even though this had not stopped him before! However, Erasmus promised Stunica that he would include the passage in his future editions if he could produce one Greek manuscript with the words. So he did. The manuscript that was finally put forward by Stunica was one produced in 1520 by a Franciscan friar, Froy, who apparently took the words from the Latin Vulgate. The whole scenario is highly suspect, and the document was almost certainly created for precisely this purpose. Nevertheless, Erasmus remained faithful to his word and included the additional words in the third (1522) and subsequent editions of his text, but did qualify its inclusion with a detailed footnote explaining that the manuscript that he derived the reading from was compiled for the specific purpose of refuting his original decision to exclude the reading based upon the absence of Greek manuscripts in support of it. **Erasmus's fifth edition** (published in 1535) was the final, definitive one, which included, in parallel columns, his most recent Greek edition, his own Latin edition, and the Latin Vulgate. In this edition, he made use of the superior Greek text employed in Ximénes's polyglot, making a number of corrections that reflected the readings in Ximénes's edition.

Erasmus had relied upon just a few twelfth- and thirteenth-century minuscule manuscripts representing the latest textual tradition, the Byzantine, often referred to as the Majority text (though technically the "majority" text is simply that text to which the majority of manuscripts point, which also happens to be the Byzantine text). Even when majuscule texts were available to Erasmus, he did not consult them. For example, he had access to the eighth-century majuscule manuscript Basiliensis (E) (also a Byzantine text). The famous reformer Theodore Beza also had in his possession copies of *Codex Bezae Cantabrigiensis* (D^{ea}) and Codex Claromontanus (D^p), two earlier Western texts (see ch. 5) that Erasmus could have consulted but did not. It was from Erasmus's text that the Authorized Version (later known as the KJV) was translated in 1611. Erasmus's text became known as the "Received Text" or the **Textus Receptus** due to a comment made in the preface of Elzevir's printed edition of the Greek NT (see below) that Erasmus's text was "received" by all.

The first published Greek edition to follow Erasmus's was published by **Colinaeus** in 1534, but the most important Greek text (next to the Textus Receptus) in the sixteenth century was the one published by Robert Estienne (Latinized as **Stephanus**) in France and later published in the Netherlands during the seventeenth century by the **Elzevir** publishing house, going through seven editions (1624-1678). The third and best-known edition of Stephanus's text (1550) was the first to include a text-critical apparatus, which cited Codex Bezae and was aligned closely with the fourth and fifth editions of Erasmus's text. Stephanus's 4th edition (1551) (a smaller sized version) was the first to add verse divisions to the Greek NT.

A new stage in the history of the Greek text is reached in the edition of the Tübingen scholar **Johann Albrecht Bengel** (1687-1752) and those who followed him. As a precursor to his edition, Bengel published in 1725 a volume detailing significant text-critical principles to be employed when *weighing* (as opposed to merely counting) the significance of textual variants according to groups and families. In 1734 he published an edition that essentially reproduced the Textus Receptus (apart from 19 places in Revelation) but indicated in the margins of his edition what he considered the relative value of each variant reading on a scale of gradation, with α on the one end representing the original reading and ε on the other end representing a very inferior reading to be rejected. The edition included three large excursuses that detailed his text-critical principles and collated various manuscripts used in an earlier edition by John Mill as well as twelve others that Mill had not used. Though Bengel was a man committed to piety and orthodoxy, he was regarded by many as an enemy of the Scriptures for calling attention to the variations and errors within the textual tradition.

In 1751-1752 **Johann Jakob Wettstein** (whose work Richard Bentley drew upon) followed a model similar to Bengel's, publishing an edition based on the Elzevir text, but making notes on which readings he thought were most likely original. Wettstein's apparatus was the first to denote majuscule manuscripts by capital Roman letters and minuscule manuscripts by Arabic numerals.

Salomo Semler (1725-1791) also built upon the work of Bengel. Developing Bengel's idea of textual groups in his reprint of Wettstein's *Prolegomena,* Semler was the first to classify the NT manuscripts in three textual recensions: (1) Alexandrian (Origen and Syriac, Bohairic, Ethiopic versions), (2) Eastern (Antioch, Constantinople), and (3) Western (Latin versions and church fathers). Witnesses from a later period tended to produce a text that mixed these recensions, according to Semler.

Finally, the synthesizing work of **Johann Jakob Griesbach** (1745-1812) brought the eighteenth-century editions of the Greek text into what would be their final form, but he too was highly dependent upon Bengel. Like Bengel, Griesbach noted distinct text-types, but spoke of the following three traditions: (1) Alexandrian, (2) Western, and (3) Byzantine. He also provided alternate readings to the Textus Receptus, but not as substantially as Bengel had done before him. Textual critics today still use Griesbach's fifteen canons of textual criticism.

The project of **Karl Lachmann** (1793-1851) marks the next major shift in the history of the printed text of the NT. Lachmann's editions (1st ed. 1831; 3rd ed. 1846) were among the first to intentionally set out a program to free NT scholarship from the Textus Receptus and the late manuscript tradition that it represented, which, Lachmann thought, was clearly inadequate. **Constantine Tischendorf** was a significant figure who moved this agenda forward by deciphering the Ephraemi Rescriptus (C) as well as discovering and publishing numerous early NT manuscripts that helped support our understanding of the textual history of the NT in its earlier periods, especially the fourth century (see ch. 4). Tischendorf also published numerous editions of the NT, culminating in his 8th edition (1869-1872). Tischendorf's eighth edition considered all of the external evidence available to him at the time and gave pride of place to Codex Sinaiticus, which he had discovered, in instances of textual variation.

Two Cambridge scholars, **Brooke Foss Westcott** (1825-1901) and **Fenton John Anthony Hort** (1828-1892), mark the next stage in the use of textual criticism to produce critical editions of the Greek NT. Unfortunately, this stage marks a step away from firsthand engagement with the ancient manuscripts and focuses more on summarizing the work of those scholars who had engaged critically with the manuscripts that went before them (esp. Tischendorf). Westcott and Hort also continued to move the focus away from the Textus Receptus and back to the text current in the fourth century. Their edition, *The New Testament in the Original Greek* (1881), and the accompanying text-critical principles that guided its production placed a great deal of emphasis upon the superiority of both fourth-century codices available to them, Sinaiticus and Vaticanus. Indeed, when these two codices agreed, Westcott and Hort insisted that this reading represented the original. Westcott and Hort's edition of the Greek NT went a long way to displace the then longstanding tradition and use of the Textus Receptus.

Eberhard Nestle (1851-1913) continues the trajectory set by Westcott and Hort, relying on other editions and scholars rather than the actual ancient manuscripts, and marks the beginning of the era of manual editions (see the next section for discussion). Beginning with his third edition, Nestle relied heavily upon three editions in the establishment of the text: Tischendorf, Westcott and Hort, and **Bernhard Weiss** (1894-1900), who assessed readings based upon internal criteria, especially contextual considerations. Where two or three of these editions agreed, Nestle incorporated that reading into his text. The apparatus contains a number of helpful early witnesses to the text, some of which were discovered in the twentieth century.

Hermann von Soden's (1852-1914) edition (1901-1913), which von Soden hoped would replace Tischendorf, represents a continued advancement of these trends in textual criticism to establish the text of the NT according to the earliest witnesses available. Von Soden developed an entirely new set of symbols denoting the various manuscripts for the publication of his editions, but scholars have generally found his system too complex and impractical for textual study. Scholars have also now rejected his view of the various recensions that support the NT and generally consider his apparatus to be industrious but unreliable. Nevertheless, von Soden's edition did influence the readings of a number of early-twentieth-century editions.

It would be Nestle's version that would eventually provide the basis for the development of the standard modern editions of the NT found in NA$^{27/28}$ and *UBSGNT*$^{4/5}$ (these two manual editions are discussed in detail in the next chapter).

The twentieth century did not see as many monumental developments in textual criticism as did the nineteenth century with the rise of the importance of the early majuscules. Nevertheless, a number of advances are worth noting. S. C. E. Legg published editions of Mark (1935) and Matthew (1940). E. C. Colwell initiated the **International Greek New Testament Project,** which hoped to be a continuation of Legg's original program. After forty years the members of the project finally published the Gospel of Luke, which seeks to provide a fairly comprehensive apparatus of external witnesses.

Even though in the twentieth and twenty-first centuries we observe a strong preference among textual critics for the Alexandrian tradition, several still remain convinced of the importance of the Byzantine tradition for establishing the original text. **Zane Hodges** and **Arthur Farstad**, for example, continue to argue for the superiority of the Majority text, leading them to publish *The Greek New Testament According to the Majority Text* (1981).

Several other projects have emerged in recent years, such as the CNTTS (Center for New Testament Textual Studies, with a digital, searchable apparatus) and the Society of Biblical Literature edition of the Greek NT (with an apparatus that compiles several editions), but continue the trend began by Westcott and Hort, where these tools often (even if not always — in the case of the CNTTS) simply rely on prior editions.

2. From Nestle to NA$^{27/28}$ and *UBSGNT*$^{4/5}$

Although several significant text-critical projects surfaced in the twentieth century, the most important development was the establishment of the standard manual editions. A **manual edition** is limited as a tool for studying the history of the NT text or in studying individual manuscripts or their tendencies (since they by no means provide comprehensive information); instead it is intended to provide a *preliminary* basis for studying what are considered to be important variants by the editors of the edition. In other words, manual editions in no way seek to provide a comprehensive apparatus of witnesses in their notes, just a sample of the more important ones. Quite a few of these manual editions have emerged over the last one hundred years, but the ones that dominated the twentieth century and continue to provide the standard text for academic study and translation of the NT are the NA and the UBS texts, which contain the exact same text in their most recent editions — regardless of where they differ in terms of formatting and the critical apparatus.

After Eberhard Nestle died, his son **Erwin Nestle** (1883-1972) took over the responsibilities for the edition. In the 13th edition (1927), Erwin Nestle made a number of revisions, most notably the inclusion of a strong text-critical apparatus that supported variant readings from Tischendorf, Westcott and Hort, Weiss, and von Soden. The format was also changed to facilitate reference and use among scholars. These changes made the Nestle edition superior to its competition and resulted in the Nestle edition becoming the predominant one used in NT scholarship.

Two nearly simultaneous developments that progressed parallel to one another would eventually result in the NA$^{27/28}$/*UBSGNT*$^{4/5}$ texts that are standard today. **Kurt Aland** began to get involved with the Nestle edition in the 1950s. Aland's job was initially to verify the accuracy of the evidence that had been used in the previous editions through a rigorous consultation of the primary rather than secondary sources (since the Nestle edition and its apparatus was originally based on other editions) in preparation for a new edition. Around the same time (1955), **Eugene A. Nida**, Translations Secretary of the American Bible Society, undertook to prepare an edition of the Greek NT designed for use by translators. Four scholars were invited to be part of the committee: Matthew Black, Bruce Metzger, Allen Paul Wikgren, and Kurt Aland. This resulted in Aland being involved in two distinct editorial projects, both designed to produce editions of the Greek NT for differing purposes. As the two committees compared their results for the Gospels, they found that the text they produced was remarkably similar. After the second edition of the UBS *Greek New Testament,* the Württemberg Bible Society gave up its plan for a 26th independent edition and agreed to consolidate their committee of scholars and the resultant text with those who were working on the *Greek New Testament* so that the text of the UBS (representing a number of supporting Bible societies, hence the "United Bible Societies"; therefore, *UBSGNT*) third edition and NA^{26} were joined together. Other issues of format, paragraph divisions, font, and punctuation, however, were only updated according to each edition's original standards. And it has remained together in the most recent (5th) *UBSGNT* and NA (28th) editions (the latest edition of each being a slight modification of the previous one with the exception of the Catholic Letters — see the next chapter).

3. Summary

In this chapter we have outlined the history of the printed Greek NT in several phases. The first phase is ushered in by the invention of the printing press. The standardization of Erasmus's Textus Receptus characterized most of this era, but the chains of the Textus Receptus were eventually broken and editions based upon manuscripts copied in the fourth century slowly became more dominant, of which Nestle's is representative. Nestle's edition and those comparable to it marked the beginning of our present era with dominance of the manual edition and the now widely used NA$^{27/28}$ and the *UBSGNT*$^{4/5}$.

KEY TERMINOLOGY

Gutenberg Press
Gutenberg Bible
Francisco Ximénes de Cisneros
Complutensian Polyglot
Desiderius Erasmus
Johann Froben
Diego Lopez de Zuñiga
Stunica
Erasmus's fifth edition
Textus Receptus
Colinaeus
Stephanus
Elzevir
Johann Albrecht Bengel
Johann Jakob Wettstein
Salomo Semler
Johann Jakob Griesbach
Karl Lachmann
Constantine Tischendorf
Brooke Foss Westcott
Fenton John Anthony Hort
Eberhard Nestle
Bernhard Weiss
Hermann von Soden
International Greek New Testament Project
Zane Hodges
Arthur Farstad
manual edition
Erwin Nestle
Kurt Aland
Eugene A. Nida

BIBLIOGRAPHY

Aland, Kurt, and Barbara Aland. *The Text of the New Testament: An Introduction to the Critical Editions and to the Theory and Practice of Modern Textual Criticism.* Trans. Erroll F. Rhodes. 2nd ed. Grand Rapids: Eerdmans, 1989.

Baird, William. *From Deism to Tübingen.* Vol. 1 of *History of New Testament Research.* Philadelphia: Fortress, 1992.

Clarke, Kent D. *Textual Optimism: A Critique of the United Bible Societies' Greek New Testament.* JSNTSup 138. Sheffield: Sheffield Academic Press, 1997.

Metzger, Bruce M. *The Text of the New Testament: Its Transmission, Corruption, and Restoration.* 4th ed. Rev. Bart D. Ehrman. Oxford: Oxford University Press, 1992.

Porter, Stanley E. *How We Got the New Testament: Text, Transmission, Translation.* Grand Rapids: Baker, 2013.

CHAPTER 12

A Guide to the Text and Apparatus
of the *UBSGNT*⁴/⁵ and NA²⁷/²⁸

In this chapter we provide an introductory guide to using the two standard manual editions for NT study and translation: *UBSGNT*⁴/⁵ and NA²⁷/²⁸. The aim is to introduce the reader to the basic conventions needed to understand and use the text and apparatus of these two editions. It is not exhaustive, but it does endeavor to cover all of the commonly employed conventions. Abbreviations for the classes of manuscripts (e.g., papyri [𝔓], majuscules [capital letters and/or numbers beginning with 0]) and most significant manuscripts in those classes (e.g., 𝔓⁴⁶, ℵ) have already been introduced (see ch. 4). A comprehensive list of conventions and abbreviations used in *UBSGNT*⁴/⁵ and NA²⁷/²⁸ is found in the introductions of the respective editions. In this chapter we will also seek to highlight the distinctive features of each edition. Unique features reflect the purpose and intended functions of the two editions. *UBSGNT*⁴/⁵ purports to be primarily intended for translators, whereas NA²⁷/²⁸ is said to be intended for exegetical scholars and specialists in textual criticism. However, the differences in terms of actual content between the two turns out to be quite insignificant, and NA²⁷/²⁸ is really more of a manual edition, best for all-around use, not for specialized text-critical work. For the latter purpose, Tischendorf's 8th edition is still the best choice. The International Greek New Testament Project (IGNTP) attempts a comprehensive apparatus for each NT book, but so far only one NT book has been produced (Luke's Gospel). NA²⁸ incorporates the *Editio Critica Maior* for the Catholic letters, along with making some changes in the apparatus for these books (including the elimination of bracketed readings). Since the textual changes in the Catholic Letters are surprisingly minimal (only about 30 in all), students need not rush out and buy this updated edition, if they already have the 27th edition, as in some ways the

27th edition is more consistent than the 28th (see below). The same applies to the *UBSGNT*[5] in relation to the *UBSGNT*[4].

1. Distinctive Features of NA[27/28]

Distinctive features of NA[27/28] include the use of inner and outer margins, its own unique textual apparatus, and a number of distinct characteristics pertaining to issues of format.[1]

a. Inner Margins

In NA[27/28] the user will find a set of numbers in the **inner margins** in the Gospels. These are **Eusebian section and canon numbers**. Eusebius, the fourth-century church historian, developed an excellent system for classifying Gospel parallels in which he divided the Gospels up into ten canon tables or collections of parallel material. These canons are recorded in many of the traditional Greek manuscripts and editions since they would have been useful for scribes and readers. They provide, in effect, an early synopsis of the Gospels, as they indicate where the individual Gospels have parallel passages in the others. NA[27/28] continues this tradition. Canon I includes the parallel pericopes/paragraphs that are represented in all four Gospels. Canons II-IV contain parallel pericopes found in three Gospels. Canons V-IX contain par-

---

1. We are ambivalent on whether the student should adopt either the newer NA[28] or the *UBSGNT*[5] editions of the Greek New Testament. In some ways, the changes to both texts/apparatuses are relatively minor and only slightly updated. For example, the papyri included in the discussion now extend from P117 to P127. However, the seven so-called Catholic Letters now follow the *Editio Critica Maior* (ECM) and introduce over 30 changes to the prior editions. This, then, makes the two editions inconsistent, as the editors admit (*UBSGNT*[5], IX and NA[28], Vorwort and Foreword), because of the introduction of a different set of text-critical principles. At least in this way, some might view the new editions as a step backward due to the inconsistencies now present. Further, several useful features in the NA[27] have been removed from the NA[28] (e.g. subscriptions for NT books and comparison with other editions, e.g. Tischendorf, Westcott-Hort, and others), which takes a step back in different ways. For further ways in which the NA[28] is potentially inferior to the NA[27], see David Trobisch, *A User's Guide to the Nestle-Aland 28 Greek New Testament* (Atlanta: Society of Biblical Literature, 2013), 46-54. We, therefore, discuss the *two* most recent editions for both the NA and UBS texts of the Greek New Testament as we are not always convinced that the new editions are steps forward at this stage.

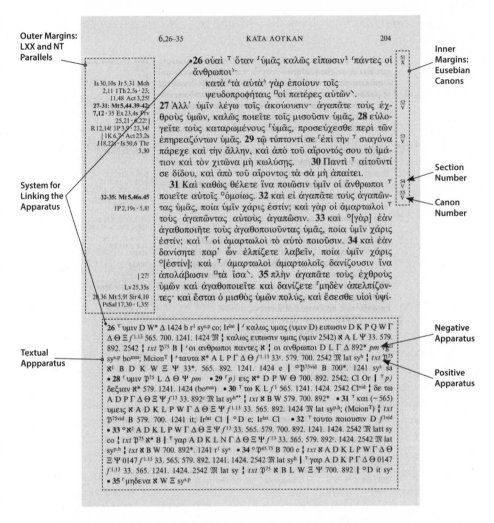

Figure 12.1: Explanation of NA²⁸ Text, Margins, and Apparatus

allel pericopes found in two Gospels, and canon X contains pericopes that are unique to one Gospel. In NA²⁷/²⁸ these canons (and where they occur) are marked in the inner margins. The Arabic number above the line refers to the section number of a particular canon and the Roman numeral below the line refers to the canon number. This information will be of historical interest to the student, but is intended by the editors primarily for the use of specialists in the study of the text and history of early Christianity.

b. Outer Margins

In addition to an apparatus at the bottom of the page, NA²⁷/²⁸ uses its **outer margins** to make note of parallel expressions and citations of the OT and NT. This also includes information about specific parallels in Greek translations of the OT (e.g., Aquila or the OT portion of Codex Sinaiticus). NA²⁷/²⁸ provides a far more extensive selection of parallel passages than *UBSGNT⁴/⁵*. The following conventions are used in NA²⁷/²⁸ outer margins in this way:[2]

p)	Refers to parallel passages in the Gospels, which are listed in the margin at the beginning of the pericopes.
(L 2,7) (22,3) (12)	Notice the use of shorter German abbreviations for biblical books and the different way of referring to biblical books with a comma rather than a colon (e.g., L 2,7 rather than Luke 2:7). A parenthetical reference to a passage standing before a variant reading refers to a parallel passage in another NT book (cf. the reference to Luke 2:7 at Matt 1:25). If the parenthetical reference does not name a book (e.g., Luke 22:3), the parallel is found within the same book (cf. the reference to Acts 22:3 at Acts 21:39), or the same chapter (cf. the reference to v. 12 at Matt 2:13).
(19 *v.l.*)	A parenthetical reference to a verse with *v.l.* standing before a reading suggests that the reading derives from a variant reading in the verse indicated (cf. Matt 2:13, which refers to the same transposition at 2:19).
(Jr 38,15𝕲)	A reference to a passage in the LXX standing before a variant suggests a parallel expression in the LXX text (cf. the reference to Jer 38,15 𝕲 at Matt 2:18).

---

2. The definitions for signs and abbreviations given in these sections for NA²⁷/²⁸ are quoted, adapted, and/or expanded from the introduction in NA²⁷, 44*-83*, and NA²⁸, 46*-88*.

c. Text and Critical Apparatus

The critical apparatus is the section of notes that occurs at the bottom of each page of the Greek NT. The verse numbers that the notes are associated with are in bold. NA$^{27/28}$ uses a selection of symbols to indicate how much text is being commented upon. The introduction to NA$^{27/28}$ should be consulted for a comprehensive list of these symbols and their meanings, although many of them are covered below by virtue of summarizing, expanding, and commenting on the explanations found in the introduction. Some manuscripts are of greater significance than others. NA$^{27/28}$ includes significant as well as less significant manuscripts since these latter manuscripts can often give the interpreter insight into the history of the text. In order to distinguish these two classes of evidence, NA$^{27/28}$ contains both a positive and negative apparatus. The **positive apparatus** lists all of the variants in the external evidence that are substantial for establishing the original text. The positive apparatus contains readings *for* and *against* the reading found in the text. The **negative apparatus** lists variants that are significant only for understanding the history of the text (e.g., how and for what reasons the text might have been altered). The negative apparatus only lists readings *against* the text. Therefore, when manuscripts are listed in support of a given reading, but the evidence in support of the text is not mentioned (indicated by the sign *txt*; see below), you know that the variants are not important for establishing the original text, but may give insight into its history. The *txt* abbreviation, then, is an indicator that one is dealing with the positive apparatus. This can admittedly be confusing for students or those first introduced to the edition.

In order to provide the maximum amount of information within the apparatus, modern editions use abbreviations and symbols in order to facilitate the representation of a wide range of data into a small amount of space. The abbreviations and symbols used in NA$^{27/28}$ are as follows:

NA$^{27/28}$ uses both double and single brackets in the following way (apart from the elemination of square breackets in the Catholic Letters in NA^{28}):

[ ]   Square brackets ([ ]) signify that the enclosed reading is one that the committee could not reach a certain decision on so they include the text in brackets to indicate doubt. For example, in Phil 1:24, we find [ἐν] τῇ σαρκὶ, where the brackets indicate

that ἐν is an uncertain reading. In the NA[28], however, this correction is used everywhere with the exception of the Catholic Letters (see explanation below on the diamond ♦).

We find this rather bizarre. If the UBS committee is editing the text, and they cannot decide, they are in effect deferring judgment by including these points of indecision in bracketed text. We think that editors should make a decision, but indicate that the evidence is what it is in the apparatus without introducing confusion or uncertainty into the main text. We think this current bracketing method is not helpful, especially to a student, and also to many scholars who are not specialists in textual criticism. Nevertheless, this is the convention that is used, so the student should be familiar with it.

♦ The ♦ (diamond) indicates passages where the guiding line is split in the second edition of the ECM, because there are two variants which in the editors' judgment could equally well be adopted in the reconstructed initial text. In the ECM apparatus the alternative variant is marked with ♦ as well. In the NA[28] edition the diamond precedes the reference sign of the respective variant passage and the variant text in the apparatus. This does not mean that the editors regard the text as definitively established in all other passages. However, square brackets and other signs are no longer seen as suitable for expressing different degrees of reliability in the reconstructed initial text.

⟦ ⟧ Double brackets are perhaps even more problematic. They indicate that the text (⟦ ⟧) within the enclosed words (often long portions of text) is *definitely* not part of the original. These include passages like Mark 16:9-20 and John 7:53-8:11 that played an important role in the development of the (esp. KJV) English Bible, but which have very little manuscript support.

We do not believe it is helpful to include this material in the main text at all; but, again, this is the convention and those using this edition should be familiar with it.

The following critical signs are used most frequently in the text and are correlated to the notes below within the text-critical apparatus:

Figure 12.2: Symbols in NA$^{27/28}$ for Linking the Text to the Apparatus

Abbrev.	Meaning	NT Example
°	The *word* following in the text is *omitted* by the witnesses cited.	°καὶ (Titus 1:16)
⸆ ⸌	The *words, clauses or sentences* following in the text are *omitted* by the witnesses cited. The sign ⸆ marks the beginning and the sign ⸌ marks the end of the omitted text.	⸆τῆς δόξης⸌ (2 Cor 4:6)
⸀	The *word* following in the text is *replaced* with one or more words by the witnesses cited.	⸀κρίνει (Rom 2:16)
⸀ ⸁	The *words* following in the text are *re-placed* with other words by the witnesses cited. The sign ⸀ marks the beginning and ⸁ marks the end of the replaced text. Frequently this involves the transposition of words. To the extent the words are identical with those in the text, they are indicated by italic numerals in the apparatus corresponding to their position in the printed text.	⸀οἱ ἀκούοντες⸁ (Rev 1:3)
⸋	This sign marks the location where *one or more words*, sometimes a whole verse, are *inserted* by the witnesses cited.	⸋πᾶσιν (Gal 3:10)
⸂ ⸃	The *words* following in the text are *transposed* (a different order) by the witnesses cited. The sign ⸂ marks the beginning and the sign ⸃ marks the end of the portion of text transposed (change of order).	⸂μόνον ἀκροαταὶ⸃ (Jas 1:22)

There are a few other notations that students may want to familiarize themselves with. Centered dots (see first example below) and superscript numerals distinguish between multiple occurrences of the same kind of variant within a single unit of the apparatus. A raised colon (˸) indicates a variation in punctuation.

The following conventions are employed in organizing the text:

- A large dot followed by a bold verse number opens each new section of the apparatus. Critical signs do not occur twice within a single section; their repetitions are distinguished by the addition of centered dots or italic numerals. Apparatus sections usually span a single verse; when variants extend over several verses, this is made explicit by the reference following the large dot (cf. Luke 22:17-20).

| A solid vertical line separates the instances of variation from each other within a single verse or section of the apparatus.

¦   A broken vertical line separates the various alternative readings from each other within a single instance of variation. These readings taken together make up a group of readings, or a variant-unit.

txt   This sign (= *textus*) introduces the list of witnesses supporting the text of this edition. It always occurs as the last member of a group of readings, or variant-unit. This can be rather confusing since the *txt* comes after the variants, a convention not followed in the *UBSGNT⁴ᐟ⁵* text.

NA²⁷ᐟ²⁸ usually spells out the variant within the apparatus. However, in certain cases, it is more space efficient to use abbreviations when variants only relate to word order or minor issues of variation (e.g., spelling). (Users of the NA are also referred to Appendix II, which lists minor variant readings.) In these cases, the following symbols are used:

   Only the distinctive element of a variant form may be given, whether it is the first part of a word (cf. Luke 19:43) or the last (cf. Luke 19:37; Matt 2:23 –ρεθ). No symbol is used other than the abbreviated form of the word.

...   Three periods (...) represent the text of the edition where the variant form cited is in agreement with it (cf. Luke 20:25).

2 3 1 4 5   Variants of word order are represented by italic numerals that correspond to the order of the words in the text (*1* = the first word in the text, etc.), a feature not found in NA²⁸ (see below).

( )   Witnesses that show only minor differences are noted in parentheses ( ), along with the witnesses for the main variant.

[ ]   Brackets [ ] enclose conjectures with regard to both the text and its punctuation.

The witnesses are always presented in the same order: Greek manuscripts (papyri, majuscules, minuscules, lectionaries), versions, patristic citations. Patristic citations are separated by semicolons (;). It is sometimes necessary to qualify the listing of a witness, often because of a correction, in which case the following superscripts are used (e.g., $\aleph$*):

*	identifies the original reading when a correction has been made.
c	identifies a correction made by a later hand, but sometimes also by the first hand.
$D^{1.2.3}$	Superscript numeral identifies a correction made by the first, second, or third corrector.
v.l.	(= *varia lectio*) indicates a reading recorded in a manuscript as an alternative reading (*v.l.* is coordinated with the superscript sign *txt*).
txt	(= *textus*) as a superscript sign indicates the reading in the text of a manuscript that also records an alternative reading (*txt* is coordinated with the superscript sign *v.l.*).
mg	(= *in margine*) indicates a reading in the margin of a manuscript without being identified as either a correction or an alternative reading.
s	(= *supplementum*) indicates a reading derived from a later addition to a manuscript, usually replacing a lost folio or section of a manuscript.
vid	(= *ut videtur*) indicates that the reading attested by a witness cannot be determined with absolute certainty. So, for example, if a papyrus has been damaged and the reading is reconstructed to the best of the editor's ability, this abbreviation will be used by the manuscript notation.

The symbol $\mathfrak{M}$ represents the Majority text reading. Manuscripts from the Syrian text-type (often referred to as the Byzantine text-type) that make up the Majority text are not cited in NA[27/28] independently unless they are distinct from the collective testimony of the Majority text. When the Majority text is equally or near equally divided, the sign *pm* is used to introduce both sets of witnesses for the Majority text. Of course, it will only occur once in cases where the negative apparatus is presented.

Since NA[27/28] does not provide a comprehensive apparatus of textual witnesses, NA[27] employs a set of abbreviations that helps to give the interpreter an idea of the amount and quality of the uncited evidence — a feature not employed in NA[28]. These occur after the Greek witnesses have been cited:

pc	= *pauci*: a few manuscripts, other than those explicitly mentioned for a given reading, that differ from the Majority text. This convention is abandoned in NA²⁸.
al	= *alii*: some manuscripts (more than represented by *pc*), other than those explicitly mentioned for a given reading, that differ from the Majority text.
pm	= *permulti*: a large number of manuscripts, when the Majority text is divided (see above).
rell	= *reliqui*: the rest of the manuscript tradition (including 𝔐) supporting *txt* (cf. Luke 5:39); a few especially authoritative witnesses may precede *rell* (cf. John 8:16).

In NA²⁷ but not in NA²⁸ a cross (†) introduces a reading in the apparatus; it "marks a change in the text from the 25th edition. . . . These passages always represent very difficult textual decisions."[3]

The citation of the church fathers follows a set of conventions as well. In addition to the abbreviations for the names of the fathers (e.g., Ambrosiaster is abbreviated Ambr), the following conventions are observed:

( )	The quotation supports the given reading, but with some slight variation.
ms,mss	The father indicates knowledge of one or more NT manuscripts supporting the given reading.
txt-com	In citing patristic commentaries the distinction is drawn between the *text commented on* (txt), called the lemma, and the text of the father ascertained from the *commentary proper* (com).
lem	The reading represents the *lemma*, i.e., the running biblical text of a commentary. This sign is used when the text of a father cannot be reconstructed from the commentary proper, and advises a degree of caution.
pt/pt	(partim/partim) The father cites the particular passage more than once and in more than one form. This sign comprises a complementary pair, and both elements are always shown whenever possible. When one is not shown, this is either because the evidence for the reading in the text is not cited in the

3. Ibid., 14*.

	apparatus, or because the father is witness to a further reading that is not cited in the apparatus.
vid	(*videtur*) The witness of a father for the reading given is *probable,* but not completely certain. Note the same ^{vid} abbreviation above when listing manuscripts. This is a distinct ^{vid} abbreviation for church father witnesses.
v.l.	(*varia lectio*) In the manuscript tradition of the father, *one or more manuscripts support the reading given.*
1739^{mg}	Patristic evidence noted in the margin of the Greek manuscript 1739 (e.g., Eph 3:18).

When a church father is known only indirectly through another church father, the abbreviation for the church father through whom we know the church father is placed in superscript with the abbreviation of the church father responsible for the citation. For example, if we know of a citation by Marcion through Tertullian, the abbreviation Mcion^T is used.

It should be noted that lectionaries are often summarized in NA$^{27/28}$ due to the belief of the editors that lectionaries often reflect the late Syrian tradition. The following conventions are used to summarize the data from lectionaries (with the last four based on important letters in the Greek words they abbreviate):

l^a	a lectionary with the text of the Apostolos (Acts, Catholic Letters, and Pauline Letters)
l^{+a}	a lectionary with the text of the Apostolos and the Gospels
U-*l*	an uncial lectionary
*l*e	a lectionary with readings for the weekdays
*l*esk	a lectionary with readings for the weekdays from Easter to Pentecost, and for the Saturdays and Sundays of the other weeks
*l*sk	a lectionary with readings only for Saturdays and Sundays
*l*sel (Jerus.)	a lectionary with readings for select days (selectae) according to the Jerusalem order

There is also a helpful set of abbreviations that aids in weighing certain internal considerations and factors that may have contributed to the development of the history of the text. The following symbols are employed for these purposes as well as others:

(!)	= *sic!* indicates an accurate transcription of an apparently absurd reading.
h.t.	(= *homoioteleuton*) indicates an omission due to the similar endings of successive words, phrases, or sentences (a visual error: the scribe's eye skips from the first to the second, in effect omitting the text between them).
add.	= *addit/-unt,* add(s)
om.	= *omittit/-unt,* omit(s)
pon.	= *ponit,* place(s), transpose(s)
a.	= *ante,* before
p.	= *post,* after
id./ead.	= *idem/eadem,* the same wording
ex err.	= *ex errore,* erroneously, by scribal error
ex itac.	= *ex itacismo,* by itacism, the substitution of letters with the same phonetic value
ex lat?	= *ex versione latina?* apparently derived from a Latin reading
bis	(= twice) immediately following a critical sign refers to two similar words in the text and their variant(s) that are exceptionally identified by the same critical sign.
?	indicates that the reading found in this manuscript should be checked or verified against the original source.

A number of other abbreviations are used for the purposes of reference as well. These abbreviations are usually based on their Latin equivalents, not English, so that they are not always obvious to the English language user:

a	before
acc	accent or breathing marks
apud	in, according to
Aqu	Aquila
c	with
cf	compare
cj/cjj	infer/infers
cod/codd	manuscripts
del	removes, deletes
dist	separates/differentiates
ex lect	influenced by lectionary use
glossa	explanatory note

hab	has/have
hic	here, at this place
huc	here, to this place
i.e.	namely, that is
illeg	unreadable
incert	uncertain
interp	punctuation
it	likewise
κτλ	etc.
lac	gap/hiatus
loco	in place of
mut	damaged
nihil	nothing
obel	critical sign used in manuscripts for additions
ord inv	inverted order
pon	put/transpose
pro	in place of
rectius	more correctly
sec	according to
sed	but
sim	like/similar
sine	without
s/ss	following
sq/sqq	sequences following
Symm	Symmachus's Greek translation of the OT
tantum	only
ter	three times
test	witness(es)
Theod	Theodotion's Greek translation of the OT
totaliter	completely
usque (*ad*)	as far as, up to
v	see
v(e)l	or
verss	early versions
vs/vss	verse/verses

We may now turn to the apparatus itself and illustrate how the various symbols work together with the text of NA$^{27/28}$ and its apparatus. Luke 6:26 appears as follows in NA$^{27/28}$:

26 οὐαὶ ⸆ ὅταν ⸉ὑμᾶς καλῶς εἴπωσιν⸊ ⸂πάντες οἱ ἄνθρωποι⸃· κατὰ ⸄τὰ αὐτὰ⸅ γὰρ ἐποίουν τοῖς ψευδοπροφήταις □οἱ πατέρες αὐτῶν⸌.

The corresponding apparatus for this passage reads (the apparatus for this passage in NA^{28} is expressed slightly differently, but contains essentially the same information):

• 26 ⸆ υμιν D W* Δ 1424 *pc* b r^{1} sy$^{s.p}$ co; Ir^{lat} | † ⸉ *2 1 3* (D) Q W Θ Ξ *f*$^{1.13}$ 𝔐 ¦ *2 3 1* ℵ A L Ψ 33. 579. 892. (2542) *al* ¦ *txt* 𝔓^{75} B | ⸂ *2 3 1* ℵ ¦ *2 3* D L Γ Δ 892* *pm* vg^{cl} sy$^{s.p.}$ bo^{mss}; Mcion^{T} | ⸄ ταυτα *v. vs* 23 | □ 𝔓^{75vid} B 700*. 1241 *pc* sy^{s} sa

The first variant-unit (marked by ⸆) involves the insertion of ὑμῖν between οὐαὶ and ὅταν in D W* Δ 1424 *pc* b r^{1} sy$^{s.p}$ co; Ir^{lat}. Recall that the capital Greek and Roman letters (plus one Hebrew letter for Sinaiticus [ℵ]) are used to denote majuscules, numbered manuscripts not beginning with 0 are used for minuscules, and *pc* indicates that there are a few other Greek manuscripts besides those explicitly cited that differ from the Majority text but that also support this reading. In the introduction of NA$^{27/28}$ the user will discover that "a,b,c, etc." stands for individual Old Latin manuscripts. Manuscript r^{1} is the siglum for the Latin codex Usserianus 1. The semicolon separates the versional evidence from citations in the church fathers, in this case a Latin translation (thus the superscript ^{lat}) of Irenaeus. The solid vertical line (|) marks the end of this section of the apparatus. This is an example of the negative apparatus since the *txt* abbreviation is not present. As one can see, the evidence for this reading is quite minimal, being supported by primarily Western witnesses.

The second variant-unit spans three words: ⸉ὑμᾶς καλῶς εἴπωσιν⸊. The symbols used here (⸉ ⸊) indicate a transposition or change of ordering. This change of order is indicated by the italicized numbers. Therefore, (D) Q W Θ Ξ *f* 𝔐 read καλῶς ὑμᾶς εἴπωσιν and ℵ A L Ψ 33. 579. 892. (2542) *al* read καλῶς εἴπωσιν ὑμᾶς. The cross (†) denotes that this reading was changed from the text of the 25th edition, and thus indicates a difficult textual decision for the committee. D is in parentheses, which means that D is different in some minor way, but generally agrees with the reading that is marked in the text. The broken vertical (¦) line separates alternative readings for a single instance of variation. So here another possible reading is being offered to the one found in the text, and this is set apart from the previous alternative with the broken line. The manuscript 2542 is in parentheses, denoting a slightly different reading. The abbreviation *al* follows the list of Greek manuscripts, indicating that some other manuscripts from the Majority text support this reading. This set of variants is part of the positive apparatus since the *txt* symbol introduces 𝔓⁷⁵ and B in support of the reading found within the text. The use of the positive apparatus indicates that the variants listed here may have some bearing on establishing the original text.

The third variant unit also spans three words: ⌐πάντες οἱ ἄνθρωποι⌐. The signs used (⌐ ⌐) indicate that the text is replaced by other words in certain manuscripts. Again, the italicized numbers indicate a transposition so that א reads οἱ πάντες ἄνθρωποι and D L Γ Δ 892* *pm* vg^{cl} sy$^{s.p.}$ bo^{mss}; Mcion^T only read οἱ ἄνθρωποι. The minuscule 829 has an asterisk superscript (*), marking the original hand of the manuscript. After the Greek manuscripts are listed, *pm* is used to indicate that "some" other manuscripts support this reading from the Majority text. Then three versions supporting this reading are listed (vg^{cl} sy$^{s.p.}$ bo^{mss}) followed by a citation from Marcion according to Tertullian, separated by a semicolon. Again, since the *txt* abbreviation is not used, we are dealing with the negative apparatus.

The fourth variant unit covers two words: ⌐τὰ αὐτὰ⌐. The superscripted dot inside the symbol that indicates that the words are replaced by other words (⌐ ⌐) just indicates that this sign has already been used in this verse. In other words, this is the second unit of variation in this verse in which words are replaced. The *v.* stands for Latin *vide,* "see," and *vs* stands for "verse." So the apparatus refers the reader to verse 23 of Luke 6, where the same variant occurs.

The final variant-unit, again separated by the unbroken vertical line (|), has the sign for the deletion of words, clauses, or sentences, and here spans three words: ⌐ οἱ πατέρες αὐτῶν ⌐. The square (⌐) indicates deletion and the inverted line (⌐) marks the end of the text marked for deletion. Therefore, 𝔓⁷⁵ᵛⁱᵈ B 700*. 1241 *pc* sy^s sa delete the word group οἱ πατέρες αὐτῶν. The superscript ^{vid} (attached to 𝔓⁷⁵ above) indicates that this reading cannot be confirmed with certainty, possibly because the papyrus has broken away or is unreadable at this particular place. We have another asterisk on the minuscule manuscript 700 above, noting the original hand, and *pc* following the list of Greek manuscripts indicating a few other manuscripts from the Majority text.

There are a few differences between NA^{27} (the basis for the example we have just utilized) and NA^{28} (fig. 1, at the beginning of this section) that should be noted—we use both in this chapter to illustrate similarities and differences. First, in the example from Luke 6:26 above, we notice that NA^{27} utilizes *pc* (a few manuscripts that differ from the Majority text but are not cited) and other abbreviations to indicate the existence of other witnesses not cited (see above) whereas NA²⁸ (pictured in fig. 1) does not. The list of manuscripts is now a bit more comprehensive (see below), which may seem like an improvement; however, the abbreviation system of NA²⁷ is still preferable, we think, since it indicates, and consistently reminds the reader, that a comprehensive list is not provided while also providing some indication of what witnesses have not been included. The NA²⁸ means of indicating the evidence may leave the impression that a comprehensive list has been provided when it has not. NA²⁸ has also removed use of the cross (†) to indicate a change from the 25th edition. This is a helpful update as space can now be used for something other than tracking the history of the editions. Gone from the NA²⁸ is also the numbering system for indicating differences in order (transposition) with the different word order being indicated now with the Greek wording itself.

In the above example, for the variant ⁵ὑμᾶς καλῶς εἴπωσιν˨ in Luke 6:26, ⁵ 2 1 3 (D) in NA²⁷ becomes ⁵καλως υμας (υμιν D) ειπωσιν in NA²⁸ (see below on why accents are not used in the apparatus), and this format (as can be observed in the picture in fig. 1) is followed throughout the apparatus. We like this format change since it allows readers to see the Greek text rather than numerical representations. A few more later manuscripts are listed in NA²⁸ as well. Again, drawing from the example above, support for ⁵καλως υμας (υμιν D) ειπωσιν in NA²⁷ Q W Θ Ξ $f^{1.13}$ 𝔐 becomes D K P Q W Γ Δ Θ Ξ $f^{1.13}$ 565. 700. 1241. 1424 𝔐 in NA²⁸. Having the additional evidence is good, but could give the misconception that all the evidence is cited without the abbreviation system that NA²⁷ employed. So we see pros and cons between NA²⁷ and NA²⁸. The student may, then — at least in some ways — still be best served by NA²⁷ (see n. 1 above).

d. Citation, Orthography, Punctuation, and Font

The convention of NA²⁷/²⁸ for citing the OT is to put the citation in *italics*. It also uses capital and lower-case Greek letters in a distinct way. To mark direct speech, it has a colon followed by a lower-case letter. In previous editions, the punctuation differed between *UBSGNT* and NA versions, with NA following what is intended to represent Greek punctuation and *UBSGNT* following English conventions. The punctuation in *UBSGNT*⁴ was brought into conformity with NA²⁷ and remains the same in *UBSGNT*⁵ and NA²⁸. It should be noted, however, that the accenting in the apparatus still differs, since NA$^{27/28}$ does not use accents and *UBSGNT*$^{4/5}$ does. In this respect, NA$^{27/28}$ supposedly leaves more discretion to the interpreter since accents are a later convention not found in the earlier manuscripts. However, there are accents in many early manuscripts, and these are not indicated, so the problem is not really solved. Many modern text-critical articles and monographs follow this same convention: they do not include accents when discussing variant readings in hopes of not artificially prejudging the issue. Last of all, NA$^{27/28}$ uses a bold or upright square Greek font.

2. Distinctive Features of *UBSGNT*$^{4/5}$

The *UBSGNT*$^{4/5}$ also has a set of distinct features that the student should be aware of, including three levels of apparatus and a system of gradation that indicates the committee's level of certainty for the reading found within the text. Like NA^{28}, *UBSGNT*^{5} also uses the *Editio Critica Maior* for the Catholic Letters, with similar changes to the apparatus.

a. Differences in Abbreviations

The *UBSGNT*$^{4/5}$ generally follows the same system of abbreviations that NA$^{27/28}$ does in its apparatus. Both follow the Gregory-Aland numbering system for manuscripts. The following differences, however, should be noted. *UBSGNT*$^{4/5}$ uses *v.r.* to indicate "variant reading" instead of *v.l.* as in NA$^{27/28}$. *UBSGNT*$^{4/5}$ also uses *supp* instead of ^{s} to indicate a "supplement" or later addition to a manuscript, but one which is not of significant value. In *UBSGNT*^{4} the question mark (?) also has a different meaning. It indicates the uncertainty of a reading, not just that a manuscript should be verified against its original source. The Syrian (or Byzantine) tradition is represented by 𝔐, *pc,* and *pm* in the NA$^{27/28}$, but *UBSGNT*$^{4/5}$ uses *Byz* for the majority of the Byzantine tradition and *Byz*^{pt} for part of the manuscripts in the Byzantine tradition. So, to summarize, in addition to the lists of abbreviations mentioned above for NA$^{27/28}$, one should make note of the following abbreviations for *UBSGNT*$^{4/5}$:[4]

---

4. Definitions for symbols and abbreviations in these sections on the *UBSGNT*$^{4/5}$ are quoted, adapted, and/or expanded from the introduction in *UBSGNT*^{4}, 1*-52*, and *UBSGNT*^{5}, 1*-63*.

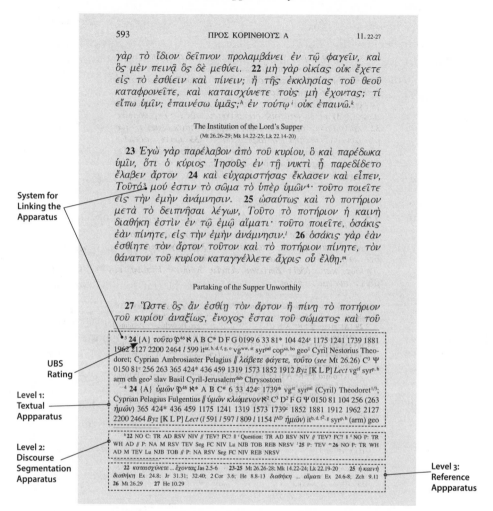

Figure 12.3: Explanation of *UBSGNT*^{4} Text, Margins, and Apparatus

v.r.	variant reading
supp	supplement added by a later hand that is not of much value for determining the original
?	the citation of the edition is uncertain and does not clearly support the reading
Byz	the majority of the Byzantine tradition
Byz^{pt}	part of the Byzantine tradition

The citation of church fathers in $UBSGNT^{4/5}$ is different in certain ways. To begin with, $UBSGNT^{4/5}$ spells out the name of the church father, whereas $NA^{27/28}$ uses (often) quite condensed abbreviations for the names of the fathers. The following conventions are unique to $UBSGNT^{4/5}$ and should be observed as well:

supp	a portion of a church father's text *supplied* by a later hand where the original is missing (e.g., Origen's *Commentary on John*).
ms,mss	*manuscript(s)* of a church father's text when differing from the edited text.
mss[acc. to Origen]	variant readings of manuscripts according to a church father's witness.
1/2, 2/3, 5/7 etc.	Superscript fractions indicate the statistics for *variant readings in multiple instances of a passage*. The second number of the fraction indicates the number of times the passage occurs in the church father's writings; the first number indicates how many times the reading attested is supported.
pap	a reading from the *papyrus stage* of the tradition of a church father's text when it differs from an edition (usually now dated) of the father.
ed	the reading from an *edition* of a church father when it differs from a reading in the papyrus tradition of his text.
gr	a citation from a Greek fragment of the work of a Greek church father that is preserved complete only in a translation.
lat,syr,arm,slav,arab	a Latin, Syriac, Armenian, Slavonic, or Arabic translation of a work by a Greek church father that has not survived in its original form.
acc. to	*according to:* indicates the source of a citation by a church father which is preserved only indirectly, i.e., through quotation by another church father.
dub	a citation from the work of a church father, to whom its attribution is dubious.

Lectionaries are also represented differently in $UBSGNT^{4/5}$. $UBSGNT^{4/5}$ is able, with its system, to provide a more comprehensive assessment of the evidence here. The following conventions are employed for citing lectionaries:

Lect	the *majority* of the selected *lectionaries* together with the lectionary text of the Greek Church (i.e., the text of the edition published by Apostoliki Diakonia, Athens).
l 68, etc.	individual lectionary manuscripts when they differ from the reading of the majority.
Lect^{Pt}	a part of the lectionary manuscript tradition (at least ten manuscripts) that differs from the rest (also designated Lectpt). This symbol always appears in pairs in the critical apparatus.
Lect^{Pt,AD}	a part of the lectionary manuscript tradition in agreement with the lectionary text of the Greek Church (i.e., the text of the edition published by Apostoliki Diakonia, Athens).
l^{AD}	a reading of the lectionary text of the Greek Church (i.e., the text of the edition published by Apostoliki Diakonia, Athens).
l 866^{½}	The superscript fraction after the symbol for a lectionary manuscript shows the *relative frequency* of a reading in the *multiple occurrence* of the same passage in a single lectionary manuscript. The second number of the fraction indicates the number of times the passage occurs in the manuscript; the first number indicates how many times it supports the reading attested.

In addition to a knowledge of the value, date, and abbreviations for the most significant classes of manuscripts (e.g., papyri [𝔓]) and most significant manuscripts in those classes (e.g., 𝔓⁴⁶, ℵ; see ch. 4), becoming familiar with the NA²⁷/²⁸ conventional symbols and abbreviations and then noting these major differences should provide one with facility in using both editions.

b. Critical Apparatus

The first level of apparatus in *UBSGNT⁴/⁵* is the **critical apparatus,** where units of textual variation are noted. Instead of summarizing the tradition in the broadest way possible, as with NA²⁷/²⁸, the *UBSGNT⁴/⁵* apparatus contains a very limited number of what are considered to be important variants for translators and then goes into more detail on the manuscript support for these variants even if it is not always clear *how* this practice helps translators. Besides this major methodological and functional difference, an important distinctive feature of the *UBSGNT*[4/5] apparatus is the system of gradation that is given to the readings regarding the committee's level of certainty that the reading in the text reflects the original. The grades are based on a four-letter system progressing from an **A rating** (certain) to a **B rating** (almost certain) to a **C rating** (the committee had difficulty determining which variant should be in the text) to a **D rating** (the committee is uncertain as to which variant should be in the text), progressing from most to least certain.[5] In the Catholic Letters the ♦ (diamond) is used where no ranking can be determined due to textual uncertainty. This is the least certain rating. These letters are enclosed in the following style of brackets {} (e.g., {A}) and introduce the first reading (the reading found in the text) and its support. This system will be discussed in greater detail below. The alternative readings for a single unit of variation are separated by double diagonal lines // in the apparatus instead of a broken vertical line, as with NA[27/28], and instead of using an unbroken vertical line to separate variant-units for the same verse, these are divided by separate footnotes. A final important difference worth highlighting is the way in which the text is linked to the critical apparatus in *UBSGNT*[4/5]. Instead of employing a series of symbols that mark off units of text, as with NA[27/28], *UBSGNT*[4/5] uses a system of footnotes. Numbers are used for the text-critical apparatus and lower case letters are used for the punctuation apparatus (see below).

For example, in *UBSGNT*[4/5], 1 Cor 11:24 is represented as follows:

24 καὶ εὐχαριστήσας ἔκλασεν καὶ εἶπεν, Τοῦτό[3] μού ἐστιν τὸ σῶμα τὸ ὑπὲρ ὑμῶν[4]· τοῦτο ποιεῖτε εἰς τὴν ἐμὴν ἀνάμνησιν.

The corresponding apparatus in *UBSGNT*[4] (similar in *UBSGNT*[5]) connected by the footnotes is displayed as follows:

5. The reader should know that the definitions of these ratings has changed over the years, and there has been grade inflation, so that now the A means certainty, whereas earlier it meant something somewhat less than that. Another problem involves giving an A rating to a text that is certain. What does this imply? That these parts are more or less certain than the parts that have no variant listed? We know that there are many more variants not listed, so what does this indicate? Space should be used for rating instances where the text is less certain. This system also has other shortcomings and should not be relied upon heavily, in our opinion.

³24 {A} τοῦτο 𝔓⁴⁶ ℵ A B C* D F G 0199 6 33 81* 104 424ᶜ 1175 1241 1739 1881 1962 2127 2200 2464 *l* 599 itᵃʳ, ᵇ, ᵈ, ᶠ, ᵍ, ᵒ vgʷʷ,ˢᵗ syr ᵖᵃˡ copˢᵃ,ᵇᵒ geo¹ Cyril Nestorius Theodoret; Cyprian, Ambrosiaster Pelagius//λάβετε φάγετε, τοῦτο (*see* Mt 26.26) C³ Ψ 0150 81ᶜ 256 263 365 424* 436 459 1319 1573 1852 1881 1912 1962 2127 2200 2464 *Byz* [K L P] *Lect* vgᶜˡ syrᵖ,ʰ arm eth geo² slav Basil Cyril-Jerusalemᵈᵘᵇ Chrysostom

⁴24 {A} ὑμῶν 𝔓⁴⁶ ℵ* A B C* 6 33 424ᶜ 1739* vgˢᵗ syrᵖᵃˡ (Cyril) Theodoretˡ/³; Cyprian Pelagius Fulgentius//ὑμῶν κλώμενον ℵ² C³ D² F G Ψ 0150 81 104 256 (263 ἡμῶν) 365 424* 436 459 1175 1241 1319 1573 1739ᶜ 1852 1881 1912 1962 2127 2200 2464 *Byz* [K L P] *Lect* (*l* 591 *l* 597 *l* 809 *l* 1154ᴬᴰ ἡμῶν) itᵇ, ᵈ, ᶠ², ᵍ, ᵒ syr ᵖ, ʰ (arm) geo slav Basil Chrysostom Nestorius Theodoretˡ/³; Ambrosiaster//ὑμῶν διδόμενον (*see* Lk 22.19) it⁽ᵃʳ⁾, ᶠ*, ᵒ vgᶜˡ, ʷʷ copˢᵃ, ᵇᵒ eth

Footnote 3 is attached to 1 Cor 11:24 displayed above from *UBSGNT⁴*. The text itself is different from NA²⁷/²⁸ in a number of ways. The first difference worth mentioning is the capitalization of τοῦτο since it introduces direct speech. The note system rather than the symbol system for connecting the text to apparatus is also distinct. Numbered footnotes in *UBSGNT⁴/⁵*, instead of a dot as in NA²⁷/²⁸, are used for each variant-unit in the apparatus, as in 11:24. The letter {A} is the rating that the UBS committee assigned to their choice to include the reading found within the text, another unique feature of the *UBSGNT⁴/⁵* apparatus. And instead of the *txt* abbreviation, the UBS apparatus spells out the reading found in the text. Unlike NA²⁷/²⁸, the reading of the text is first instead of last. The list of variants included in *UBSGNT⁴/⁵* is far more extensive than those found in NA²⁷/²⁸. The list of later manuscripts and those representing the Byzantine (Syrian) tradition receives much more detailed treatment in *UBSGNT⁴/⁵*. Instead of treating this information by listing specific manuscripts, NA²⁷ uses abbreviations to summarize this tradition. The abbreviation *Byz* is also employed above to represent that the majority of other Byzantine manuscripts supports the given reading. The critical apparatus for *UBSGNT⁴/⁵* only includes a positive apparatus. This is consistent with its purpose to comment only on variants meaningful for establishing the original text.

The first variant-unit involves a decision regarding whether λάβετε φάγετε introduces the demonstrative pronoun (τοῦτο). The committee is certain that the additional words did not appear in the original and therefore give τοῦτο alone an A rating. That is why the reading is introduced by an A and followed by the manuscripts that support this reading, starting with Greek manuscripts: papyri first, then majuscules, then minuscules, and finally lectionaries. The minuscules are not separated by periods as they are in NA²⁷/²⁸. Next, the versions are listed, and finally the church fathers. As discussed above, the double diagonal lines // mark the introduction of an alternative reading not found in the text, in this case λάβετε φάγετε. It becomes immediately obvious why the *UBSGNT*⁴/⁵ committee gave the reading found in the text an A rating. Most of the support for the alternative reading comes from later manuscripts, and the support for the reading found in the text has extremely early testimony (esp. 𝔓⁴⁶ ℵ B).⁶

The second unit of variation connected with verse 24 is introduced by footnote 4 corresponding to the reading ὑμῶν found within the text. A few observations can be made here that help highlight the difference in conventions between NA²⁷/²⁸ and *UBSGNT*⁴ (and *UBSGNT*⁵). Notice that Theodoret has a ¹/³ fraction superscript beside his name. In *UBSGNT*⁴/⁵ when a fraction such as this is used with the name of a church father, it indicates how many times this citation occurs in that father (in this case 3) and how many times it supports the attested reading (in this case once). The reading found in the text is supported by ℵ*, but the first alternative reading (ὑμῶν κλώμενον) is supported by ℵ². ℵ² indicates that this is the reading of the second corrector's hand. ℵ* signifies the presence of a corrector, but the original reading of the manuscript. Therefore, ℵ* is the older reading. Also notice the way that the parentheses are used to indicate slightly different readings. For example, we find the lectionary reading *Lect* (*l* 591 *l* 597 *l* 809 *l* 1154ᴬᴰ ἡμῶν). This means that these lectionary manuscripts have ἡμῶν κλώμενον instead of ὑμῶν κλώμενον. The slight difference then is the change from a second person plural pronoun to a first person plural pronoun. The last of these manuscripts has the ᴬᴰ superscript, indicating a lectionary of the Greek Church.

The *UBSGNT*⁵ includes an additional feature in the apparatus of citation from a selected group of modern Bible translations in English, German, French, and Spanish to indicate where major translations vary from the UBS Greek text.

---

6. But the bigger question is why did they spend the extra space on it at all, when there are other variants that are not A level that they left out.

c. Discourse Segmentation Apparatus

The second level of apparatus in *UBSGNT*[4/5], the discourse segmentation apparatus, is designed specifically for translators. The **discourse segmentation apparatus,** therefore, contains variations on punctuation in a number of Greek editions of the NT (e.g., Textus Receptus, Westcott and Hort) as well as several modern translations (e.g., Luther's German Translation, ASV, RSV). Since this tool is created for translators, not textual specialists, it is not included in NA[27/28]; but most Bible scholars are translators at some level or another and so should be concerned with this discourse segmenting as well, in our opinion. In any case, this is the convention for *UBSGNT*[4/5] and it is important to be familiar with it. The discourse segmentation apparatus has been revised in *UBSGNT*[5]. The major structural abbreviations are as follows:

P or *NO P*	The letter P indicates that a paragraph break occurs in the editions or translations cited, and *NO P* indicates that no paragraph break occurs in the editions or translations cited.
SP	The letters *SP* indicate that a subparagraph break occurs in the editions or translations cited. (This segmentation marker is not used in *UBSGNT*[5].)
S or *NO S*	The letter *S* indicates that a section heading or section break occurs in which several paragraphs are grouped together to form a larger segment of discourse. *NO S* indicates that the editions and translations cited do not segment the text into a new section of discourse. (The segmentation marker *NO S* is not used in *UBSGNT*[5].)
MS	The letters *MS* indicate that a major section heading or break occurs in which a number of separate sections are grouped together to form a larger segment of discourse, e.g., the breaks at the end of Romans 8 and Romans 11 in some translations. (This segmentation marker is not used in *UBSGNT*[5].)
C or *NO C*	The letter *C* indicates a break that occurs between clauses or words in the editions or translations cited. Such differences in segmentation result in different words and clauses being grouped together with a change of meaning from that in the UBS text. *NO C* indicates that no break

between clauses or words occurs in the editions or translations cited.

The following signs are also used:

?   indicates that the citation of a particular edition or translation
is doubtful, since the evidence does not clearly support one or
another alternative.

()   Parentheses indicate minor differences of detail in segmentation, while the authority supports in general the segmentation
for which it is cited.

mg   a marginal reading in one of the translations.

When punctuation like periods, commas, dashes, or colons causes
segmentation, these are written out. The function of how the conjunction
ὅτι is translated is also written out: *Direct, Indirect,* or *Causal.* When parentheses cause segmentation, these are abbreviated with *parens.* When
quotation punctuation is used, the conventions *Begin quotation* and *End
quotation* are employed. *Poetic structure* and *Traditional material* are noted
when they are marked off in various editions or translations (consult the
UBSGNT[4/5] introduction for further abbreviations).

In order to illustrate how the discourse segmentation apparatus is
used, we may use an example from Rev 2:25:

25 πλὴν ὃ ἔχετε κρατήσατε ἄχρι[ς] οὗ ἂν ἥξω.[w]

The corresponding section of the discourse segmentation apparatus is as
follows (in *UBSGNT*[4], not in *UBSGNT*[5]):

[w]25 SP: NA//P: M Seg NIV

The footnote *w* at the end of verse 25 is linked to the number 25 representing the corresponding verse number in the segmentation apparatus.
We know from the introduction to *UBSGNT*[4] that NA stands for NA[26],
but in *UBSGNT*[5] for NA[28].[7] Therefore, NA[26] has a subparagraph marker
here (indicated by SP, as explained above). This verse marks the end of a
subparagraph. As in the critical apparatus, the double diagonal lines //

7. See *UBSGNT*[4], 44*; *UBSGNT*[5], 50*.

mark a separation between alternatives (in this case, alternative paragraph breaks). P indicates that the Seg (*La Nouvelle Version Segond Revisée,* a standard French translation) and NIV have full paragraph breaks here in their translations.

d. Reference Apparatus

The third level of apparatus in *UBSGNT*⁴/⁵ is the **reference apparatus**, which contains a cross-reference system of parallel passages and citations from the OT and NT. It contains similar information to what is found in the outer margins of NA²⁷/²⁸, but it is far less extensive. The *UBSGNT*⁴/⁵ reference system, however, does contain a number of important NT parallels. It includes indices of OT quotations and allusions (two separate indices) as well.

The apparatus works by introducing the cross reference with which the verse is associated (footnotes are not used at this level of apparatus) and then spells out the parallel wording directly following the verse number and cites the NT and OT texts where relevant parallels exist. For example, in Jude 5, we read:

5 Ὑπομνῆσαι δὲ ὑμᾶς βούλομαι, εἰδότας [ὑμᾶς] πάντα ὅτι [ὁ] κύριος ἅπαξ λαὸν ἐκ γῆς Αἰγύπτου σώσας τὸ δεύτερον τοὺς μὴ πιστεύσαντας ἀπώλεσεν,

The parallel passages for this verse are displayed in the reference apparatus at the bottom of the page in *UBSGNT*⁴ (*UBSGNT*⁵ is similar) in the following way:

5 Ὑπομνῆσαι ... πάντα 2 Pet 1.12 ὁ κύριος ... σώσας Ex 12.51 τοὺς ... ἀπώλεσεν Nu 14.29-30, 35; 1 Cor 10.5

The parallel wording is introduced (the ellipsis points ... stand for the text in between the two words) and followed by the verse(s) where the parallel is found. As with NA²⁷/²⁸, *UBSGNT*⁴/⁵ has a distinct way of citing biblical passages using shortened abbreviations and a period rather than a colon or a comma to separate chapters and verses.

e. The UBS Rating System and Textual Optimism

Although *UBSGNT*[4/5] does provide a potentially helpful letter system for rating the certainty of their readings, the rigor and consistency of this system from edition to edition has recently been called into question. **Kent Clarke** has demonstrated that the UBS committee's certainty concerning their selected variants increases from edition to edition.

Commenting upon the nature of additions and omissions in the *UBSGNT* text and the associated letter ratings given to the status of the certainty of the text, Clarke summarizes the data as follows:

> First, there are a greater number of variants with improving or upgraded letter-ratings (598) over against variants with decreasing or downgraded letter-ratings (30) in the *UBSGNT*[4]. Secondly, there are a greater number of new A rated variants added to the *UBSGNT*[4] (168) than any of the three other letter-rating groups, or even the combined total of these three groups (B = 62, C = 55, D = 0). . . . This reveals that a greater number of A rated variants, rather than C rated variants, are preserved within the *UBSGNT*[4]. These . . . factors continue to confirm . . . that there has been an extensive upgrade in the quality of the text presented in the *UBSGNT*[4].[8]

Moisés Silva makes similar remarks in commenting upon the upgrades in letter-rating between *UBSGNT*[3] and *UBSGNT*[4].

> [T]he rating for most passages has been raised. For Romans through Galatians, 19 passages were already given an A in the third edition and thus could not be raised. Out of the remaining 152 passages (206 minus 19 As minus 35 deletions), a full 105 are given a higher evaluation, that is, 69 percent. Specifically, 15 were raised from D to C, 41 from C to B, and 37 from B to A; and as if that were not enough, 2 passages were raised from D to B, a full 10 from C to A! Out of the 43 variation units added to the fourth edition, no fewer than 24 are given an A. How radically different is the resulting complexion of the material can be seen

---

8. Kent D. Clarke, *Textual Optimism: A Critique of the United Bible Societies' Greek New Testament* (JSNTSup 138; Sheffield: Sheffield Academic Press, 1997), 120.

by comparing the third and fourth editions: Third Fourth A 20 93 B 62 63 C 99 55 D 25 2. . . . .[9]

This phenomenon is referred to by Clarke as **textual optimism**. In most cases, according to Clarke, the enhancement of the letter ratings has not been justifiable in any obvious way on the basis of the textual evidence. In other words, the textual evidence even in those instances where the grade has been raised is usually virtually the same as it was when the grade was lower. This is a valuable lesson to learn. It will not do to simply rely on the rating assigned by the UBS committee or the rationale for the specific letter rating provided in Metzger's *Textual Commentary* (as has been the unfortunate tendency of many modern commentators!)—the evidence must be evaluated on its own terms. The grading system and textual commentary are potentially valuable tools, but students of textual criticism must learn to develop their own text-critical instincts in weighing and evaluating the nature of the evidence.

f. Citation, Orthography, Punctuation, and Font

In *UBSGNT*$^{4/5}$ the citations of the OT are in **bold** rather than *italics,* as they are in NA$^{27/28}$. In *UBSGNT*$^{4/5}$ a colon followed by a *capital letter* is used to begin direct speech, and punctuation *is* used in the apparatus—both of these features distinguish it from NA$^{27/28}$. The more italicized and cursive font of *UBSGNT*^{4} has become more upright and square in *UBSGNT*^{5}. *UBSGNT*$^{4/5}$ also includes section divisions in its text, which are lacking in NA$^{27/28}$.

The chart in figure 4 summarizes the important differences between these two editions that have been discussed in this chapter. This chart includes some information from chapter 11.

---

9. Moisés Silva, "Review Symposium of GNT^4," *Bible Translator* 44 (1994): 352, quoted in Clarke, *Textual Optimism*, 120.

Figure 12.4: A Comparison of *UBSGNT*$^{4/5}$ and NA$^{27/28}$

Features	UBSGNT$^{4/5}$	NA$^{27/28}$
First Edition	1966	1898
Intended Use	Intended primarily for translators and students. But we believe that some of its distinct translation features would be beneficial for scholars as well.	Intended exclusively for specialists in textual criticism. However, we see it more as a manual edition and specialists will still be better served by Tischendorf's 8th edition.
Margins	margins are unused	*inner margin:* Eusebian canon and chapter numbers found in traditional Greek manuscripts and editions. *outer margin:* Cross reference system for parallel passages
Critical Apparatus	Lists more evidence for fewer variants (1.6 per page). Evidence listed is intended to be nearly exhaustive (though why this is a feature for *translators* remains unknown). Does use punctuation and accents linked to text by numbers. Only positive apparatus the reading in the text is spelled out. The support for the reading in the text is introduced first. Evidence is evaluated through a letter-graded system: A, B, C, D.	Lists less evidence for more variants (20 variants per page). Evidence listed is intended to be representative and summarized. Does not use punctuation or accents (we believe the reasons for this are inconsistent). Linked to text by symbols positive and negative apparatus. The reading in the text is symbolized by *txt* when the positive apparatus is used, but not otherwise. The support for the reading in the text is introduced last evidence is not explicitly evaluated.
Discourse Segmentation Apparatus	Indicates section, paragraph, subsection, and various punctuation breaks in Greek editions and versions.	Not included.

Features	UBSGNT[4/5]	NA[27/28]
Reference Apparatus	Includes parallel passages and citations.	Although a reference apparatus is not included, parallels are referenced in outer margins.
OT Citations	Cited in bold, relatively *less* extensive reference to parallel passages in the reference apparatus.	Cited in italics, relatively *more* extensive reference to parallel passages in the outer margins.
Direct Speech	Introduced with a colon and a capital letter.	Introduced with a colon and a lower-case letter.
Section Headings	Included.	Not included.
Font	Italicized, cursive ([4]), upright, square ([5]).	Bold, square ([27]), upright, square ([28]).

3. Summary

In this chapter we have attempted to introduce some of the distinctive features of the text and apparatus of the two standard manual editions for the study and translation of the Greek NT: NA[27/28] and *UBSGNT*[4/5]. We have also sought to provide a guide to the conventions used in these critical editions, especially those concerned with documenting external evidence.

KEY TERMINOLOGY
inner margins
Eusebian section and canon numbers
outer margins
positive apparatus
negative apparatus
critical apparatus
A rating
B rating
C rating
D rating
discourse segmentation apparatus
reference apparatus
Kent Clarke
textual optimism

BIBLIOGRAPHY

Aland, Kurt, and Barbara Aland. *The Text of the New Testament: An Intro-duction to the Critical Editions and to the Theory and Practice of Modern Textual Criticism.* Trans. Erroll F. Rhodes. 2nd ed. Grand Rapids: Eerd-mans, 1989.

Clarke, Kent D. *Textual Optimism: A Critique of the United Bible Societies' Greek New Testament.* JSNTSup 138. Sheffield: Sheffield Academic Press, 1997.

Greenlee, J. Harold. *The Text of the New Testament: From Manuscripts to Mod-ern Edition.* Peabody, MA: Hendrickson, 2008.

"Introduction." Pages 1*-40* in *Novum Testamentum Graece.* Ed. Barbara Al-and et al. 27th ed. Stuttgart: Deutsche Bibelgesellschaft, 1993. Pages 46*-88* in 28th ed. 2012.

"Introduction." Pages 1*-53* in *The Greek New Testament.* Ed. Barbara Aland et al. 4th rev. ed. Stuttgart: Deutsche Bibelgesellschaft, 1993. Pages 1*-63* in 5th rev. ed. 2014.

Trobisch, David. *A User's Guide to the Nestle-Aland 28 Greek New Testament.* SBLTCS 9. Atlanta: Society of Biblical Literature, 2013.

CHAPTER 13

Text and Translation

A final major issue that needs to be considered is the relationship between the Greek NT text and its translation. Since this book is created for English speakers and due to the rich heritage of the English Bible, English Bible translations will occupy this chapter's focus. We shall begin by offering a brief history of the English Bible, followed by a consideration of the issues involved in choosing a base text for translation, as well as how textual variation is displayed within Bible translations. The chapter concludes with a brief overview of translation theory and makes some suggestive remarks toward how to choose a good Bible translation.

1. A Brief History of the English Bible

There are two major phases of Bible translation in the history of the English Bible. The first phase is marked by the rise of vernacular translations that in many ways supported the efforts of the Protestant Reformation, which included William Tyndale (1526), Miles Coverdale (1535), Thomas Matthew (finished by a man named John Rogers, it was the completion of the OT of Tyndale's Bible, 1537), the Great Bible (1539), the Geneva Bible (1560), and the Bishops' Bible (1568). These English versions were used in various ways, especially Tyndale's, in the translation of the **Authorized** (or **King James**) **Version** (**AV/KJV**) of the Bible (1611). Due to its numerous excellent qualities, its strong support, and its heavy reliance upon the remarkable translational work of Tyndale, the AV became the translation that dominated this first phase of the English Bible's history. The second major turning point is marked by the rise of modern English versions, beginning around the end of the nineteenth century with the English Revised Version and the American Standard Version.

What caused the turning point in the nineteenth century? The simple answer is textual criticism. By this time a number of early manuscripts had been discovered (most significantly, codices Sinaiticus and Vaticanus), and Westcott and Hort and other textual critics had made substantial advances in developing canons for weighing this textual evidence, according to both external and internal criteria. These advancements, as well as the previous pioneering translation efforts of individuals like John Wesley (1775), Noah Webster (1833), and Henry Alford (1869), set the stage for the formation in 1870 of a committee that hoped to revise the AV. The committee was composed of British and American scholars from a wide variety of denominations. The **Revised Version (RV)** of the NT was published in 1881, the OT in 1885, and the Apocrypha in 1895. The NT essentially followed the text of Westcott and Hort (see ch. 11). This updated text ended up causing controversy for two major but different reasons: (1) it moved certain cherished texts (e.g., 1 John 5:7) to the margins, thus apparently "changing" the Bible, and (2) the translation of the original Greek language into English was more rigid ("literal"; see below) than the AV had been, and so the Bible had supposedly lost some of its sacred grandeur. The American version of the RV was published as the **American Standard Version (ASV)** in 1901, without the Apocrypha. It met with more popularity than its British counterpart. Although these translations ultimately failed in their attempts to replace the AV, they did succeed in paving the way for the numerous modern versions that emerged in the twentieth century and continue into the twenty-first century. Initially, this translational project provided incentive for a number of personal translations in the first half of the twentieth century, such as those of James Moffatt (1903), J. B. Phillips (1958), and Gerrit Verkuyl (known as the Berkeley Translation; 1959). Translational projects were slow in developing, however, all the way up through the early twentieth century, due to the admiration, even veneration, that many still had for the AV, which had been used almost exclusively in English-speaking congregations for centuries.

These personal translations, however, gave new impetus to the possibility of success for committee-based translations, often sponsored by Bible societies, in the second half of the twentieth century. The **Revised Standard Version (RSV)** — which was a revision of the ASV that began in 1937 by a committee now known as the National Council of the Churches of Christ, and was finally fully published (i.e., both OT and NT) in 1951 — is by far the most significant committee-produced Bible translation since it resulted in numerous later projects that sought to imitate its efforts. This translation was based upon the Masoretic Hebrew text (with some supplementation from the Dead Sea Scrolls, esp. in Isaiah) of the OT and upon the 16th (1936) and 17th (1941) editions of Nestle's Greek NT, while making reference to other Greek texts as well. In terms of translation, one of the major revisions in this version involved an updating of some Old English forms of expression (e.g., thou, thee) to more current English vernacular (at least for 1950). Although it initially met with mixed reactions (some were uncomfortable with the way that theology was expressed in the translation), the RSV was the predominant English translation for the next twenty-five years until the NIV was published. The committee, continuing to update the translation, especially regarding gendered language, published a thoroughly revised version in 1989 called the **New Revised Standard Version (NRSV)**. This version continued to weed out remaining antiquated English expressions, seeking a fully updated English vocabulary and syntax while employing the most recent Greek text available, *UBSGNT*[3] (which is similar to NA[26]), with knowledge of the soon-to-be-released 4th edition.

In addition to several advances in Europe, the Lockman Foundation — a conservative American Bible society — was especially concerned that in these newer translations the original virtues of the ASV were being lost. Some were convinced that this was a good thing, but the Lockman Foundation apparently was not. They embarked therefore upon a translation project designed to revise the original 1901 ASV. The final product was published as the **New American Standard Bible (NASB)** in 1971 (revised in 1995 under the title the **New American Standard Bible 1995 Update** [NAU]). The translation itself sought to be **intentionally** literal, resulting in a very useful translation for personal Bible study and for students of the original languages but one less readable as a modern English version.

Another important committee-based translation published around this time was **Today's English Version (TEV)**, now known as the **Good News Bible (GNB)** or **Good News Translation (GNT)**. This translational product was spearheaded by the linguist and Bible translator Eugene Nida, who sought to apply a number of translation principles that he and his associates had developed to emphasize translating the biblical meaning into a modern cultural equivalent (see below). The project was sponsored by the American Bible Society, and the entire Bible was published in 1976 (with an edition including the Apocrypha in 1979). The OT was translated from Rudolf Kittel's *Biblia Hebraica* (3rd ed. 1937) by a small body of translators. The NT was translated by Robert Bratcher from *UBSGNT*[1] (in that sense, the NT of the TEV is a personal translation). Reflecting a similar translation philosophy and using *Biblia Hebraica Stuttgartensia* (1977) in translating the OT and *UBSGNT*[3 and 4] for the NT, the **Contemporary English Version** (**CEV**) was published in 1995, providing a more recent translation that was conceived along similar lines as the GNT. Both translations met with mixed reception and were criticized for inaccuracy in translation (which really meant difference in translation methodology, in most cases — see below). Nevertheless, due to the support of the Bible societies and its ease for reading, the GNB/GNT especially has been widely used.

The **New International Version** (**NIV**) was yet another extremely significant translation project that was completed during this time. This version grew out of the concern of a number of American denominations to have an all-purpose Bible, similar to the AV, but one that was translated into contemporary English. Being displeased with the RSV, a committee was drawn up in 1965 to begin working on this version, which hoped to recruit the help of numerous scholars, both from Europe and North America. According to the preface, this conservative committee of translators is "united in their commitment to the authority and infallibility of the Bible as God's Word in written form." After overcoming numerous difficulties in what turned out to be a very slow, complex, and difficult process (esp. due to the number of people involved), the whole Bible was published in 1978. It was based upon the Masoretic Hebrew text and a critical Greek text, very similar to the *UBSGNT* and NA texts in use today. Essentially, it offered a conservative alternative to the RSV while (bravely!) breaking away, in many places, from the traditional renderings of the AV. The NIV committee attempted to publish a gender-inclusive edition in the 1990s, but their efforts were thwarted at least in the United States by some vocal opponents who decried such efforts as being contrary to the purpose of the translation, until they finally were able to publish **Today's New International Version** (**TNIV**) in 2005. This again met with strong opposition in some circles. So in 2011 the NIV committee issued a revised version that utilized gender-inclusive language. This is now the standard NIV translation.

In 2001 the **English Standard Version** (**ESV**) was published. This translation is a revision of the RSV (whose copyright was bought by a conservative publisher), with an estimated 6 percent changed by a group of conservative scholars to correct it doctrinally. As a result of its strong roots in the RSV, this version is more literal than the NIV (which had been criticized by some for being too "loose" or "interpretive") yet not as wooden and literalistic as the NASB/NAU. This literal translation and conservative commitment of the revisers has been a significant draw for some pastors and teachers emerging from particular theological contexts.

In 2010 for the NT and in 2011 for the entire Bible, the **Common English Bible** (**CEB**) was published. The product of the work of 120 different translators and scholars, this version attempts to provide a readable Bible for contemporary readers. It is mostly designed for those who are more theologically mainstream than the readers of the ESV, and who are perhaps less familiar with traditional theological language. It fully embraces nongendered language, as well as making more relevant (not always successfully) technical theological language.

A final group of projects worth noting is the recent development of web-based translations. The most substantial of these translations is the **NET Bible** (NET stands for New English Translation). The most noteworthy feature of this Bible is its extensive (though sometimes repetitive) footnotes related to translational, grammatical, text-critical, historical, and theological issues. It is especially designed for those familiar with the original languages and textual criticism. It is available in both print and electronic forms (the electronic edition can be accessed for free at http:// net.bible.org/home.php). As with the NIV and ESV, the NET Bible is distinguished by the fact that its translators are from conservative evangelical backgrounds, consistently reflected in the study notes. The translation itself, as with the NIV, breaks away from the traditional translations of the AV in many places and often reflects a quite interpretive translation philosophy (see below).

2. The Textual Basis of Modern Translations

In the OT the textual basis of translations has remained fairly fixed. The Masoretic text has been used as the basis for virtually every Western translation since its composition in the medieval period (the exceptions being Roman Catholic Bibles based upon the Latin Vulgate and Orthodox Bibles based upon the LXX). The Dead Sea Scrolls, especially in Isaiah, have been taken into consideration in newer translations, but the Masoretic tradition continues to be the major basis for Hebrew texts and the modern translations based upon them. This distinguishes the OT text from what has become the dominant practice in NT studies, since the Masoretic Hebrew text is a single continuous text whereas the text typically used in NT scholarship has been an eclectic text in one form or another.

There has been much more sustained debate over the Greek text that is to be used as the basis for producing editions and translations. As we discussed in chapter 11, in a race to print the first printed Greek edition of the NT before Cardinal Ximénes de Cisneros could publish his Complutensian NT (printed in 1514, but not formally published until 1522), Erasmus published his Greek text in 1516, followed by a revision in 1519 and three additional revisions before he died. Erasmus's text was based on a few late Byzantine manuscripts (essentially two, with reference to three or four others that dated to around the twelfth century). Some final portions of Revelation were not available in the Greek manuscripts that Erasmus had available to him so he actually translated the Latin texts that he had back into Greek. It was from Erasmus's text that the AV NT was translated in 1611. Erasmus's text became known as the "Received Text" or Textus Receptus due to a comment made in the preface of the Elzevir printed edition of the Greek NT (1633) that Erasmus's text was "received" by all. And this text was received as the text for NT scholarship until the nineteenth century, especially with the publication of Westcott and Hort's edition (1881), when the textual basis for NT study and translation began to shift toward texts grounded in a much earlier tradition of manuscripts, for the most part representing the Alexandrian text-type.

This shift was due to two major developments: (1) the publication of the fourth- and fifth-century codices (esp. Sinaiticus and Vaticanus) and (2) the discovery of the Greek papyri (which were not fully appreciated until later). Constantine Tischendorf (see ch. 4) was extremely instrumental in this process, editing more Greek manuscripts than any single person before or after him. Westcott and Hort reflected these developments in their establishment of a system of textual criticism designed to support their production of an eclectic text (see chs. 7, 11). So scholars of the late nineteenth century, then, began to draw upon these developments in the production of their translations.

These developments resulted in the use of essentially four kinds of Greek texts (on the development of Greek editions, see ch. 11) in the translation of the NT, apart from the few dissenting scholars who chose to remain reliant upon the Textus Receptus. First, the RV and ASV, as well as Phillips, relied primarily upon Westcott and Hort's edition. Second, Hermann von Soden's text was used by Moffatt in his translation of the NT. Nestle's eclectic text, revised by Kurt and (then later) Barbara Aland and others, is the third major text that has been used. The latest revisions of this text in the NA form are the basis for most of the modern translations. The RSV seems to have used the 16th/17th editions of this text. The NRSV used NA[26]/*UBSGNT*[3]. The NASB is translated from NA[23]. A fourth category is occupied by a few others who saw it necessary to create their own eclectic texts for translation. These include translations like the New English Bible (1964), which also included a publication of the Greek text that was created and used, along with notes on textual decisions.

While most scholars and translators saw it necessary to incorporate the discovery of early manuscripts and supporting text-critical principles in producing eclectic texts based upon them, a few scholars insisted upon the importance of retaining the Textus Receptus as the basis for NT study and translation. Some have gone as far as to suggest that the AV is still the most suitable English translation (as noted in previous chapters). It is surprising in some ways that people continue to hold this position in light of the fact that the basis for this text is so limited and evidence for the Syrian textual tradition (upon which these translations are based) dating before the fourth century is lacking (for further treatment of the textual issues involved here, see chs. 5 and 9). In our view, this major underlying textual distinction makes the AV as well as the **New King James Version** (an attempt to bring the AV into a more modern form of English) inferior to the modern English versions since, at least in the NT and at the level of textual support, these translations are based upon an inferior manuscript tradition. Nevertheless, as Gordon Fee and Mark Strauss remark, "the sum total of manuscript differences still make up a relatively small percentage of the biblical text and seldom affect important points of doctrine."[1]

3. Presentation of Textual Variation in Translations

Another issue that impacts translation is whether textual variation is presented and, if it is presented, how it should be noted. Most translations use a combination of brackets and footnotes to highlight (esp. major) divergences in the manuscript tradition. John 7:53–8:11, the episode of the woman caught in adultery (on this passage see ch. 12), provides a suitable

---

1. Gordon D. Fee and Mark L. Strauss, *How to Choose a Translation for All Its Worth: A Guide to Understanding and Using Bible Translations* (Grand Rapids: Zondervan, 2007), 113-14.

case study. The ESV has a bracketed comment above chapter 8 that reads, "[The earliest manuscripts do not include John 7:53–8:11]," with a footnote that reads, "Some manuscripts do not include 7:53–8:11; others add the passage here or after 7:36 or after 21:25 or after Luke 21:38, with variations in the text." Similarly, the NAU contains a footnote that reads, "Later mss add the story of the adulterous woman, numbering it as John 7:53–8:11." The NET Bible has a thorough (several paragraphs) — some might argue, overboard — discussion of the problem. This becomes a rather interesting translational decision. NT textual scholars almost universally believe that this passage is not original, but translators leave it in anyway. Why? There is no compelling reason for doing so, except for tradition and a (perhaps misguided) desire not to cause possible upset among those who are textually not well informed. We recognize that the versification was added during medieval times and has now been relatively standardized in church and academic usage. However, we do not think that this is sufficient reason for including the pericope and providing a footnote that indicates the reason for the move from John 7:52 to 8:12. The footnote is also a place to possibly include the deleted passage and to explain that even though later church tradition has retained it (esp. in some later manuscripts), as have earlier translations, it is best not to include it in the text of the NT and hence in the translation. The same is true of other major textual problems, such as the long ending of Mark (16:9-20).

4. Introduction to Translation Theory: Form and Function

Once an appropriate base text is established, including if and how to represent textual variation within a translation, issues related to how the **original** or **source language** (the language that a text is translated *from*) is best transferred into the **receptor language** (the language that a text is translated *into*) must be addressed. Some theories focus more on rendering the form of the text in translation while others focus more on rendering its function. Theories that emphasize carrying over as much of the form of the original language as possible are often referred to as **formal** or **literal equivalence translations**. As much as possible, these translations attempt to preserve the tone, vocabulary, syntax, and style of the original language within the receptor language. Formal equivalence translations include the NASB, NAU, KJV/NKJV, RSV/ESV, and NRSV (in order from more to less formal). On the other side of the spectrum, **dynamic** or **functional**

equivalence translations focus on conveying the function of the original language in translations. In other words, they attempt to understand the meaning of the original language and then to render that meaning with an appropriate linguistic equivalent in the receptor language. These include versions like the Holman Christian Standard Bible (HCSB), NET, NIV, TNIV, New Living Translation (NLT), CEV, and The Message (in order from less to more functional). Rather than understanding Bible translations as either strictly formal or functional, we notice a scale of more and less formal/functional Bible translations:

Formal   →   →   →   →   →   →   →   Functional

NASB, NAU, KJV/NKJV, RSV/ESV, NRSV, HCSB, NET, NIV, TNIV, CEB, NLT, GNT, CEV, The Message

Translations on the far right side of the spectrum are often considered paraphrases. **Paraphrases** are typically viewed as a very close interpretation of the text rather than a translation in the proper sense of the term. Nevertheless, most of these (excluding, for example, The Message) are still usually guided by finding linguistic-cultural equivalents for the original language in the receptor language and so should not be quickly dismissed as useless for Bible reading and study (and the term *paraphrase* should probably not be used pejoratively as a way of dismissing such a translation). A further examination of functional equivalence theory will reveal how these principles are intended to operate.

Dynamic equivalence theory is a fairly recent development and should be understood against the background of the more traditional formal equivalence view. The most significant figure in contributing to the movement away from the traditional model by a number of Bible translators is **Eugene A. Nida.** In 1964 he published a book that attempted to consolidate work that he had been doing in translation for the previous twenty years entitled *Toward a Science of Translating.* This was followed by a number of other works by Nida and his colleagues, especially Charles Taber and Jan de Waard. In these publications, Nida assumed a linguistic model that is similar to the linguist Noam Chomsky's early work (e.g., *Syntactic Structures,* published in 1957), which posits two levels of linguistic structure: deep structure and surface structure. **Deep structure** refers to universal meaning, whereas **surface structure** concerns how universal meaning is expressed in a variety of different languages. Languages are merely the surface structure realization of the underlying deep structure of meaning that all languages attempt to communicate in their own ways. Nida was critical, therefore, of the traditional theory's attempt to translate the surface structure of one language (Hebrew, Aramaic, or Greek) into the surface structure of another language (e.g., English). What Nida proposed is that the translator first determine how the original language is expressing deep structure through its surface structure. In Nida's terminology, the translator was to find the **kernel sentence** or underlying meaning in the original language: that is, the deep structure meaning that the surface structure is communicating. Then the translator is to ask how that kernel sentence in the original language is best expressed using the surface structure of the receptor language. For example, the clause "God is love," expressed literally in the original language, might be translated "God loves" in the receptor language.

Nida's classic example for illustrating the helpfulness of his theory is Mark 1:4, often translated literally as "John the Baptist appeared in the wilderness preaching a baptism of repentance for the forgiveness of sins" (NAU). According to Nida, "baptism of repentance" and "forgiveness of sins," while conveying a literal expression of the Greek language, have little significance for the contemporary reader. He sees the verse broken into five kernel sentences: (1) John preached something (the following phrases fill out the content), (2) John baptizes people, (3) people repent, (4) God forgives something, and (5) the people sin. From these five kernels, he suggests the translation: "John preached, 'Repent and be baptized, so that God will forgive the evil you have done.'"[2]

Many would disagree with Nida's assumption that transferability of meaning is helpful or possible in translation. Particularly problematic are instances in which the meaning of a passage is debatable. This model of translation requires more interpretation, increasing the possibility that informed Bible readers may disagree with the underlying interpretation that is reflected in a translation. The more interpretation that a translation has, the greater margin there is for error. On the other hand, all translation involves interpretation. No translation is completely literal. Such a rendering would be unintelligible.

Another issue that may factor into method in Bible translation and may be an important consideration for some in choosing a translation of the Bible is the issue of gender and translation. A number of recent translations have sought to use gender-inclusive language. The NRSV and the Revised

2. Cf. Eugene A. Nida, *Toward a Science of Translating* (Leiden: Brill, 1965), 66; Nida and Charles R. Taber, *The Theory and Practice of Translation* (Leiden: Brill, 1969), 51-52.

English Bible (revision of the New English Bible) were the first to do this. Several translations followed suit, most recently the TNIV and now NIV since 2011 and the CEB. This strategy to bring the Bible's language into more contemporary manners of expression that do not marginalize women through the language used has caused serious concern in some quarters. Besides tradition or downright prejudice, one reason for this concern is that the biblical languages are grammatically gendered languages and to make translations gender-inclusive may be difficult or even thought to be untrue to the original (grammatical gender means that some languages indicate the gender of certain words, usually but not always following natural gender categories). Changing gendered language may also seem to prohibit people who genuinely desire to come to terms with the world in which the original text was composed. However, even though readers need to know that the original languages were grammatically gendered (and those studying the original languages are aware of this), we believe that the primary purpose of a translation is to communicate the message of the Bible to its readers, and so we believe that translations should be gender-inclusive where appropriate to reflect the inclusive nature of what is being discussed. Thus use of "brothers and sisters" is appropriate to reflect a word that in previous translations would have been rendered "brothers," if Paul is speaking to a church congregation that includes both men and women.

Which is the best translation then? We think this is the wrong question to ask. A better way to think about choosing a Bible translation is in terms of function. Before the dawn of the AV, in which a single Bible translation was standardized and used for most purposes, people were accustomed to hearing the Great Bible (1539) read in public and using the Geneva Bible (1560) for private study. Our day and age is similar in the sense that there are multiple Bibles to choose from, which can each helpfully serve a different function in the believer's life. Translations such as the NASB, NAU, and RSV/ESV serve as helpful Bibles for detailed study and analysis, especially when working with the original languages. More mediating translations, such as the NIV and HCSB, function as good all-purpose Bibles. As we move closer to the right of the above formal-functional scale, translations like the CEB and GNT are perhaps better for easy, smooth reading of large portions of the text. Translations at the far right end of the spectrum may help as references when one desires a fresh angle on the text or is unclear about its meaning, but these will be less close to the original and so the reader must keep in mind that the margin for interpretation here remains greater.

5. Summary

The purpose of this chapter has been to introduce the major issues and relationships between establishing the Greek text and translating it into English. After a quick survey of the development of the English Bible, we have noted the differing textual bases between the AV tradition of the English Bible, which relied upon the Textus Receptus, and modern translations, which are typically based upon eclectic texts that incorporate the earliest and highest quality manuscripts available today. We have also briefly considered issues related to the representation of textual variation, before finally outlining an introduction to translation theory and some comments on issues to look for in translations.

KEY TERMINOLOGY
Authorized Version/King James Version (AV/KJV)
Revised Version (RV)
American Standard Version (ASV)
Revised Standard Version (RSV)
New Revised Standard Version (NRSV)
New American Standard Bible (NASB)
New American Standard Bible 1995 Update (NAU)
Good News Bible/Translation (GNB/T) or Today's English Version (TEV)
Contemporary English Version (CEV)
New International Version (NIV)
English Standard Version (ESV)
Common English Bible (CEB)
NET Bible (NET)
New King James Version (NKJV)
original/source language
receptor language
formal/literal equivalence translations
dynamic/functional equivalence translations
Eugene Nida
Toward a Science of Translating
deep structure
surface structure
kernel sentence

BIBLIOGRAPHY

Beekman, John, and Kathleen Callow. *Translating the Word of God.* Grand Rapids: Zondervan, 1974.

Bruce, F. F. *History of the Bible in English.* 3rd ed. Guildford: Lutterworth, 1979.

Carson, D. A. *The King James Version Debate: A Plea for Realism.* Grand Rapids: Baker, 1979.

Daniel, David. *The Bible in English: Its History and Influence.* New Haven: Yale University Press, 2003.

Fee, Gordon D., and Mark L. Strauss. *How to Choose a Translation for All Its Worth: A Guide to Understanding and Using Bible Versions.* Grand Rapids: Zondervan, 2007.

Hill, Harriet. *The Bible at Cultural Crossroads: From Translation to Communication.* Manchester: St. Jerome, 2006.

Metzger, Bruce M. *The Bible in Translation: Ancient and English Versions.* Grand Rapids: Baker, 2001.

Nida, Eugene A. *Toward a Science of Translating.* Leiden: Brill, 1964.

Nida, Eugene A., and William D. Reyburn. *Meaning Across Cultures.* Maryknoll, NY: Orbis, 1981.

Nida, Eugene A., and Charles R. Taber. *The Theory and Practice of Translation.* Leiden: Brill, 1969.

Porter, Stanley E. "Modern Translations." Pages 134-61 in *The Oxford Illustrated History of the Bible.* Ed. John Rogerson. Oxford: Oxford University Press, 2001.

———. *How We Got the New Testament: Text, Transmission, Translation.* Grand Rapids: Baker, 2013.

Waard, Jan de, and Eugene A. Nida. *From One Language to Another: Functional Equivalence in Bible Translating.* Nashville: Nelson, 1986.

White, James R. *The King James Only Controversy: Can You Trust the Modern Translations?* Minneapolis: Bethany House, 1995.

Tools for Further Text-Critical Study

A number of tools form a vital part of text-critical research. These tools range from commentaries on the textual tradition of the Greek text to biblical commentaries to collections and/or editions of individual manuscripts to a number of digital and Web-based tools.

1. Textual Commentaries

Textual commentaries essentially provide a verse-by-verse commentary on the textual tradition behind the NT and offer the rationale for a committee's or an individual's text-critical decisions regarding specific passages. Bruce M. Metzger's *Textual Commentary on the Greek New Testament* (London: UBS, 1971; corr. ed. 1975), commenting on *UBSGNT*[3], and the 2nd edition (London: UBS, 1994) commenting on *UBSGNT*[4], is certainly the best known of these types of resources. This is an important commentary as it provides insights into the rationale that governed the committee that created the two editions discussed in chapter 12. There are tensions within the committee revealed by comparing occasional comments from one edition to another. The comments need to be used with discretion. An expanded edition for Bible translators is Roger L. Omanson's *A Textual Guide to the Greek New Testament* (Stuttgart: Deutsche Bibelgesellschaft, 2006). However, other commentaries are arguably just as good, if not better, and should be consulted in the text-critical process. Philip Comfort's *New Testament Text and Translation Commentary* (Carol Stream, IL: Tyndale House, 2008) is another important textual commentary. It is much more thorough than Metzger and offers implications for translation as well — a very helpful tool. Daniel Wallace includes a textual commentary for the Greek text of the NET Bible as an appendix in the NET Greek diglot edition as well.

2. Biblical Commentaries

Many biblical commentaries include sections on textual criticism or address text-critical issues within the narrative of their commentaries. Commentaries such as the Word Biblical Commentary (WBC), International Critical Commentary (ICC), and the New International Greek Testament Commentary (NIGTC) attempt to emphasize text-critical issues, but in many cases these merely resort to citing Metzger's textual commentary as the authority on text-critical decisions. The student will want to look for biblical commentaries that engage with the manuscripts themselves and are text-critically competent, revealed on at least one level by the abilities of commentators to make their own evaluations of the evidence. Otherwise, these are not a second kind of tool at all — just a restatement of the *UBSGNT*'s textual comments.

3. Journal Articles, Chapters, and Monographs on Textual Criticism

Those desiring to do further work on textual criticism or writing a research paper on a text-critical issue will certainly want to familiarize themselves with the relevant journal articles, collections of individual chapters, and monographs pertinent to their interests. Most of the major academic journals focusing on biblical studies or the NT specifically welcome articles on textual criticism. These include, but are by no means limited to:

> *Biblica* (*Bib*)
> *Filología Neotestamentaria*
> *Journal for the Study of the New Testament* (*JSNT*)
> *Journal of Biblical Literature* (*JBL*)
> *Journal of Greco-Roman Christianity and Judaism* (*JGRChJ*)
> *New Testament Studies* (*NTS*)
> *Novum Testamentum* (*NovT*)

TC: A Journal of Biblical Textual Criticism (an online journal devoted exclusively to textual criticism)
Tyndale Bulletin (*TynBul*)

The articles that appear in these journals typically focus on a specific variant or manuscript and represent cutting-edge work within the field. The following is a good example of a journal article dealing with an important text-critical matter:

Peter M. Head, "The Date of the Magdalen Papyrus of Matthew (P. Magd. Gr. 17 = P64): A Response to C. P. Thiede," *TynBul* 46 (1995): 251-85.

Head is assessing the date of a Matthew manuscript held at Magdalen College in Oxford in response to another textual scholar, Carsten Peter Thiede.

Collections of individual chapters are also a means of presenting work on textual criticism. Sometimes these collections bring together the work of a single scholar, and sometimes they are by various scholars.

A collection of one author's work is found in the following:

Eldon Jay Epp, *Perspectives on New Testament Textual Criticism: Collected Essays, 1962-2004* (NovTSup 116; Leiden: Brill, 2005).
James Keith Elliott, *New Testament Textual Criticism: The Application of Thoroughgoing Principles: Essays on Manuscripts and Textual Variation* (NovTSup 137; Leiden: Brill, 2010).

A collection of essays by various authors is found in the following:

Bart D. Ehrman and Michael W. Holmes, eds., *The Text of the New Testament in Contemporary Research: Essays on the Status Quaestionis* (2nd ed.; Leiden: Brill, 2013).

A *monograph* is a specialized academic work focusing on a specific area of study — think of it as a number of coordinated journal articles or scholarly chapters on the same topic. We may contrast a monograph with the volume you are reading, which is a textbook (a summary and necessarily abbreviated statement of scholarship with the student particularly in mind). Monographs in textual criticism have a considerable range. They may encompass the treatment of the textual history of a particular book, as we find in:

Tommy Wasserman, *The Epistle of Jude: Its Text and Transmission* (ConBNT 43; Stockholm: Almqvist and Wiksell, 2006).

Or they may focus on the textual history of a single chapter or section of a NT book, for example:

Harry Y. Gamble, *The Textual History of the Letter to the Romans: A Study in Textual and Literary Criticism* (SD 42; Grand Rapids: Eerdmans, 1977).

Gamble's study really focuses on Romans 14, 15, and 16 and tries to resolve the original form of Romans, since we have various versions (some manuscripts with Rom 1–14, some with 1–15, and some with 1–16) represented in the textual history.

Monographs may also tackle a topic within textual criticism, as we find in:

Kent D. Clarke, *Textual Optimism: A Critique of the United Bible Societies' Greek New Testament* (JSNTSup 138; Sheffield: Sheffield Academic Press, 1997).

Students interested in further study in textual criticism will want to take a look at some of these studies to see how modern textual criticism is done.

As with journals, some specific monograph series are especially rich with text-critical study. These include, but are by no means limited to:

Texts and Editions for New Testament Study (TENTS) (Brill)
New Testament Tools and Studies (NTTS) (Brill)
New Testament Tools, Studies and Documents (NTTSD) (Brill)
Studies and Documents (SD) (Eerdmans)
Journal for the Study of the New Testament Supplement (JSNTSup) (Sheffield)[1]

These are vital sources for cutting-edge, book-length, text-critical research.

---

1. The series is now published by Bloomsbury and has been renamed Library of New Testament Studies (LNTS).

4. Manuscript Editions and Transcriptions

More important than the various commentaries, articles, and books written on the evidence is the evidence itself — the actual manuscripts, or at least editions of them. Too often text-critical work is reduced to merely consulting one of the textual commentaries or a journal article or monograph dealing with the relevant textual issue. This merely amounts to citing text-critical works and not doing fundamental textual criticism. Several editions and transcriptions enable access to the biblical manuscripts (or least reproductions of them) in print form. Transcriptions for most of the earliest manuscripts, including several papyri and early majuscules, can be found in:

Philip W. Comfort and David P. Barrett, *The Text of the Earliest New Testament Greek Manuscripts* (Wheaton, IL: Tyndale House, 2001).

Several others can be found in:

Stanley E. Porter and Wendy J. Porter, *New Testament Greek Papyri and Parchments: New Editions.* Vol. 1: *Texts* (Mitteilungen aus der Papyrussammlung der Österreichischen Nationalbibliothek n.s. 29; Berlin: de Gruyter, 2008).

Hendrickson has recently released a handsome facsimile of Codex Sinaiticus (Peabody, MA: Hendrickson, 2010) that can be consulted by those wanting to further investigate that manuscript. There are many others besides, but these give an idea of what is available for those desiring to access and evaluate the original manuscripts in printed form.

5. Digital and Web-based Tools

Finally, we turn to digital tools. Logos, Accordance, and BibleWorks — the three major biblical software platforms — have all emphasized the availability of text-critical resources. Both Accordance and BibleWorks offer images and transcriptions of most of the major codices, with Logos the least developed in this regard. One limitation of these image collections, however, is that they contain only the NT portions of the manuscripts, not the Septuagint or Apostolic Fathers. Logos is catching up, having released transcriptions for Codex Bezae and, most recently, Sinaiticus — both made available for free by the Institute for Textual Scholarship and Electronic Editing (University of Birmingham). One can also access a number of text-critical tools within each software program. BibleWorks and Accordance lead the way since they make available the *Center for New Testament Textual Studies' New Testament Critical Apparatus,* an extensive digital-only text-critical apparatus that its producer (New Orleans Baptist Seminary) claims contains the equivalent of over seventeen thousand pages of printed textual information. Each software platform also makes available the NA$^{27/28}$ text and apparatus as well as Tischendorf's 8th edition of the Greek NT. These highly annotated texts should not be used early on as they will almost certainly impair the student in acquiring text-critical skills.

Many Web sites exist that aid in textual research. One noteworthy achievement is:

http://www.codexsinaiticus.org/en.

Users can view the entirety of Codex Sinaiticus at this site, along with a running transcription.

Codex Alexandrinus, along with several other important manuscripts housed at the British Library, can be viewed here:

http://www.bl.uk/manuscripts/FullDisplay.aspx?ref=Royal_MS_1_d_viii

Images of Codex Ephraimi Rescriptus can be viewed here:

http://gallica.bnf.fr/ark:/12148/btv1b8470433r/f1.image

Images of several of the earliest papyri, including $\mathfrak{P}^{46}$, can be examined here:

http://www.earlybible.com/manuscripts

Images of several manuscripts and transcriptions can be viewed at the University of Münster's virtual manuscript room:

http://ntvmr.uni-muenster.de

Images and transcriptions of the Mingana Collection of Middle Eastern Manuscripts held at Special Collections in the University of Birmingham can be viewed here:

http://vmr.bham.ac.uk

The Center for the Study of New Testament Manuscripts has photographed and hosts images of significant NT manuscripts, which can be viewed here:

http://www.csntm.org/manuscript

There are many other Web sites as well, but these provide an entry point for the student who desires not only to read the text-critical studies of others, but to engage with the biblical manuscripts themselves.

Index of Modern Authors

Index of Ancient Sources